The Origins of Citizenship
in Ancient Athens

The Origins of Citizenship
in Ancient Athens

Philip Brook Manville

PRINCETON UNIVERSITY PRESS

PRINCETON, NEW JERSEY

To My Teachers

Parents, Professors, and Family

Copyright © 1990 by Princeton University Press
Preface to the paperback edition
Copyright © 1997 by Princeton University Press

Published by Princeton University Press, 41 William Street,
Princeton, New Jersey 08540
In the United Kingdom: Princeton University Press, Chichester,
West Sussex

Library of Congress Cataloging-in-Publication Data
Manville, Philip Brook.
The origins of citizenship in ancient Athens / Philip Brook Manville.
Includes bibliographical references and index.
1. Citizenship—Greece—Athens. I. Title.
JC75.C5M36 1990 323.6'0938'5—dc20 89-70119
ISBN 0-691-09442-X
ISBN 0-691-01593-7 (pbk.)

This book has been composed in Linotron Sabon

Princeton University Press books are printed on acid-free paper and
meet the guidelines for permanence and durability of the Committee
on Production Guidelines for Book Longevity of the Council
on Library Resources

Second printing, with corrections, 1992
Third printing, and first paperback printing, 1997

Printed in the United States of America
by Princeton Academic Press

3 5 7 9 10 8 6 4

CONTENTS

PREFACE TO THE PAPERBACK EDITION

THE ISSUANCE of a less expensive paperback edition of this book is intended to widen its availability to students, and to more casual readers of topics within the domain of ancient Greek history. It is also hoped that this publication can make a contribution to contemporary discussions among policymakers, commentators, and general audiences interested in the themes of community formation and membership in democratic society, of which ancient Athenian citizenship is a (literally) classic case. The favorable reception of the original volume has confirmed my belief that the topic of citizenship cuts across many of the central issues of ancient Athenian history; also that it is a useful touchstone in any discussion about democratic theory and practice and, more broadly, about the role that community plays in defining the character and identity of the individual.

For reasons of cost and expediency, this paperback edition reprints largely verbatim the original text of 1990. On re-reading it today, now myself six years older and (in some ways) wiser, I would have ideally changed a few things and added many more. The philosopher Heraclitus said that no one can step into the same river twice, and this topic, like all others, has moved along swiftly since I completed the first manuscript. But, the overall thesis of this volume is still something I stand behind, and it remains a reasonable story of the rise and development of the Athenian polis and citizenship through the archaic and pre-classical age.

More ambitious readers will want to supplement the reading of this monograph with treatments of the topic included in any of several relevant articles and books published since 1990. The exploding interest in democratic institutions and culture in recent years has led to a similar growth of useful discussions of classical Athenian citizenship, both as a central focus of inquiry and within the broader context of work on democratic institutions and culture. Those of particular note include: Alan Boegehold and Adele Scafuro (eds.), *Athenian Identity and Civic Ideology*; David Cohen, *Law, Violence, and Community in Classical Athens*; Charles Fornara and Loren Samons, *Athens from Cleisthenes to Pericles*; Victor Hanson, *The Western Way of War* and *The Other Greeks*; Mogens H. Hansen, *The Athenian Democracy in the Age of Demosthenes*; Virginia Hunter, *Policing Athens*; Donald Kagan, *Pericles of Athens and the Birth of Athenian Democracy*; Nicole Loraux, *The Children of Athena*; Oswyn Murray and Simon Prince (eds.), *The Greek City from Homer to Alexander*; Josiah Ober, *The Athenian Revolution*; Josiah Ober and Charles Hedrick (eds.), *Dēmokratia: A Conversation on Democracies Ancient and Modern*; Paul Rahe, *Republics Ancient and Modern*; Jennifer Roberts, *Athens on Trial*; Eli Sagan, *The Honey and the Hemlock*; and Barry Strauss, *Fathers and Sons in Athens*. The collected essays edited by Boegehold and Scafuro, and those by Ober and Hedrick each include an article by me reflecting some of my further work on this general topic in the last few years. Enthusiasts may also want to pursue some of the reviews of my original book which add to the thinking about Athenian citizenship and the polis (as listed in *L'Année Philologique*). Two substantial critiques are offered by Raphael Sealey (*Ancient History Bulletin* 5.3 [1991]: 75–80) and Pericles Georges (*International History Review* 15 [1993]: 84–105). As I wrote in 1990, this is a topic about which there is always a lot left to say.

Princeton, September 1996

PREFACE

When I first began this project, the subject of ancient Greek citizenship had received little recent attention from scholars. As my work progressed, I thought a lot about why. Partly, I supposed, because the subject seemed so obvious. Many historians of the past and current generations may have felt that there was little to say about a topic whose legal details had been dissected endlessly since the nineteenth century; and those who would focus on broader themes might have believed there was little to add to the long tradition of modern writers who celebrated "the glory that was Greece" and "the genius of ancient democracy."

But there may have been another, deeper reason. If one believes, as I do, that every generation studies the past on the basis of its own concerns, it is understandable that citizenship in Athens might not have received the same treatment as some other themes of greater contemporary interest, such as the role of women in ancient society, Greek homosexuality, or other aspects of ancient private life. If indeed scholarship mirrors the trends and themes of the society in which it is pursued, the slight attention paid to the subject of citizenship may be the academic reflection of a decline of civic consciousness. That decline—or at the very least, confusion about what citizenship means—in our own society might explain the relative neglect of the topic among historians in the last decades.

This is not the forum to discuss such decline, but if this book has a larger purpose beyond pure scholarship, it is to help the reader think about the why and what of citizenship today. That is a large and elusive topic, but one, it is hoped, that might occasionally visit the thoughts of this audience. Some humanistic perspective on the origins and concept of membership in a democratic *polis* might stimulate thought about what it means to belong—or not to belong—to a modern "democratic" state. Thus, if scholarship reflects contemporary social themes, I would also hope that it can play a role in helping to create new ones, or in renewing those of the past.

In fact, my interest in citizenship is increasingly finding good company among historians of ancient Greece. If the subject has been relatively ignored by the last generation, the qualification "relatively" comes in the face of several important studies of the most recent years on various aspects of civic life. I have benefited from a great deal of excellent work in this area, much of it published in the 1980s. Whether my mentors and co-workers on ancient civic themes are indeed reflective of a resurgent interest in modern citizenship, I leave to future history to judge. We are just perhaps beginning to enter a new era in our society marked by "a commitment to public action, idealism and reform, [and] a high degree of popular participation."[1] If so, let this book be seen as one tiny part of that trend.

As I have humbly discovered over the last several years, Athenian citizenship is a complex and difficult topic. This book began life as a graduate seminar paper in the Yale Department of Classics, developed further as a Ph.D. dissertation in the Department of History, and matured over the course of four years of research and teaching in classics and humanities at Northwestern University. It has taken me a long time to write, and I know now that there is still a good deal left to say. To understand citizenship, even as I have defined it, has required a grasp of many more diverse forms of knowledge than certainly I first imagined.

Accordingly, this book reflects a synthesis of political, social, and intellectual history—subdisciplines that ought never be, but in the last two decades often have been, treated separately by historians. The range and philosophy of my research into the Athenian citizen and his world in many ways coincides with the perspective on Greek political history offered by W. R. Connor in a recent, thoughtful essay:

[1] The quotation is from Arthur Schlesinger (1989), advancing his cyclical theory of American politics.

> Politics, in the approach I am suggesting . . . keeps close to its
> etymological home, the *polis*, but sets for itself the task of trying
> to understand how people came to shape a civic order, to feel
> that they belonged to it and it to them and to derive part of their
> identity from its existence. . . . The problem of access to power
> and control of state apparatus, upon which so much traditional
> Greek political analysis depends, retains its importance, but not
> its exclusive claim on our attention. We must see it not in isola-
> tion, but as one of the ways in which citizens expressed and even
> created a sense of belonging to a *polis*. It must be understood as
> part of a cultural complex that included cult, processions, festi-
> vals, the creation of tribal structures, market and festival days,
> and even the roads that brought people from outlying villages to
> the public space of the inner city.[2]

Such an approach, of course, demands that in writing a narrative one must take a stand on a wide array of problems and
issues, many ideological as well as historical. That I have indeed done, and it is therefore unlikely that anyone will agree
with all that follows; my methods and ideas may even trouble
certain readers. But the risk is well worth taking if this work
helps foster debate about what I believe to be one of the more
important topics in the study of Western civilization.

As those who have ever produced this kind of book will
know, many thanks are owed to many people by the time of
final publication. I would begin by acknowledging my grati-
tude to Donna Tingen and Adrienne Mayor, for their help in
preparing my manuscript, and to the staff of Princeton University Press for their careful and professional attention to the
production of this volume; special thanks goes to Ms. Joanna
Hitchcock, my sponsoring editor. I am also indebted to the
College of Arts and Sciences and the Department of Classics
at Northwestern University, who generously supported much
of my research with faculty fellowships and teaching leave.

Further thanks are due for much counsel and advice from
several scholars along the way. My investigations of Greek cit-

---

[2] Connor (1986), 347.

izenship have been significantly enhanced by discussions with Victor Bers, John Davies, Moses Finley, Michael Gagarin, Mogens Hansen, Charles Hedrick, Alan Kantrow, Peter Krentz, Cynthia Patterson, Paul Rahe, Raphael Sealey, Anthony Snodgrass, and Bob Wallace; and as a practical matter, I collectively acknowledge the helpful comments of scores of other friends and colleagues who patiently discussed this project with me during years I spent in New Haven, Oxford, Cambridge, and Evanston, Illinois. I here express the earnest hope that if I have chosen sometimes to disagree with their spoken or published points of view, it has been through no disrespect for the many kind generosities offered.

There are also many other scholars to whom I owe a more personal debt for continuing advice and suggestions over the long term of this book's gestation. Earlier drafts benefited from the generous scrutiny of Tony Andrewes, Paul Cartledge, George Forrest, Dan Garrison, John Herington, Ramsay MacMullen, Josh Ober, Martin Ostwald, and Barry Strauss. And that said, there remain two very special thanks for extraordinary support and encouragement above and beyond the call of mortal duty: to Don Kagan, without whose help this book never would have begun; and to Margarita Egan, without whose help this book never would have been.

April 1989

A NOTE ON REFERENCES AND ABBREVIATIONS

REFERENCES to all modern scholarship are cited by author and date of publication, with multiple works published by the same author in any one year further distinguished by a, b, c, etc. Full listings appear alphabetically by author in the References.

Citations of ancient authors, texts, and other edited sources for the most part follow abbreviations and conventions as listed in the *Oxford Classical Dictionary* (2d ed.; Oxford, 1970). For the benefit of the nonspecialist, those appearing most frequently, plus a few additional abbreviations, are listed below:

Aeschin.	Aeschines
Aesch.	Aeschylus
Andoc.	Andocides
Ar.	Aristophanes
Arist.	Aristotle
Ath.	Athenaeus
Ath. Pol.	Aristotle, *Athēnaiōn Politeia**
Dem.	Demosthenes
Dig.	*Digesta Iustiniani*
Din.	Dinarchus
Diod. Sic.	Didorus Siculus
Diog. Laert.	Diogenes Laertius
Dion. Hal.	Dionysius Halicarnassensis
DK	H. Diels and W. Kranz, *Die Fragmente der Vorsokratiker*, 6th ed., 1951–52
Eur.	Euripides

* In this book, I follow the view held by many scholars that the *Athēnaiōn Politeia* is an authentically Aristotelian work. For a defense of the philosopher's authorship, see Keaney (1980). The enduring controversy is succinctly summarized by Rhodes (1981), 58ff., who takes the other side.

FGrH	F. Jacoby, *Fragmente der griechischen Historiker*, 1923–58
Hdt.	Herodotus
Hes.	Hesiod
Hom.	Homer
IG	*Inscriptiones Graecae*, 1873–
Isae.	Isaeus
Isoc.	Isocrates
Kock	T. Kock, *Comicorum Atticorum Fragmenta*, 1880–88
Lycurg.	Lycurgus
Lys.	Lysias
LSJ	H. G. Liddell and R. Scott, *A Greek-English Lexicon*, 9th ed., revised H. S. Jones, 1940
Nauck	A. Nauck, *Tragicorum Graecorum Fragmenta*, 1889
Pind.	Pindar
Pl.	Plato
Plut.	Plutarch
Ps. Xen. *Ath. Pol.*	Pseudo-Xenophon, *Athēnaiōn Politeia*
SEG	*Supplementum epigraphicum Graecum*, 1923–
SN	E. Ruschenbusch, *Solonos Nomoi*, 1966
Soph.	Sophocles
Strab.	Strabo
Theophr.	Theophrastus
Thuc.	Thucydides
Xen.	Xenophon

The Origins of Citizenship
in Ancient Athens

Chapter One

INTRODUCTION: WHAT WAS ATHENIAN CITIZENSHIP?

For the Athenian people, although they hold ultimate authority over all things in the state and have the power to act however they see fit, nonetheless regarded their citizenship to be something so worthy and august that they passed laws strictly prescribing its bestowal—laws which now [the defendant and her consort] are dragging through the mud. (Dem. 59.88)

THE SCENE is an Athenian court, about 345 B.C.[1] The speaker is expressing his outrage that a foreign prostitute and her Athenian "husband," through their wanton behavior and illegal registration of children, have disgraced the laws of Athenian citizenship, something "worthy and sacred" (*kalon kai semnon*). A rhetorical exaggeration? Not really. A good deal of evidence from the classical age suggests that Athenians did consider their citizenship something very valuable. It was, for example, only sparingly granted to foreigners, particularly in the fifth century.[2] And as this speaker from the Athenian court notes, the people passed laws regulating it—not only for the enfranchisement of deserving aliens but also for the proper enrollment of Athenians themselves. The penalties for breaking

[1] Hereafter, all century dates and three-digit year dates are B.C., unless otherwise noted. References to the nineteenth and twentieth centuries are A.D. Translations of ancient texts cited throughout this study are my own, except as indicated.

[2] Evidence collected and analyzed by M. Osborne (1981), (1982), (1983); cf. Hansen (1982a), 173–79; Bordes (1982), 49–77. On Athenian reluctance to extend citizenship, Gauthier (1974); Sinclair (1988), 24–27.

such laws involved large fines and enslavement.[3] One further indication that citizenship was indeed serious business: the Athenians periodically revised their civic registers with an eye toward limiting the number of "true" or "legal" or "full" citizens.[4] Who was and who was not a citizen frequently stood at the center of political debate.

Why was citizenship considered "worthy and sacred," argued about, jealously guarded, and carefully maintained by Athenians in the classical period? What in fact was Athenian citizenship, and how did it come to be? The pages that follow represent an attempt to answer these questions of origin and development and to understand something that was simultaneously an institution, a concept, an ethic.

The primary (and difficult) task is one of terminology and definition. Let me first be clear about the meaning of "citizenship" in English, a word that can be glossed over too casually. According to Webster, citizenship is "the status of being a citizen."[5] A more expansive definition is offered by Marshall in a well-known essay on the subject. Citizenship, he says, is "a status bestowed on those who are full members of a community. All who possess the status are equal with respect to the

---

[3] On the enrollment of foreigners, M. Osborne (1983), 143ff.; on Athenians, MacDowell (1978), 67–70. Cf. Hansen (1987b), 114 on the importance of honorary grants of citizenship in the work of the *ekklēsia*.

Athenians proposed for enrollment in a deme at age eighteen (discussed below) were probably sold into slavery if a subsequent scrutiny or appeal found them to be of unfree birth; the enrolling demesmen could be fined for accepting candidates below age (*Ath. Pol.* 42 with Rhodes [1981], 493–503), and aliens who illegally adopted the status of citizens could be imprisoned, prosecuted, and sold into slavery if convicted (Dem. 24.131 [with schol.]; Dem. *Ep.* 3.29). Cf. also the penalties for contraventions of Perikles' citizenship law (Plut. *Per.* 37.2–4; *Ath. Pol.* 26.4) involving enslavement, fines, confiscations, and loss of citizen rights (Dem. 59.16, 52 with Harrison [1968], 26–28).

[4] Scrutiny of citizens: *Ath. Pol.* 13.5 (510/9); Plut. *Per.* 37.4; *FGrH* 328 F 119 (445/4); Isae. 12; Dem. 57 (346/5). Attempts to limit the *politeia:* Plut. *Per.* 37.2–4; *Ath. Pol.* 26.4 (Perikles' citizenship law of 451/50); Thuc. 8.67–98; *Ath. Pol.* 29–33 (oligarchic revolutions of 411/10); *Ath. Pol.* 34–41.1 (rule of the Thirty, 404/3).

[5] *Webster's Third New International Dictionary* (1961).

rights and duties with which the status is endowed."[6] Now if citizenship can be described as a status of membership, with specific rights and duties, the term in English also carries another connotation. Again to quote Webster, it can alternatively mean "membership in a community; the quality of an individual's adjustment, responsibility, or contribution to his community."[7] Thus, for example, an individual is sometimes rewarded for his "citizenship," his (good) service to the community, that is, a positive response to the society to which he belongs. By and large the two cited definitions in English are not commonly confused, nor do the meanings really overlap in the minds of most people today.[8] The first has a juridical sense of status and is potentially passive (one may have the status of citizenship and do nothing with it, beyond fulfilling certain minimum legal requirements); the second must be active, for it depends on action within, and with regard to, the community to which one belongs.

The analogous term for citizenship in Greek (*politeia*) can have similar legal (passive) and social (active) meanings, but it is much less easy to draw a distinction between them.[9] That is because the status of membership in the Athenian community could not really be separated from the role the citizen played in it; politeia appears in texts as "the condition and rights of a citizen" but also as "the daily life of the citizen," with both senses often implied at the same time. For the classical period, it is difficult to talk about a purely "passive" meaning of politeia, that is, as an abstract legal status, because Greek citizenship was defined by the active participation of the citizen in public life.[10] An illustration of this often-stated point is provided by the procedures outlined in Athenian decrees granting

[6] Marshall (1964), 84.

[7] Ibid.

[8] Oddly, the *Oxford English Dictionary* does not even cite the second definition. On the distinction between the two meanings, see Gettys (1934), 1.

[9] See Ehrenberg (1969), 39–52; and Bordes (1982), 13ff. for the discussion of politeia that follows.

[10] Gauthier (1981); and Sinclair (1988), 23ff. Cf. Ehrenberg (1969), 42ff.; and Mossé (1979a).

citizenship to foreigners. In the fifth and fourth centuries, all such decrees, even those only "honorary," always included the proviso that the recipient be enrolled in a tribe and a deme, the membership corporations that (after the Kleisthenic reforms of 508/7) comprised the bodies of actual and practical involvement in the state.[11]

"State" itself is a word also often used casually, so some understanding of what it really implies must be established in the context of ancient Greece. "State" is another possible translation of politeia (as are "commonwealth," "republic," "constitution," etc.), and at first that concept may seem very different from the legal status and daily life of a citizen. If so, modern perceptions are again getting in the way. Today, the state is often considered a formal, independent entity, in conflict with the individual and ultimately aloof from the citizens (and non-citizens) in its domain. For the Greeks, membership in the state and the state itself were closely related.[12] In fact, the state—the *polis*—was its citizens, as, for example, the Athenian general Nikias reminded his troops in Thucydides' account of the Sicilian campaign in the year 413: "*andres gar polis, kai ou teichē oude nēes andrōn kenai*" ("Men make the polis, not walls or a fleet of crewless ships": Thuc. 7.77.7).[13] For the same reason, literary and epigraphic sources never refer to the Athenian polis as "Athens"; Athens was only the name of a place. What we would call the state was always represented as *hoi Athēnaioi* ("the Athenians") meaning the political community of citizens. Thus, together with "state," "citizen body" is yet another of the many possible nuances of politeia; citizenship and the polis were interdependent.

[11] M. Osborne (1983), 147–48. I follow Whitehead (1986a), 34–35, 97–104 in believing that the formal deme registration procedures seen in *Ath. Pol.* 42, if not established by the reforms of Kleisthenes (see below chapter 7), "had their roots in some basic regulations laid down with the same end in view, by Kleisthenes" (p. 35), *contra* Patterson (1981), 13–28.

[12] Ehrenberg (1969), 88–89; Bordes (1982), 17; Meier (1984), 20ff.; Vernant (1986), 227–28; Morris (1987), 3ff.; and others. On the polis and "state" see chapter 2.

[13] Cf. Alkaios F 22; Soph. *OT* 56; Aesch. *Pers.* 349; Dem. 18.299; etc. Cf. C. Smith (1906–7).

This background allows a more precise definition of Athenian citizenship, the necessary beginning of this investigation. In short, citizenship was membership in the Athenian polis, with all that this implied—a legal status, but also the more intangible aspects of the life of the citizen that related to his status. It was simultaneously a complement of formal obligations and privileges, and the behavior, feelings, and communal attitudes attendant upon them. To be an Athenian citizen, as an Athenian himself might say, was to be someone who *metechei tēs poleōs*: someone who "shares in the polis."[14] What did this really mean in the classical age?

During much of the fifth and fourth centuries, Athenian citizenship was membership in a polis defined by a democratic constitution. To sketch a general picture, we might start with the imprecise but workable assumption of a basically stable and continuous set of democratic laws and institutions in Athens between about 450 and 322.[15] Against this background, the scattered evidence relating to citizenship per se can be drawn together to present a coherent outline of its legal characteristics in this period.[16]

Except for the small percentage of foreigners granted Athe-

---

[14] Lys. 6.48; *Ath. Pol.* 26.4; and cf. Dem. 21.106 for a use of *polis* in itself equivalent to "citizenship." For other various formulas (*metesti moi tēs poleōs, metechein tēs politeias*, etc.), see Bordes (1982), 491–92 and references.

[15] Thus Sinclair (1988), 22–23, and many others. The earlier date represents an approximate but normally agreed-upon starting point for when the "full democracy" was in place, and the later is its conventional end, corresponding to the end of the so-called Lamian War and the imposition on Athens of a Macedonian-backed oligarchic government.

In reality, of course, there were several legal and institutional changes throughout the approximately 130 years of the democracy, all with practical implications for the citizenship of Athenians. See, e.g., Hansen (1987b), passim who focuses on changes in the *ekklēsia*, but notes (124) the overall importance of the assembly in the civic affairs throughout the period, despite its loss of absolute sovereignty in the fourth century. For some further comments about changes in the ethos of public life during the democratic age, Humphreys (1983c). See also chapter 8.

[16] Recent general treatments: Jones (1957); Davies (1977–78); MacDowell (1978), 67–83; Vamvoukos (1979); Finley (1981a) and (1983), 70ff.; Patterson (1981) passim; Sealey (1987), 5–31; Sinclair (1988).

nian citizenship by decree (which entailed its own criteria and formal procedures),[17] the citizens of the polis were native Athenian males who had reached the age of eighteen,[18] and who had been duly registered in the same local Attic village unit, or deme, to which their fathers belonged. That registration embodied a formal and multistepped process.[19] Candidates were scrutinized by fellow demesmen to ensure that they were eighteen, freeborn, and legitimate with regard to the lawful marriage of two Athenian parents. If the candidate was challenged, appeal to a jury court (*dikastērion*) was possible, and in all questionable cases a further scrutiny (*dokimasia*) by the democratic council (*boulē*) was required.

Successful candidates' names were inscribed in a list kept by the deme, the *lēxiarchikon grammateion*.[20] Once entered into legal adulthood,[21] citizens could expect to (and might be expected to)[22] exercise a variety of specific prerogatives: to participate in Athenian cults, festivals, and worship;[23] to attend, speak, and vote in the popular assembly (*ekklēsia*);[24] to serve

---

[17] M. Osborne (1983), 141ff.

[18] For the debate about the age of majority see arguments and literature cited by Rhodes (1981), 497–98.

[19] For details of deme registration see Whitehead (1986a), 97–109; and Rhodes (1981), 493–510 whose reconstruction I follow, particularly regarding the likelihood that the *boulē* and *dikastēria* could have examined both the age and free status of enrolled candidates.

[20] For the problem of the origin, nature, and meaning of the *lēxiarchika grammateia*, Whitehead (1986a), 35 n. 130; but cf. the valuable caution against overly legalistic interpretations of these registers in R. Osborne (1985a), 72. See also Hansen (1985b), 14–16.

[21] There is some debate about the age of full legal adulthood because of the normal requirement (at least in the fourth century) that newly registered citizens serve as "military cadets" (*ephēboi*) between the age of eighteen and twenty (discussed later). On the question of their access to the *ekklēsia*, and the possibility of a second registration in a special roster of the assembly (*pinax ekklēsiastikos*) in their demes, Rhodes (1981), 494–95; Hansen (1985b), 14–21, 49ff.; (1987b), 7.

[22] Sinclair (1988), 53 correctly notes that the notion of obligation should not be interpreted too narrowly; the boundary between Athenian social values and "legal" responsibilities was not sharply drawn.

[23] Mikalson (1975); Parke (1977); Sinclair (1988), 53ff.

[24] Jones (1957), 108–33; Hansen (1977a), (1977b), (1978), 127–41;

(after the age of thirty) as a juror in the law courts (*dikastēria*);[25] to vote and (depending on age and eligibility) stand for elected and allotted offices (*archai*);[26] to seek redress and receive protection under the laws;[27] to have the capacity to own land in Attika;[28] to receive public disbursements, whether for services provided, as special distributions, or as maintenance for hardships.[29] The loyal Athenian might also be rewarded with public burial at state expense if he sacrificed his life on behalf of the polis.[30]

The chief obligation of citizens was to obey the laws of the polis.[31] Indeed, appropriately the penalty for not doing so was often the loss of one's civic rights and privileges within the law (*atimia*).[32] Military service and taxation were other obvious obligations, though these, just as certain privileges, fell to varying degrees upon citizens, in accordance with an individual's census rank.[33] All citizens except those of the lowest

---

(1979a), (1982b), (1983a), 43–48; (1983b), (1987b); Sinclair (1988), 31, 65ff.

25 MacDowell (1978), 33–40; Hansen (1978), 127–43; Sinclair (1988), 31, 65ff. On the qualifications and selection of jurors, *Ath. Pol.* 24.3, 27.4, 62–69 with Rhodes (1981), esp. 689–735.

26 *Ath. Pol.* 43–62 with Rhodes (1981), 510–697; Hansen (1980b).

27 MacDowell (1978), passim; Sinclair (1988), 72–73.

28 Harrison (1968), 236–38; Pečírka (1966), 137ff.

29 On pay for service in *ekklēsia*, *dikastēria*, *boulē*, military, and *archai* see *Ath. Pol.* 41.3, 27.2–5, 32.1, 24.3, 62.2 with Rhodes (1981). For additional references and commentary see Pritchett (1971–85), 1:3–29; Hansen (1979b), (1980a), (1987b), 46–48; Gabrielsen (1981); Finley (1981a), 88–90; Markle (1985). For special distributions, see, e.g., *Ath. Pol.* 22.7 (proposed); 43.1 with Rhodes (1981), 514–15; Plut. *Per.* 37.4; Plut. *Mor.* 843 D–E; Buchanan (1962); Latte (1968), 64–75; Humphreys (1978), 145. For hardship maintenance such as, e.g., care of orphans, see Dem. 43.75; Aeschin. 1.158; Thuc. 2.46; Lys. F 6; Stroud (1971); MacDowell (1978), 93–98.

30 Pritchett (1971–85), 4:102ff.; Clairmont (1983).

31 Sinclair (1988), 49; on "obligation" in the ancient Athenian context, see above, n. 22. The classic text on this issue is, of course, Plato's *Crito*, though the precise interpretation of the Socratic argument is open to much debate. See Kraut (1984), esp. 154ff. for its relationship to citizenship.

32 Harrison (1971), 169–71; Hansen (1976), 55ff.; Manville (1980).

33 Finley (1981a), 88ff. discusses the social implications; see also generally Sinclair (1988), 54–65.

order (*thētes*) were liable for service in the hoplite army or cavalry. By the latter part of the fourth century, Athenian males between eighteen and twenty years of age were also obliged to undergo two years of preparatory military training (*ephēbeia*).[34] Upon completion, they were required to supply the necessary (and costly) equipment demanded by their regular military duty. *Thētes* served in the Athenian navy, typically on a voluntary but occasionally mandatory basis.[35] Taxes in the Athenian polis were mostly indirect, and those such as harbor dues and import duties affected all citizens.[36] Direct taxes (*eisphorai*) were levied from time to time, but were restricted to citizens of a certain minimum wealth (probably a net worth of 2,500 drachmas).[37] The wealthiest men were also responsible for various liturgies (literally, "work on behalf of the community"), such as the command and maintenance of warships or the financing of festivals for the polis.[38] Finally, any man who served in public office was required, at the end of his duties, to have his performance scrutinized and his financial dealings audited. Thus, all those who exercised any civic authority were *hypeuthynoi*, that is, subject to the legal examinations called *euthynai*, and fully accountable for the course of their public service.[39]

Despite some differential privileges and obligations based

[34] *Ath. Pol.* 42.3–5, 53.4–5. On the origins and practice of the Athenian *ephēbeia:* Pélékidis (1962); Vidal-Naquet (1981). I follow Rhodes (1981), 503 and others that *ephēboi* were drawn only from the top three census orders since their training was primarily for hoplite warfare. For the view that *thētes* were also included in the fourth century, Ruschenbusch (1978); (1981). Hansen (1985b), 48–50 points out that in any case not all citizens necessarily served in the *ephēbeia* since some who were physically unfit for service were excused. On citizens' hoplite service, see Andrewes (1981).

[35] See de Ste. Croix (1981), 207 with n. 8, 581; Rhodes (1981), 327. Cf. Meiggs (1972), 439–41; Hansen (1985b), 22. For discussion of pay for military service, Pritchett (1971–85), 1:3–29.

[36] Jones (1974), 153; de Ste. Croix (1981), 206.

[37] On *eisphorai*, de Ste. Croix (1953), (1966); Fisher (1976), 24–27; Davies (1981), 147ff.; Rhodes (1982); Sinclair (1988), 62–63.

[38] Davies (1971), xx–xxxi; (1981), 25–37; Rhodes (1982); Sinclair (1988), 61–65.

[39] See de Ste. Croix (1981), 285; 601 n. 11; Sinclair (1988), 77–82.

on rank, Athenian citizenship embodied an overall legal status, defined by identifiable boundaries. The boundaries become most clear when we compare citizenship to the status of various groups of non-Athenians in Attic society.[40] Classical law distinguished Athenians from foreigners (*xenoi*), resident aliens (*metoikoi*), and slaves (*douloi*). Unlike the citizen, the *xenos* could not hold public office, own Attic land, or marry an Athenian woman; if he wished to trade in the public marketplace, he had to pay a special tax (*xenika*). His rights and access to justice in the Athenian courts were severely limited.[41]

The foreigner who wished to settle permanently in Attika as a *metoikos* had to be sponsored by an Athenian citizen (*prostatēs*) and be willing to pay a yearly tax on his inferior status, the *metoikion*.[42] Once registered, the *metoikos* gained a certain legal advantage over other foreigners, though he still shared many of their disabilities, such as a prohibition against marriage with an Athenian woman. Moreover, *metoikoi* were also liable for two serious responsibilities of citizens, military service and (if wealthy enough) the obligations of liturgies and taxes such as *eisphorai*. In the courts, the *metoikos* stood at marked disadvantage to the Athenian. In addition to certain procedural disadvantages (e.g., inability to act as a prosecutor in public indictments or *graphai*), *metoikoi* might suffer what no citizen feared: torture to extract judicial testimony.[43]

Slaves also could be tortured for testimony, which is not surprising given their even more lowly status under Athenian law.[44] Like other items of property, and unlike all free men

---

[40] Cf. Finley (1981a), 80ff. on the inverse relationships of privileges and disabilities among status groups. Whitehead (1984a) offers a valuable overview on the evolution of distinctions between citizens and immigrant groups. See also Hansen (1985b), 8ff. for discussion of the legal concept of the citizen; Sinclair (1988), 28–33.

[41] Laws and evidence summarized in MacDowell (1978), 75–76.

[42] On the status and procedures of *metoikia*, see MacDowell (1978), 76–78, and 78–79 for special dispensations from disabilities, such as *enktēsis*, *ateleia*, *asylia*, etc. Gauthier (1972), 108ff.; Whitehead (1977), 6–96.

[43] Whitehead (1977), 95 with n. 167; Sinclair (1988), 31.

[44] Dem. 30.35–37 with MacDowell (1978), 245–47. Fisher (1976), 21 notes, however, that the practice is not securely attested in surviving evidence.

and women in society (citizens or others), *douloi* could be bought, sold, hired out, bequeathed, or given away by their owners. With few exceptions, slaves were the responsibility of their masters in any legal action and had no official identity of their own.[45]

The superior status of the full citizen of the polis is manifest in homicide law. The known procedures and penalties indicate that the murder of any non-Athenian counted for less than the murder of an Athenian. The man who slew a citizen (or his Athenian daughter or wife) was tried before the court of the Areopagos, and could receive the death sentence; the man who slew a *metoikos, xenos,* or *doulos* went before a lesser court, the Palladion, and was liable only to exile.[46] Athenian law held Athenian life dearer and maintained a firm separation between members and nonmembers of the polis. The kinds of sentiments behind this boundary are obvious in the comments of the Athenian Euxitheos, on trial to defend his own civic status in the year 345:

> In my opinion, gentlemen of the jury, you ought to treat severely those who are proved to be *xenoi*, who, without either asking or having been granted the right, now share in Athenian sacred rites and public privileges by dint of trickery and violence. And in the same way, you ought to render aid and salvation to those men who have suffered misfortunes but can show themselves to be citizens. (Dem. 57.3)

Two other Athenian groups, women and children, deserve brief mention because of their ambiguous position in the society.[47] Athenian women were members of the Athenian com-

---

[45] Harrison (1968), 168–83; MacDowell (1978), 79–83.

[46] *Ath. Pol.* 57.3 with MacDowell (1963), 69, 125–27; and Harrison (1968), 170 with n. 1 for evidence and argument that the penalty for first degree murder of a non-citizen was equivalent to the penalty of manslaughter of a citizen. For several revisions of the orthodoxies about homicide courts, however, see Sealey (1983a).

[47] The status of a third ambiguous group, *nothoi* ("bastards") has been debated for centuries; Rhodes (1981), 496–97 summarizes the controversy succinctly; since then see Hansen (1985b), 73–76. I have little to add to the old arguments about whether or not *nothoi* could be "citizens," except to say that

munity, but belonged to the polis in a legal sense only indirectly—through their relationship with a father, husband, or other male relative who acted as their master and guardian (*kyrios*) in all important affairs. Athenian women, and a fortiori Athenian girls, could not own or inherit property, enter into contracts, or take independent action to marry or divorce; through their *kyrios*, however, they enjoyed the full protection of any citizen under the law.[48] Male children held a status similar to that of Athenian women. Until they came of age and entered adulthood, Athenian boys were wholly dependent on a *kyrios* (normally the father) for their legal identity in the polis.[49]

If Athenian citizenship in its various legal aspects can be described as a formally instituted status group, what can be said of its more intangible qualities in the classical age? Attempting to describe the values, behavior, and communal attitudes of the citizens themselves is tricky, given the paucity and nature of the evidence and the problem of trying to generalize from it. Still, an analysis that fails to take account of some of the supralegal qualities of politeia risks both undervaluing and misunderstanding it.

An obvious starting point, and indeed the veritable *locus*

---

because the institution of citizenship evolved over time, and only took concrete form after the reforms of Kleisthenes (the thesis of this book), the question is irrelevant before about 500. Thereafter, I would hazard that the ambiguous status that bastardy represented in the oikos continued as an ambiguous status in the polis: the illegitimately born were something more than *xenoi*, but something less than *Athēnaioi*, though in practice many *nothoi* probably did behave and were treated as if they were citizens. "Shades of gray" of membership existed throughout society (e.g., women, children, *metoikoi* with certain privileges that others did not have); why try to make this group "black" or "white"? For a similar view, see Lotze (1981).

[48] On the legal status of women, MacDowell (1978), 84–89; Gould (1980). On their place in demes, Whitehead (1986a), 77–81. On their place in phratries, and the rites of initiation of both girls and boys, S. Cole (1984). See also, generally, Loraux (1981), 7–153 who explores from a structuralist perspective the ambiguities and social contradictions of women in the Athenian male-dominated culture; and Humphreys (1983b).

[49] MacDowell (1978), 85–95. On the status and social role of children in Athenian society in general, M. Golden (1981).

classicus of Athenian citizenship, is the funeral oration delivered by the statesman Perikles in 431/30 (Thuc. 2.34ff.). The speech, with its interrelated themes of Athenian customs, political institutions, and manner of living reflects the richness and complexity of citizenship in the democratic polis.[50] As Perikles first tells his audience, he intends to discuss the greatness of Athens, and the political organization and way of life from whence the greatness came (*meth' hoias politeias kai tropōn ex hoiōn*: 2.36.4).

The speech, as passed on by Thucydides, is an elegant blend of tradition, contemporary commentary, and moral principles.[51] Perikles reminds the audience of its ancient ancestry ("the same people have always lived in our land, from generation to generation": 2.36.1), their past military exploits (36.2–4), and their special form of politeia, unique in the Greek world:

> Our government is called a democracy, because its conduct is in the hands of the many, and not just a few. There is equality for all under the laws with regard to the settlement of private disputes; as for the value placed on men, when someone is put forward for public responsibilities, preference depends on personal merit rather than social class; nor because of poverty is any man held back in obscurity, as long as he has some benefit to contribute to the polis. (37.1)

Athenian virtues, and by implication, the virtues of a good citizen, are variously praised: discretion in private dealings with neighbors (37.2); courage in battle (35.1, 39.4, etc.); love of beauty and wisdom (40.1); prosperity with moderation

---

[50] Bordes (1982), 20–21, 214–18 who *inter alia* defends the Periklean (rather than Thucydidean) application of politeia to the themes; here, as elsewhere, I adopt the view of Gomme (1937) and followers (e.g., Kagan [1975]) that speeches in Thucydides represent essentially accurate reports of what was said by the speaker on the occasion of their delivery (cf. Thuc. 1.22). On the tradition of such speeches, and an interesting structuralist interpretation of the Periklean oration, Loraux (1986).

[51] The interpretation that follows owes much to the unpublished remarks of Kagan (1982a) which he graciously shared with me.

(40.1); grace and versatility (41.1); and respect and obedience for order and authority, both human and divine.

> While in our private lives we conduct ourselves without offense, in our public lives our reverent respect restrains us from lawlessness, for we obey both persons in authority and the laws (*nomoi*), especially those established for the aid of people who have been wronged, and those which, although unwritten, bring a shame on men who break them that everyone recognizes. (2.37.3)

Throughout the speech, Athenian virtues and successes are related to the particular manner of life of their politeia: recreation with contests and sacrifices (38.1); a city open to the goods and peoples of the world (38.2–39.1); education and military training free from oppressive discipline (39); the custom of debating policy before taking action (40.2). Perikles finishes the oration by suggesting that the benefits of membership in the polis are a spur to moral action among its members (46.1): "Where the rewards for excellence (*aretē*) are the greatest, there are found the best citizens (*andres aristoi politeuousin*)."

One of the most telling parts of Perikles' speech concerns the relationship between private and public life. The two spheres are several times distinguished (37.1–2; 40.2; 42.3), but a central theme of the oration is the Athenians' perception of the interdependence between the two and the citizen's willingness to transcend the purely personal sphere and involve himself in the matters of the polis:

> You will find united in the same people an interest both in personal matters and public affairs (*oikeiōn hama kai politikōn epimeleia*), and even those mostly occupied with their own endeavors know a good deal about political matters (*ta politika*). For we alone regard the man who takes no part in such things not as one who minds his own business (*apragmona*), but as one who has no business here at all (*achreion*). (2.40.2)[52]

---

[52] Cf. also Thuc. 2.60.

This merging of private and public spheres and Perikles' insistence upon the preeminence of the affairs of the polis in the Athenian's daily life are reflected elsewhere in the speech. First, consider the premise of its delivery: an oration on the occasion of the burial of the dead (2.34), traditionally the obligation not of the polis but of the *oikos* or family unit.[53] In the same spirit, at the end of the speech, Perikles notes another traditional family function that the polis was now taking over: the raising of children, in this case public maintenance for the offspring of the fallen soldiers (41.1).[54] These are small examples, perhaps, but they are symbolic of a crucial underlying principle of the democratic politeia—the polis superseding and incorporating the affairs of private life.[55]

Perikles' oration is an eloquent statement of such a philosophy, but it is open to the charge that it was only that, philosophy (some would say rhetoric) removed from the reality of the day.[56] To what extent did Athenians actually direct their private lives to public matters? How much did Athenians under the democracy really care about *ta politika*, and is there any measure of such an attitude among the many members of the polis? The answers to such questions would be clearer if we had (which we do not) an accurate knowledge about the identity and motives of those who attended, for example, the various bodies of the democratic government throughout the

[53] Cf. the "public" obligation of demarchs to oversee the normal burial of a deceased member of a deme, should the duty fail to be discharged by the oikos: Dem. 43.57–58; Whitehead (1986a), 137–38.

[54] Cf. the restriction of the practice to only legitimate children in 403/2: Stroud (1971). Note that Perikles also mentions (Thuc. 2.44.3) the value to the polis of citizens bearing children.

[55] On the themes of public and private interests in general, and argument that the distinction between the two first appeared in the classical period, Humphreys (1983a), (1983c), (1983d). See also Rahe (1984); Goldhill (1986), 69–74; Garner (1987), 12ff.; Herman (1987), 1–9, 116ff. Cf. Sinclair (1988), 50ff., who rightly emphasizes, public and private notwithstanding, that the maintenance of the oikos was always fundamental to the values of every Athenian citizen.

[56] See Loraux (1986), 263ff. for an interpretation synthesizing the "real" and the "ideal."

period. The issue is further complicated by changes throughout the time span considered here, for it is easy to imagine that citizens' participation and their reasons for doing so were different in different years.[57] For example, comparisons between the fifth and fourth centuries traditionally portray political life of the latter marked by "less patriotism, less unity, and a reduced sense of community."[58] This plausible interpretation has been seriously challenged in recent years; yet few would doubt that the character of public life in the Athenian polis after the end of the Peloponnesian War (404/3) was different than before.[59]

Of course, during any period of the democracy, the social class, financial security, and distance a citizen lived from Athens would have affected both his ability and willingness to participate in the *ekklēsia*, *dikastēria*, or *boulē*. Generalizations based on the limited evidence of the fifth century are difficult.[60] Recent prosopographical analysis for the fourth century, however, has demonstrated that the majority of the most politically active men belonged to the wealthier classes of society, and tended to come from demes either in or near the

---

[57] Sinclair (1988), 22–23, 191–92, and passim handles this sensitively.

[58] Quotation from Fisher (1976), 45.

[59] See above, n. 15. On the issue of contrast/continuity between the fifth- and fourth-century democracy, see also generally Jones (1957), 23ff.; Mossé (1973), 5ff.; Davies (1978), 165ff.; Rhodes (1980); Hansen (1987b); Strauss (1987); Ober (1989), 91ff.

[60] Sources such as Ar. *Vesp.* and Ps. Xen. *Ath. Pol.* 2–6 are often cited to uphold the belief that members of the assembly and courts were full of "poor, unemployed or those with menial jobs" (Fisher [1976], 31), and certainly the political activity of such men as Kleon in the later fifth century supports this notion (on which see Connor [1971], 87ff.). Interpretation of literary evidence for the fourth century, despite more plentiful references, has its own share of problems; some texts seem to reflect a lower-class bias in the democratic audiences of speakers (Isoc. 7.54; Dem. 14.24–27, 21.182), whereas others seem directed to men who are materially comfortable and even well-to-do (Dem. 1.6, 2.24, 21.83ff., 22.47ff.). Doubtless different circumstances and occasions drew different audiences: see Fisher (1976), 31–45; and Sinclair (1988), 106ff. For some sound criticism of the view that the courts were an arena of continuing class struggle between leisured and working classes, Garner (1987), 64–66.

city.[61] It is also clear that throughout the classical period, though the *ekklēsia* reputedly embodied "all Athenians," in practice it was certainly attended by less than all.[62] Probably many poorer, rural men, especially those from distant demes, could not or did not regularly participate in the centralized decision-making and judicial processes of the community.[63]

Nonetheless, the frequency of meetings of the *boulē* (nearly daily), *ekklēsia* (at least forty times a year), and *dikastēria* (several days per month throughout the year) would have provided many opportunities for even the rural Athenian to join in *ta politika*, though perhaps he would have done so only on an occasional basis.[64] The sheer numbers of people needed to

[61] Members of the *boulē*: Rhodes (1972a), 4–6, stressing a "bias towards the rich" (and projecting the same for the fifth century). Proposers (*rhētores*) in the assembly: R. Osborne (1985a), 65–72, stressing the power of a "restricted and wealthy social group." *Rhētores, stratēgoi*, dikasts: Hansen (1983b), stressing relative proximity to Athens. For a more extreme view of the latter see Kluwe (1976), 298. Cf. also the remarks of Ruschenbusch (1985); Hansen (1985b), 59–60; (1987b), 8–12; Garner (1987), 64ff.; Sinclair (1988), 106–14. Markle (1985) and Ober (1989), 127ff. offer more "democratic" interpretations.

[62] Hansen (1982b) cites Ar. *Ach.* 1–25; Thuc. 8.72; Lys. 12.75; Aeschin. 3.125–26, Dem. *Ep.* 1.1; and argues for the spatial limitations of the Pnyx. See also Hansen (1987b), 8–19.

[63] The point is stressed by R. Osborne (1985b), 64ff. who also discusses literary evidence such as Ar. *Georgoi* F 1 and Theophr. *Char.* 4 for the non-political mentality of rural farmers. For arguments along similar lines see Carter (1986), 78–98; Bleicken (1986), 355ff.; Sinclair (1988), 114–19; *contra* Forrest (1966), 31ff.; Strauss (1987), 59ff.; and others. My point here is not whether poor, rural citizens *ever* participated in the public affairs of Athens (clearly they did), but whether they did so with great regularity (which I doubt, as do those just cited). Hansen offers an important corrective to the belief that such men *never* attended, for example, the assembly: see (1983b) and (1987b), 8ff. arguing (against modern assumptions) for the likely willingness of rural Athenians to walk several hours in a day to participate in the *ekklēsia*. Hansen (1987b), 16ff. is also persuasive in arguing that, because most *ekklēsiai* did not last an entire day, and, in the fourth century, pay for attendance seems to have been reasonable compensation (see also Markle [1985]), the burden of participation depicted by many scholars may be exaggerated. Indeed, by Hansen's view more citizens in the fourth century attended the assembly than citizens in the age of Perikles.

[64] Meetings of the *boulē*: *Ath. Pol.* 43.3 with Rhodes (1972a), 30; (1981),

staff the different bodies in any given year also argue for significant participation. The combined total of the quorum for the *ekklēsia* (6,000), the annual panel of jurors (6,000), annual *bouleutai* (500), and the 700 different domestic *archai* mentioned by *Ath. Pol.* 24.3 gives one pause when measured against an adult male population of only about 40,000 in 431 and perhaps half that number in the fourth century.[65] In the

---

521; Mikalson (1975), 196–98. *Ekklēsia: Ath. Pol.* 43.3–4 with Rhodes (1981), 521–31; and Hansen (1977a) who argues for even greater frequency because of the demands of *eisangelia* trials. (In [1987b], 20–24, 196ff. Hansen presents a more complex picture, segmented according to different periods of the democracy, and *contra* Harris [1986].)

Meetings of the *boulē* were probably less frequent before the reforms of Ephialtes (462/1); the increase thereafter was perhaps paralleled by an increase in the number of meetings of the *ekklēsia*, which had originally only convened once per prytany: see Rhodes (1981), 521 for references. Cf. Hansen (1978), 143; and (1985b), 63 for a challenge to the view. On the ongoing business of the courts, Ps. Xen. *Ath. Pol.* 3.6, 3.8 with Rhodes (1981), 658; see Thuc. 1.77.1 and Ar. *Vesp.* on the Athenian love of litigation. Hansen (1979d) argues that courts sat approximately 150–200 days a year, on the same days each month except for annual festival days. For discussion of the Athenian "working days" and the demands made by service in the juries and *boulē*, see also Sinclair (1988), 225–26; on the general role of the courts in fostering civic participation, Maio (1983).

[65] Quorum of *ekklēsia:* Hansen (1982b) and (1987b), 14–18; cf. (1976b), 115–34. Annual jury panel: Rhodes (1981), 702–3. *Boulē:* Rhodes (1972a), 1–48. *Archai:* Hansen (1980b) who stresses the part-time nature of many officials' responsibilities. The list of staffing omits, of course, the various overseas officials and military personnel also mentioned by *Ath. Pol.* (though there were probably not 700 of them, as claimed in the text: Rhodes [1981] 305). At the same time, in fairness it must be mentioned that the requirements of the various democratic bodies did not necessarily call for separate groups of Athenians since, for example, the same citizen might serve as an officer and attend the assembly.

For population figures, see Hansen (1982a). Patterson (1981), 29ff., in an excellent demographic analysis, proposes a population of 40,000–45,000 in the year 450 B.C. (with references to older literature on the subject); Strauss (1987), 73 reckons about the same for the year 431. For the fourth century, see also Ruschenbusch (1981) and Rhodes (1984a). In (1985b), (1987b), and (1988) Hansen argues that the number of citizens living in fourth-century Attika was closer to 30,000, down from about 60,000 in the 450s. See Strauss (1987), 70ff. for specific treatment of the impact of the Peloponnesian War on the fifth-century population. Even if Hansen's higher fifth-century number

case of the *boulē*, for example, when one figures in the requirement that members had to be over thirty years old, calculations of the available age cohort on the basis of preindustrial
population models indicate that it was "possible just barely to
run the council constitutionally" in the fourth century; almost
all citizens above thirty must have served a year at least once
in their lives.[66]

If Perikles' speech about the Athenians' willingness to partake of public life represented an ideal, it was nonetheless an
ideal that many men would have been able to at least approach under the democracy. Everything about the democratic constitution encouraged an ethos of public participation—the selection of most officials by lot, their accountability
before the people, the decision-making power of the *dēmos*,
popular jury courts, and pay for public service.[67] Furthermore, even if the "typical" citizen's involvement in the civic
bodies in Athens was neither constant nor regular, there were
still many other possible manifestations of his sharing in the
polis. Military service, attendance at state cults and festivals,
and participation in the assemblies and duties of one's local
deme all contributed to the citizen's active role in the politeia.[68]

Some additional indication of the meaning and significance
of the public sphere can be garnered from contemporary attitudes about a few of the values and obligations of citizenship.
Although every Athenian lived "the life of a citizen" in his own
way, the cultural assumptions and morality of the society per-
ceptible in Attic comedy and discourse lend credence to both
Perikles' vision of politeia and what the laws themselves leg-

---

is correct (*contra* most other scholars), the requirements for civic offices and
institutions were clearly still a substantial draw on the citizen population.

[66] Quotation from Hansen (1983b), 231; cf. Rhodes (1981), (1984); Sinclair (1988), 106–14.

[67] On these "core democratic institutions" and their role in encouraging
civic participation, Sinclair (1988), 17ff.

[68] For further discussion along the same lines, Finley (1983), 70–84, 140–
41. See also Goldhill (1986), 57ff. who paints a vivid picture of public life in
the classical period; Loraux (1986), 263ff.

islated about it.[69] First, the important point that those laws, and laws in general, needed to be obeyed. The good citizen of all classes is typically portrayed as displaying restraint, decency, and respect for order; contempt is heaped on the man who engages in illegal and antisocial behavior, *paranomia*.[70] The speaker in Lysias' speech *On the Murder of Eratosthenes* appealed to popular sympathies when he reported his final words to the adulterer caught in his wife's bed: "It is not I but the law (*nomos*) of the polis that will now kill you. . . . You preferred to commit this foul offense against my wife and children rather than obey the laws and behave like a decent man (*kosmios*)" (Lys. 1.26).

The importance of the laws to the citizen, of course, stemmed from their moral and social value. That value, an omnipresent theme in the literature of the period, is succinctly summed up by the speaker in Demosthenes 25.17: "For two reasons, all laws are established: to hinder men from doing anything wrong (*mē dikaion*), and to ensure that the punishment of wrongdoers makes the rest of men better (*beltious*)." Moreover, for the citizen lawfulness demanded not only his obedience to the *nomoi* of the polis but also to those of the gods; Perikles had boasted of the Athenian citizen's respect for both written and unwritten laws.[71] The business of *ta politika*

[69] For an approach toward, and a defense of, interpreting popular morality on the basis of such evidence, see Dover (1974), 1–45; and Fisher (1976), 1–45 on whose work much of the following is based. See also Sinclair (1988), 191ff.

If I am guilty of oversimplifying or giving undue emphasis to certain Athenian attitudes, I offer as partial apology Dover's own defense (1974), 2: "To understand Greek morality it is certainly necessary to become capable of looking at morality through Greek eyes, but it is necessary also to switch off and become ourselves again whenever we want to know what, if anything, they thought about issues which are important to us." For a similar perspective, see also Humphreys (1983f), x and, for the Greeks' own bias in this regard (1983g).

[70] Fisher (1976), 42–45; cf. Finley (1983), 135–36.

[71] Thuc. 2.37.3, quoted earlier. That the written and unwritten laws were sometimes in conflict is a competing theme, of course: Sophokles' *Antigone* provides the most famous example, but see also Dover (1974), 255ff. for other examples and discussions.

and citizenship required the frequent swearing of divine oaths, and piety was an essential civic virtue.[72] As a typical speaker reminded the jurors who had sworn by the names of Zeus, Poseidon, and Demeter: "When you are judging a case on which a man's life depends, do not transgress the law (*paranomein*), but act piously (*eusebein*)" (Lys. F 39).

Another commonly endorsed value in the public sphere was one's military duty to safeguard the polis. Defenses against any kind of accusation routinely included an appeal to the citizen's past military service. Thus, for example, Lysias 16.17: "In all other campaigns and guard watches, I never once was absent; I always marched out in the front rank and retreated in the last. Surely it is by such criteria that you ought to judge those who live the life of the citizen with a love of honor and orderliness (*philotimōs kai kosmiōs politeuomenous*)."

Financial duties followed close behind military obligations. Although the burden of taxes evoked a certain amount of griping,[73] shouldering the burden was always a way to underscore one's contribution to the public good.[74] Similarly, dodging the burden was a cause for serious scorn: "Will you let go free the son of such parents, a man who has never been in anyway useful to the polis, no more than his father or any of his other relatives? What horse, what naval ship, what chorus, what liturgy, what special levy, what bit of goodwill, or risk undertaken on their part has our polis ever seen from any of them?" (Dem. 19.281–82).

In general, it was an accepted principle that a citizen should be "useful" (*chrēsimos*) to the polis.[75] Whether fulfilling his

[72] Civic oaths sworn on the witness of gods: heliastic oath sworn by jurors, Dem. 24.149–51 with Rhodes (1981), 696. Bouleutic oath: Rhodes (1972a), 131–32, 191–96. Oath of archons: *Ath. Pol.* 7.1, 55.5 with Rhodes (1981), 135, 620–21. Ephebic oath: Siewert (1977). On piety as a moral virtue for the citizen see Dover (1974), 250–54; and cf. Thuc. 6.27ff. on public dismay at the religious sacrilege of the herms on the eve of the Sicilian expedition in 415.

[73] Xen. *Oec.* 2.5ff.; Isoc. 8.128; Theophr. *Char.* 26.6.

[74] Fisher (1976), 26–30; Finley (1983), 37.

[75] Dover (1974), 296–99.

military or financial obligations, serving as an official, or coming forward to speak in the assembly (e.g., Dem. 18.170ff.), the "good citizen" endeavored to bring honor to himself, even at the cost of personal sacrifice. By the fourth century this striving for recognition in the public eye had become an almost formulaic concept, expressed as *philotimia*, "love of honor," but also meaning "zealous ambition on behalf of the community." The word is ubiquitous in honorary decrees and oratory.[76] The speaker of Lycurgus 1.15 characterizes his fellow Athenians accordingly: "You, men of Athens, differ above all from the rest of humanity in behaving piously toward the gods, dutifully toward your parents, and *philotimōs* toward your homeland."

The confluence of individual honor and benefit for the community represented by *philotimia* points once again to the Periklean ideal of the citizen's willingness to turn his private life to the goals of the polis. The inverse of that individual willingness to give was the public willingness to take; the democratic polis, as already noted, was capable of assuming certain traditional concerns of the family (oikos) such as burial of the dead and the maintenance of orphans. Over time, the polis' assumption of once private concerns affected each man's status and behavior as a citizen. So, for example, under the democracy personal morality ceased to be "personal" because of its perceived relevance to a man's engagement in *ta politika*. Under Athenian law, for instance, prostitution disqualified a man from all aspects of public life (Aesch. 1.19–20); similarly, a *rhētōr* (politician or proposer of a decree)[77] was forbidden to speak before the assembly if he had maltreated his parents or squandered his family inheritance. "It did not seem possible," said Aeschines, "to the lawgiver [Solon] that a man who was a scoundrel in his private affairs could be useful in public service" (1.28–30). Perhaps the ulti-

---

[76] On this concept, and other individual civic virtues such as *andragathia*, *aretē*, *dikaiosynē*, *eusebeia*, see Whitehead (1983), 243ff.

[77] For the various meanings of this word, Hansen (1983a), 37–42.

mate intrusion of the public polis into the private oikos was the classical law that prescribed the conditions for marriage and legitimacy within the politeia: Perikles' law of 451/50 mandated that Athenian citizenship would ever after depend on birth not only from an Athenian father (as before), but also from an Athenian mother, and the principle of double endogamy was upheld and strengthened in subsequent years under the democracy.[78]

Yet the intrusion of the polis into the affairs of the oikos was not total, and the relationship between public and private in the classical age, for all its overlap, also revealed a certain tension. The laws and public functions of citizenship in practice were never completely divorced from the older customs of family and regional traditions. Though it was the deme that "officially" registered a citizen at age eighteen, it was a phratry (a predemocratic kinship corporation) that "unofficially" registered most Athenian children shortly after their birth.[79] Because of this, and despite this group's unofficial standing, phratry members were sometimes called upon to substantiate the origins of a citizen challenged for his membership in the polis.[80] A prime example of the potential conflict between the

---

[78] On the setting and details of the law, Patterson (1981), 27ff.; on its status in the fourth century, Whitehead (1986b), 109–12. As is generally agreed, however, the law seems to have lapsed briefly due to manpower shortage during the Peloponnesian War: Dem. 57.30; Eumelos F 2 in Schol. Aeschin. 1.39; Patterson (1981), 140ff.; M. Osborne (1983), 152, 184; Whitehead (1986b), 109; Sinclair (1988), 24–25; *contra* Walters (1983).

[79] On phratries in general, see chapter 3. For the purpose of discussion, I have oversimplified the distinction between the "official" deme and "unofficial" phratry. Such terms an Athenian would probably never use, and they imply exactly the kind of rigid, bureaucratic state that I am laboring to set apart from the more fluid and simple world of the polis. Nonetheless, some distinction must be drawn, given the import of the Kleisthenic reforms (discussed in Chapter 7). I follow the opinion of most historians about the legal role of the deme in determining citizenship after 508/7; similarly, I assume that most, but not necessarily all, Athenians belonged to a phratry. For a concise statement of these views, with references, see Rhodes (1981), 68–71. On the (much debated) details of presentation of children to phratries, see S. Cole (1984), 233–37; Golden (1985).

[80] Dem. 57.54, 59.59; MacDowell (1978), 70.

traditions of the family and the authority of the polis' deme organization is the record of the trial preserved in Demosthenes 57.[81] The speaker Euxitheos, rejected as a citizen by the members of his deme, is at pains to prove (before a *dikastērion* in the city) his Athenian origins based on the testimony of kin, phratry members, and an appeal to ancient family tombs in Attika. The persistence of older tradition perhaps also explains why candidates for the archonship were asked not only about their demes and parents' demes, but also whether they had cults of the oikos, Apollo Patroos and Zeus Herkeios, and family tombs (*Ath. Pol.* 55.2).[82] Athens never had any central list of all its citizens, nor was it ever securely known by anyone exactly how many citizens belonged to the polis.[83]

The legacy of custom and family traditions in the politeia can be detected in other practices as well. A recent study has demonstrated the continued survival of the archaic traditions of "ritualised guest friendship" (*xenia*) among some Athenian families and those of other states during the classical period. Though by then polis loyalty had mostly superseded such "private networks" born in an earlier age, it never completely dissolved them—with the effect that "traitorous acts" per-

[81] R. Osborne (1985a), 146–53.

[82] On the archon's oath, Apollo Patroos, Zeus Herkeios, and family tombs: Rhodes (1981), 66–67, 617–18 with other references; on the purpose of this *dokimasia*, Adeleye (1983). Humphreys (1983e), in an important and thoughtful article, challenges the long-standing view traceable to Fustel de Coulanges (*La Cité antique*) that cults of ancient family tombs were an integral part of the early history of oikoi; Humphreys holds that they were a cultural phenomenon of the fourth century and later. Though many of her arguments have yet to be answered, the mention of family tombs in the archons' oath—clearly an ancient formula (cf. *Ath. Pol.* 7.1 where it is at least as old as Solon)—needs to be better explained (see Humphreys [1983e], 121) if we are to banish Fustel's assumptions about the antiquity of the practice. On a simpler level, however, even if Athenian families did not bury their dead in heroic-style cult groupings, a citizen's claim to any tradition of burial of kin in Attika would have stood as good evidence for his "native" rather than "foreign" status. On Fustel de Coulanges, see A. Momigliano's and Humphreys's edition (in translation) of *La Cité antique* (1980), ixff. On Attic family graves in the eighth century, see now Sourvinou-Inwood (1983).

[83] Hansen (1985b), 14.

formed by aristocrats such as Alkibiades on behalf of foreign guest friends could be treated with ambivalence by Athenian contemporaries.[84]

Grants of citizenship to foreigners represent another example of social traditionalism in the civic sphere. These, as already noted, provided for the honorand's enrollment in an Athenian tribe and deme. But typically (there are a few exceptions) the decrees also provided for the honorand's enrollment in a phratry—not, once again, the official or necessary credential, but probably a characteristic and traditional mark of membership in the community.[85] It is also interesting that although such grants *de iure* endowed their beneficiaries with a complement of legal rights and obligations, the standard formula of these decrees makes no specific mention of what the new status actually entailed. The award of the politeia is direct, but vague, proclaiming only *einai auton Athēnaion:* "he is to be Athenian."[86]

The simplicity of this phrase, and the nontechnical mentality behind it, harks back to an earlier age when membership in the community needed no regulation by law, and when oikos, family burials in Attika, and kinship groupings were the determining factors of "belonging" to the society of Athenians. This raises the question of what citizenship meant before the age of democracy. Thus far, I have offered a relatively static "snapshot" spanning the classical age (a compromise

[84] Herman (1987), esp. 116ff. For another example of the ambivalence, note the opposing accusations of Demosthenes and Aeschines in Dem. 18.109, 19.189–90, 248; and Aeschin. 3.224–25 with Herman (1987), 3–4.

[85] See M. Osborne (1983), 158ff. who postulates that the exceptions of no enrollment in a phratry (e.g., the enfranchisement of the Plataians in 427) were cases of block rather than individual grants (see esp. pp. 175–82). Conversely, Hansen (1985b), 74ff. argues on the basis of phratry membership specified in most grants of citizenship to foreigners that this continued as a requirement even after the reforms of Kleisthenes.

[86] M. Osborne (1983), 155–56; the formula changed sometime in the 230s (after more than 200 years!) to *dedosthai autōi kai politeian*, i.e., "he has been granted citizenship"; as Osborne notes (with references), elsewhere in Greece the formula in the classical period was *einai auton politēn:* "he is to be a citizen."

for the sake of discussion), and have treated the concept of citizenship as a reflection of the Athenian democratic ethos and institutions. Yet Athens had not always been a democracy; nor perhaps had its citizenship always been the same. Is it fair to talk about citizenship in earlier times? If so, what was it? And when did it emerge?

Most previous scholarship in this area has not addressed such questions, and tends to portray citizenship as a primarily legal institution, timeless and unchanged through history except for revisions of certain statutory details.[87] Legal distinctions did indeed exist between Athenians and non-Athenians in the classical age—but how and when did those distinctions arise? Similarly, the nonlegal qualities of citizenship are readily seen in the democratic period—in the wide range of examples of "civic spirit" and in the willingness of individuals to identify themselves with the good of the polis and not just the good of their personal and familial goals. Here again, how and when did that sensibility emerge, and can it be seen in any form before the age of Perikles?[88] If so, was early citizenship something different than just being a free male inhabitant of Attika?

CITIZENSHIP, POLIS, AND METHODOLOGY

To answer these questions, and to understand the origins of membership in the polis, one must inquire into the origins and development of the polis itself. In the pages that follow I investigate the essential qualities of the polis and evaluate the stages through which it passed before it became the classical form of "state" in Perikles' day. The analysis at the same time

---

[87] Philippi (1870); Szanto (1892); Müller (1899); Ledl (1907–8); McGregor (1973); Paoli (1976). For exceptions to this general perspective, and for valuable work stressing the continuity of Athenian legal development, see Humphreys (1983a), (1983h), (1985a), (1985b); Sealey (1987). See also R. Osborne (1985b) who offers salutary comments on the importance of understanding Athenian law in its social context.

[88] Note, e.g., how Patterson's otherwise excellent study (1981) of Perikles' citizenship law of 451/50 and its background neglects this issue.

illuminates the evolution of the concept of citizenship; as the
polis took more tangible form, so did membership in it, and
so evolved the meaning and significance of being an Athenian
citizen.[89]

Much of the inspiration of this study derives from the work
of political anthropologists who have examined the evolution
of primitive states.[90] In the course of investigating recent or
current preindustrial societies, they have observed how a diverse and unconnected population is gradually brought into
regulated political organization. Slowly, central authority
emerges; as the organization becomes more sophisticated, the
society becomes, to our way of thinking, less primitive, and
membership acquires more tangible significance. In what follows, I suggest that the same pattern can provide a guide to
help us reconstruct the history of the Athenian polis.[91]

This perspective requires further discussion, for the word
"evolution" will sound warning bells for at least some readers.
More than a few twentieth-century anthropologists have built
careers by debunking predecessors who imposed evolutionary
models on societies they studied. Many classicists today exhibit their own skepticism toward any approach that can be
similarly labeled. On such grounds alone, for example, Fustel
de Coulanges's *Ancient City* is dismissed as a naive if charm-
ing nineteenth-century period piece. Indeed, much of the criticism of the early evolutionists—Fustel, H. S. Maine, Morgan,
and others—is justified, particularly in view of the limits and

---

[89] I first set forth this idea in Manville (1979). A similar perspective also
underlies Morris (1987). On the personal significance of citizenship, cf. the
comments of Carter (1986), 1: "Because of the intimate connection between
the security of the individual and that of the city, it follows that there was no
existence outside the social existence, no reality outside the social reality;
hence the greater one's participation in that social reality, the greater one's
sense of self."

[90] E.g., R. Cohen, and Middleton (1970); Service (1975); Claessen and
Skalnik (1978); R. Cohen (1978a). Starr (1986), 42–46 follows a similar
course.

[91] For a similar approach, though with different results, see Starr (1986),
42–46. See also Runciman (1982) for another anthropological model applied
to the problem.

misconceptions of their methods: rigid, grossly connotative schema and Victorian ethnocentrism that defined the past as a slow march toward modern Christian man. As a group, they erred in devising unilineal theories that assumed all societies pass through the same stages of development.[92]

Today we know that all societies do not follow the same patterns, but this understanding does not undermine the value of an evolutionary framework for describing political development. Such is the perspective of the so-called neo-evolutionist anthropologists whose thinking has informed much of my own about ancient Athens. The emergence and advances of this school since the 1950s can be credited to the rejection of self-serving ethnocentric and unilineal theories, and to the development of more sophisticated conceptualizations of the evolutionary model. Stripped of its older connotations, "evolution" can now be understood in a general sense as a study of processes (such as a society's increased specialization or intensification of production) and, in a more specific sense, as, for example, the historical sequence of institutional forms.[93] The general and specific concepts are complementary; taken together they offer a perspective that I have found valuable in understanding the origins of the polis. The evolutionism of this book is not, categorically, intended to imply some era-by-era degeneration of noble primitives or any kind of inevitable progression of the Greeks toward modern Judeo-Christian culture. Rather, I see "evolution" as a means of discussing a series of interconnected social and historical changes that gave rise to a political innovation worthy of study, and indeed of our admiration.[94]

[92] For some representative critiques of the early evolutionists, see Leach (1982), 16–17; Lewellen (1983), 2–4; I. Lewis (1985), 36–46; cf. Momigliano and Humphreys (1980), iiff.

[93] Sahlins and Service (1960); Lewellen (1983), 9–11.

[94] Cf. Humphreys's use of the word "evolution" (legal) in her discussion of early Athenian law (1983h) to mean "a specific historical process in which changes are consciously introduced by reformers whose perceptions of the defects of existing legal institutions, and of the ways they can be overcome, are formed in definable historical circumstances and political situations" (p. 229).

Political neo-evolutionism, however, has only taken me part of the way. There are other debts to anthropology that I should acknowledge, specifically in my use of comparative material to help reconstruct a picture of archaic Attic life. To grasp the interconnected social and historical developments behind the origins of citizenship and the polis, one must attempt to imagine what early Athenian society was really like. The barrier, of course, is that the evidence for the preclassical period, especially details of social relations, is exceedingly sparse. Archaeologists have made great strides not only in unearthing and analyzing new material remains, but also in using them to think anew about the nature of archaic society.[95] Of course, the material record is usually ambiguous at best, and we are a long way from having all the artifacts needed to fully comprehend life in archaic Attika.

Yet, whatever the limitations of the new archaeologically intensive approaches, they have certainly improved upon the older, standard reconstructions of early social history. The latter, stressing mostly the sketchy literary evidence relevant to the period, produced logical but highly artificial pictures of archaic culture. For some of the traditional interpreters, life in preclassical Attika was a lineal, rational antecedent of life in the better-documented classical period; for others, it was a distinct and almost abstract social world, which, in the face of so few ancient "facts," they created out of a priori, modernistic assumptions about "the way things must have been."

As a defense against such assumptions, and as an inspiration for some that I hope are more valid, I have turned frequently to studies of other preindustrial societies. Today, any historian of archaic Greece must call upon both the (old) literary and (new) archaeological evidence, but at the same time one must also provide a context that gives meaning to the evidence. A judicious use of anthropology can serve this end. On one hand, my recourse to various ethnological monographs

---

[95] Examples include the pioneering work of Snodgrass (1977), (1980), (1986a); Coldstream (1977); Cartledge (1977), (1979); R. Osborne (1985a); and Morris (1987).

has been a constant reminder that a society's events and institutions do not necessarily match the "reason" of ours today, and that all societies do not necessarily develop along the same, "logical" lines. On the positive side, anthropological comparisons have helped me think more creatively about interpreting the preclassical evidence; in some cases, I have argued on the basis of analogy to fill out a picture of early Athenian social life beyond what a narrow interpretation of the sources would allow.[96]

This use of analogy will no doubt trouble academically conservative readers. But every historian must tell a story and the story of early archaic society has so many gaps that without some guessing there can be no narrative. If I am guilty of occasionally complementing analysis with a little anthropologically aided imagination, I have done so only when the proposed reconstruction fits well with what is securely known from the Greek literary and material record. In writing history about a period marked by so few facts, the advance of knowledge must more than usual turn on setting the terms of debate. Certainly many of the debates about preclassical Attika are in need of new frameworks; it is here that I have found anthropology to be such a valuable aid.

I readily acknowledge that in comparing different societies, one runs the risk of seeing parallels where none exist, or of misinterpreting aspects of one society and thus mismatching them to those of the second. There is an obvious danger in drawing comparisons, as for example I have done, between twentieth-century Zambian or Nigerian tribesmen and the inhabitants of preclassical Attika. In such cases, the key problem is not so much in understating the differences (those are usually clear, especially at the superficial level) but rather in overstating the similarities. In fact, the difficulties really arise in simply identifying similarities; for the process by which one does so inevitably depends on one's point of view about the

[96] On making anthropological comparisons in Greek history, Starr (1986), 18; Strauss (1989); see also the remarks of Cartledge (1985), 20–21 on comparative historical method. For some special skepticism, D. Engels (1984), 389–90; Finley (1986a), 112–18.

organizational principles of any given society, and how the observer understands them.[97]

The theoretical underpinning of observing and interpreting social organization generates its own (huge) ideological debate, one well beyond the bounds of this study. I am no professional anthropologist, and do not claim to bring any new contribution to the ongoing theoretical discussions of relevant methodology. In this book I tend to follow the thinking of one general school whose interpretation of the nature of societies I find reasonable and useful. When comparing the archaic Athenian and other preindustrial societies, I generally adopt a so-called functionalist perspective, drawing upon (and thus influenced by) several studies of functional anthropologists.

That is perhaps not surprising, given that functionalism helped pave the way for the progression from nineteenth-century theory to the political neo-evolutionism that I have also embraced. The functionalist approach, whose origins are generally credited to Edward Tylor, and which subsequently developed along different axes under Durkheim, Malinowski, and A. R. Radcliffe-Brown, takes its name from the fundamental principle that "things are what they do."[98] Social phenomena, according to this outlook, are derived from their function in the cultural context. Thus, by appreciating the functionality of social processes and institutions, one can best understand their workings, and make society-to-society comparisons toward that end. My core assumption might be stated as the following simple principle: human beings through history and around the world sometimes create simi-

[97] For a good discussion of this point, Finley (1986a), 112–18; cf. Humphreys (1983f), x.

[98] I. Lewis (1985), 60. For the purpose of this brief discussion, I do not distinguish between the various divergent subdisciplines of functionalism, e.g., structural functionalism, as embodied in the work of Radcliffe-Brown and followers, and so-called psychobiological or common sense functionalism, as in Malinowski and others. In fact, in the course of subsequent chapters, I draw from a range of functionalist studies, as anthropologically sophisticated readers will note. On the historical development of different functionalist interpretations and methods, I. Lewis (1985); Leach (1982), 24–37.

lar institutions, sometimes find similar solutions to similar problems, sometimes adhere to similar customs, especially in cultures devoid of modern technology and rigid political organization—and sometimes we can learn from such comparisons. Much of this book embodies this "habit of thought."[99]

By contrast, and against some current trends, I have not undertaken to probe my subject according to another school of anthropology, structuralism. Structuralism (derived from Lévi-Strauss, and especially as represented by the genre of semiotic interpretation) is becoming increasingly popular among historians; it is a many-faceted and rich approach to culture, focusing on "the semantic patterning of concepts which operate as normative ideas."[100] In the hands of its most able practitioners, structuralism is a tool with which one gains access to the conceptual world of a society;[101] in more radical form, it has been compared to a sort of psychoanalysis that treats "cultures as patients who expose their souls in their myth-dreams."[102]

I do not doubt that a series of lively expositions of Athenian culture related to the polis and citizenship could be written from a structuralist perspective. Indeed, a few already exist, and, although this is not a structuralist study, their influence on at least some of my thinking will be recognizable.[103] Notwithstanding, my general aim here has not been to try to uncover the more subjective "social unconscious" underlying early citizenship (an uncertain proposition, given the paucity of workable material in the preclassical period), but simply to understand, and present in a coherent story, the interplay among the institutions, human events, explicit ideas, and processes by which it came to be.

My historicist bias is obvious, and on one level is at odds

[99] The phrase is borrowed from Finley (1986a), 118.
[100] Leach (1982), 131.
[101] Geertz (1973), 24.
[102] I. Lewis (1985), 125.
[103] E.g., works ("structuralist" to varying degrees) by Detienne, Goldhill, Lévêque, Loraux, Morris, Ober, Vernant, Vidal-Naquet, Winkler, and others, cited in the References.

with the synchronic tendencies of not only structuralism but also functionalism. Synchronic interpretation can be a valuable index of social reality, but in my opinion it is not in itself history, which is what this book intends to be. Accordingly, I suggest that my use of anthropology represents an enhancement of, and not a substitute for, a narrative that chronicles a series of changes—in this case leading to what I have defined as formal membership in the special sociopolitical entity called a polis.[104]

The polis in fact represents not the end but the beginning of our inquiry, and it is to the polis that we must now turn. For until we understand what made a polis, we cannot search for its Athenian origins. Nor indeed for the origins of Athenian citizenship.

[104] I would like to count myself among those historians who have been striving to achieve a synthesis between anthropological-style synchronic analysis and "old-fashioned" political history. See my comments in Manville (1979) and those of Finley (1986a), 109–12; Humphreys (1985a), 257–59; Strauss (1989); Ober and Strauss (1990).

Chapter Two

IN SEARCH OF THE POLIS

"I AM Athenian," said the proud citizen of classical Athens; "I share in the polis." His conception and exercise of citizenship were bound intimately to the world of his polis, and we now need to examine the Athenian polis itself. As one looks for its beginnings, the quest for the origin of the community will necessarily provide clues about membership in it. When and how did Athens first become a polis?

The Athenians themselves do not provide much of an answer. No ancient commentator wrote about the historical invention of the polis, and it is likely that the average man in the agora would not have had much perspective on where it came from. If asked, he might say that as long as there had been Athenians there had been a polis—and that meant "always," since by their own legends Athenians were sprung indigenously from the soil of Attika.[1]

The historian looking back at early Greek society sees things more critically. The archaeological record reveals an earlier "Mycenaean" civilization in Attika, fundamentally distinct from the later society of the Geometric, archaic, and classical periods, and culturally separated from that latter era by the Dark Ages (approximately the twelfth to the tenth centuries) of relative "poverty, isolation, and illiteracy."[2] Though Athenians who lived in the polis of the fifth century were not conscious of any basic discontinuity in their past, it is all but

[1] Thuc. 1.2.5–6, 2.36.1; etc. See Loraux (1981), 35–73, 119–53; (1986), 148–50 for discussion and interpretation of myths of Athenian autochthony.

[2] Quotation from Coldstream (1977), 17; for a summary of arguments about the break between Mycenaean and post-Mycenaean civilization, Snodgrass (1980), 15ff.; (1982), 668–69; *contra* van Effenterre (1985), 19ff. on which see Snodgrass (1986b), whose views I hereafter follow. See also chapter 3.

certain that their particular form of community cannot be traced back (other than, perhaps, in name) to a heroic age or to the Mycenaean culture or indeed to anything that came before.[3] The polis had not "eternally existed" but came into being under real historical circumstances during some real historical period after the onset of the Dark Ages. That said, it remains to determine exactly when and why the "moment" occurred.

Here again, the question of definition arises. What in fact was a polis?[4] On purely etymological grounds, the term can be linked to *akropolis* or "citadel," and probably derived from the earlier Mycenaean form *ptolis*.[5] Classical writers used the word ambiguously, with *polis* sometimes referring to a "city" (as opposed to its surrounding countryside) and other times referring to a larger and more formal entity, usually translated as "state" or "city-state," implying a discrete but small political unit that comprised a central town and its adjacent territory.[6]

It is this latter meaning of "state" (rather than "city") that concerns us, although to invoke the word "state" can be misleading when one considers the premodern circumstances and assumptions surrounding the Greek polis. But how precisely can the polis be defined? At this point we must go beyond the *topos* of Nikias and others—the polis as its men—to say something more about the concept than the putative average Athenian in the agora. Is there some precise definition of "state" that can be applied to the city-state that will help determine when and how the polis grew out of the post–Dark Ages society?

---

[3] Andrewes (1982a), 360.

[4] For recent treatments of the subject, Ehrenberg (1969), with 256–59 for earlier scholarship and see also his classic article (1937); Austin and Vidal-Naquet (1977), 49–53; Starr (1977), 30ff. and (1986); Murray (1980), 57–68; Lévêque (1981); Gauthier (1981); Welwei (1983), 9–19; Coldstream (1984); Duthoy (1986). For a review of the German historiographic tradition of the concept, and an unconvincing attempt to portray the polis as only a modern ideal, Gawantka (1985).

[5] Morpurgo (1963), s.v. *ptolis*.

[6] Humphreys (1978), 130–35; Finley (1981b); de Ste. Croix (1981), 9–19.

Political theorists would say that there is: they have variously endeavored to develop a model of the "state" that transcends the particulars of individual historical cases. Unfortunately for our purposes, such models engender their own issues and problems, and typically stand at the center of (long-standing) ideological controversy. From Morgan to Engels to Weber to modern political anthropologists, the debate about the definition and origin of "the state" continues unresolved.[7] One school of thought (usually associated with Marxist theory, especially as formulated by Engels) sees the state as the outcome of a formation of classes in which an upper or ruling elite obtains control over the means of production; the state is the instrument for maintaining this control.[8] A second group of definitions focuses on the structure of the governmental system itself, seeing, for example, the state as a "centralized and hierarchical system of authority relations in which local political units lose their autonomy, becoming districts . . . subordinate to central government."[9] Other theorists simply define as a state any organized social system or human grouping that occupies a territory.[10]

Any of these definitions (and many others that have been proposed by theorists), could fit a city-state—but do such models really fit well enough?[11] Reading the words of such men as Perikles, and recalling the richness of such words as *politeia*, one cannot help believing that the Greek polis was something more than other states so defined, and indeed that it was even something more than other known city-states.

---

[7] E.g., Krader (1968); Finley (1981b); Claessen and Skalnik (1978); R. Cohen (1978a); Jonathan Haas (1982), 1–171.

[8] F. Engels (1891); Fried (1967), 186; (1978), 36. For a survey of this school, Jonathan Haas (1982), 34–58.

[9] Morgan (1877); Fortes and Evans-Pritchard (1940), 5–6; Service (1975), 8–9. Quotation from R. Cohen (1978a), 3, summarizing views of Hobhouse et al. (1915). See also Jonathan Haas (1982), 59–85 for a survey of related views that stress the integrative function of the state.

[10] Meyer (1921–25), 1:1, 5ff.; Lowie (1927); Koppers (1963).

[11] Starr (1986), 42ff. offers an interesting discussion of the two main models, and concludes in favor of adopting the integrative theory for the Greek polis.

Throughout history, and elsewhere in the world, peoples other than Greeks also formed themselves into city-states.[12] What was special about the Greek city-state? What were its essential characteristics?

The best source to answer these questions is Aristotle.[13] In his treatise the *Politics* he examines the character and qualities of the Greek polis, drawing upon the details of constitutions (politeiai) from several historical Greek states.[14] The *Politics*, however, is not a history of those specific states, and in the course of his discussion the philosopher comments on both the perfect form of state and imperfect, ordinary states, often without seeming to distinguish between them.[15] Such blending of the theoretical and empirical is typical of Aristotle's thought; it does not preclude our adapting his observations to determine the special nature of the historical Greek polis. For the general concept of the polis in itself represents a kind of ideal—no two historical poleis were exactly the same—and we must inevitably accept some mixture of theory and practice in a definition.[16]

"To be fellow citizens is to be sharers in one polis, and to have one polis is to have one place of residence" (*Pol.* 1260b 40–1261a 1). For Aristotle, the first requirement of the polis is that it embody a community of place, that is, members of the polis must share one locale.[17] But elsewhere in the *Politics*

---

[12] C. Thomas and Griffeth (1981); cf. Kirsten (1956).

[13] Huxley (1979); Cartledge (1980), 91–95; E. Lévy (1980); Bourriot (1984); Coldstream (1984); *contra* van Effenterre (1985), 24ff., and Farrar (1988), 271–73. Cf. Lord (1984), 22; and Snodgrass (1986b).

[14] Rhodes (1981), 1–2 with nn. 1–9; Arist. *Eth. Nic.* 1181b 12ff. On Aristotle's other historical sources; Weil (1960), 116ff.; Lloyd (1968), 246ff.; Rhodes (1981), 58–59. See also Brandt (1974).

[15] Boas (1943); von Fritz and Kapp (1950), 32–66; Weil (1965); Lloyd (1968), 248–58; Clark (1975), 130–44; Mulgan (1977), 13–14; Lord (1982), 26–28; cf. Lord (1984), 18–24. On Aristotle's mixture of the empirical and philosophical in political thought, see Irwin (1985).

[16] Austin and Vidal-Naquet (1977), 49.

[17] Newman (1887–1902) 1:90; Kornemann (1908); Ehrenberg (1969), 26–30; C. Thomas (1979). Under ideal conditions, the territory of a polis would be of only moderate size: Arist. *Pol.* 1326b 26–32, cf. Pl. *Resp.* 423b.

Aristotle makes clear that a polis need not be tied to that and only that locale, and in fact historical examples survive of citizens moving or threatening to move their polis from one site to another.

The Athenians themselves provide a famous case. In 480 an allied Greek fleet was assembled at the island of Salamis to fight the Persians. Knowing that some of the allies wanted to meet the enemy closer to their own homelands, the Athenian Themistokles confronted the Spartan commander and demanded that the Greek fleet remain near the coast of Attika as planned. If not, he warned, he would withdraw the contingent of Athenians from the allied force, and "put our families aboard our ships and sail for Siris in Italy." Herodotus tells us that the ultimatum was enough to make the Spartan commander order the fleet to stay and fight at Salamis (8.63); apparently, neither he nor the other Greeks at hand doubted that the Athenian polis could, in practice, move to a land that was not Attika. If the Athenians had carried out their threat, it would not have been the first time that an entire polis had migrated. Some sixty years before, the Ionian Greeks of Phokaia and Teos had moved their poleis (to Italian Elea and Thracian Abdera) in order to escape domination by the Persian king Cyrus (Hdt. 1.163–68).[18]

The intrinsic mobility of the polis derives from the human aspect of community implied in the "community of place." As in the famous *topos*, "it is men who are the polis," and this leads to the second condition of its nature: there must be citizens. "The polis," said Aristotle, "is a compound made up of citizens." The lengthy discussion of politeia in Book 3 of the *Politics* derives from the philosopher's perception that to understand the essence of the Greek city-state, one must first understand the nature of citizenship (1274b 38–1275a 2; cf. 1279a 21, 1295b 21).[19]

Does this second condition bring us full circle to the starting

[18] On nonterritorial aspects of the polis see C. Smith (1906–7); Hampl (1939). See also Starr (1986), 18–19 who discusses the polis-like behavior of the traveling Greek army in Xenophon's *Anabasis*.

[19] See the discussion of Mossé (1967).

point of the investigation? In seeking the origins of citizenship in the origins of the polis, perhaps it begs the question to search in turn for the polis in citizenship. That the two concepts converge remains an inescapable fact; nonetheless, this discussion can be made less circular once one appreciates an unspoken assumption behind them. Physically, the community of place implies an existence of spatial boundaries. The territory of a polis must have a definable limit that separates it from territory not part of the state. Similarly, the population of a community must be bounded in identity; the polis of citizens requires a formal standard to distinguish who is a member and who is not. In other words, if set criteria for membership in the polis are lacking, the polis itself lacks identity.[20]

In Book 3 of the *Politics*, Aristotle explores various possible definitions for citizenship, ultimately concluding that the citizen of the polis is one "who enjoys the right of sharing in deliberative or judicial office" (*Pol.* 1275b 18–20).[21] That condition might mean, for example in a democracy, a citizen's right to engage in the common assembly and public juries (*Pol.* 1274a 22–1275b 6). But Aristotle's definition also encompasses other forms of government in which citizens only selectively participate in public decision making (*Pol.* 1276b 13–17). Nonetheless, whatever the extent of citizens' privileges in a given state, Aristotle's criteria for citizenship still point to the need for a fixed standard; there must be agreed-upon rules (or laws) to determine who can and who cannot participate in the deliberative and judicial decisions.

Furthermore, two additional conditions for the polis seem to follow from Aristotle's discussion of citizenship. First, if the polis consists only of citizens, and if every citizen is an office holder (broadly defined), then the constitution that determines the holding of office will identify (and in fact define) the state.

---

[20] Boundaries of space and population for the polis and (in general) citizenship: Starr (1961), 338; R. Cohen and Middleton (1970), 15–17; Humphreys (1978), 130–35; Cartledge (1980), 92.

[21] The text is sometimes emended to make both offices a requirement. See Mulgan (1977), 143 for discussion. On Aristotle's conception of the citizen, Johnson (1984).

Thus if there is a fixed standard of citizenship, there must also be a formal constitution (both included under the term *politeia*), or the polis cannot truly exist.[22] Second, if the decision making belongs to the citizens, the polis must be autonomous—responsible for its own political affairs.[23]

In the same section of Book 3 where Aristotle defines the citizen, he proposes a concise definition of the city-state: "The polis, in its simplest terms, is a body of such persons adequate in number for achieving a self-sufficient existence" (*autarkeia: Pol.* 1275b 20–21).[24] The philosopher does not specify here exactly how many citizens make for *autarkeia*, although he suggests that the minimum number could be found in "several villages joined together in union" (*Pol.* 1252b 27–30; cf. 1325b 39ff.). More important than numbers, however, is the concept of "self-sufficiency" per se, for no matter how *autarkeia* is achieved, Aristotle perceives it to be an essential quality of the city-state. "The polis is not a mere casual group but one which is self-sufficient for the purposes of life" (*Pol.* 1328b 16–17). What does Aristotle mean by *autarkeia*?

A partial answer appears in Book 7 of the *Politics* when Aristotle discusses the services (*erga*) that every polis needs to provide in order to accomplish self-sufficiency. The *erga* comprise what might be called the economic, defensive, religious, and political functions of the state, and Aristotle lists six general needs that they must fulfill: the provision of food (*trophē*), the practice of arts and crafts (*technai*), the bearing of arms (*hopla*) for internal order and external defense, the provision of material wealth (*chrematōn tina euporian*) for domestic and military purposes, the establishment of worship of the gods (*tēn peri to theion epimeleian*), and most important, a

[22] Barker (1959), 302–7. For the various senses of politeia in Aristotle, see *Pol.* 1295a 40; 1289a 15–18; 1328a 41; Bordes (1982), 435–54.

[23] Ehrenberg (1969), 91ff.; Cartledge (1980), 92; Duthoy (1986), 7–9; cf. Arist. *Pol.* 1291a 8–10. I use the word "autonomous" here in a more general sense than the specialized meaning of *autonomia* whose origins Ostwald (1982) has traced to the relationship between Athens and her allies in the Delian League after 479.

[24] Cf. E. Lévy (1980), 229–30.

means to determine what is appropriate and what is just in men's dealings with one another (*krisin peri tōn sumpheron-tōn kai tōn dikaiōn pros allēlous: Pol.* 1328b 6–15).

On a practical level, these necessary services give further concrete meaning to Aristotle's conception of a polis. The provision of food would mean that the city-state requires a sufficient territory of arable land; that is, its area has to extend beyond the central urban settlement. The service of *technai* suggests that the society of the polis must include a division of labor to produce nonagricultural as well as agricultural necessities; the polis must be more than a community of farmers.[25] (In fact, at *Pol.* 1290b 39ff. Aristotle mentions the essential role of merchants and traders, i.e., self-sufficiency allows for the import and export of goods.)

The rest of the services all point to the need for centralized authority: a formal organization to administer an army, marshal resources, and provide for public cults.[26] There must also be centralized decision making for issues of public policy and the settlement of citizens' disputes. This final condition would similarly follow from Aristotle's definition of the citizen. If citizens have the right to participate in deliberative or judicial offices, one would expect the relevant institutions to conduct their business within easy reach of all—at a demographic (if not geographical) center of the state. Historically, of course, such business took place in the urban focus of the polis; and not surprisingly, when Aristotle postulates his ideal state, he

---

[25] In this discussion I have purposely omitted what many other historians and theorists have stressed, the integral role of slavery in the polis. The subject has generated a great deal of partisan heat in past scholarship, and the debate as to its true importance in the Greek polis continues to rage: see Finley (1980); Garlan (1982); Wood (1983) and (1988). At *Pol.* 1278a 1ff. Aristotle notes that slaves are "necessary conditions" (*hōn aneu ouk an eiē polis*) but not integral parts of the polis (cf. Farrar [1988], 271); slavery in itself need not be an essential part of our definition, and for this reason I have chosen not to include it here. Nonetheless, in chapter 6 I follow Finley (1980), 86ff. and others in believing in the general use of slavery in Attika after about 600, and its significant contribution to formation of boundaries between citizen and non-citizen.

[26] Coldstream (1984), 9–11 stresses the latter.

assumes that the central city will be the site of all political activities (*Pol.* 1330a 24–b 2).[27]

Autarkeia, with these provisions and their implications, thus provides additional key conditions for the Greek city-state; these are elements, says Aristotle, "without which the polis would not be" (*Pol.* 1328b 2–3). Yet Aristotle's conception of *autarkeia* cannot be reduced to only economic, military, and political functions. For Aristotle the self-sufficiency of the polis goes beyond mere survival (he notes that less-developed forms of society might achieve that for its members); it also implies the achievement of "the good life," a life ethically and spiritually good.[28]

The philosopher maintains, in other words, that the state must meet both material and moral needs; its institutions must be directed to a benign purpose, or the polis will not truly be a polis. But does this condition in any sense apply to the historical—and not merely a philosophically conceptualized—polis? To answer that question, we must first look at the principles underlying Aristotle's view of the state as an ethical way of life.

In the *Politics*, Aristotle argues teleologically that the polis exists by nature; it developed out of simpler forms of society, evolving toward its ultimate goal of "the good life" (*Pol.* 1252a 24–1252b 35). As a kind of association (*koinōnia*) the polis unites and harmonizes the functions of its members for their mutual benefit, and all members thus have a common aim and partake in common actions. Further, it is a special kind of association: not a mere alliance, but a *koinōnia* consisting of rulers and ruled whose final common purpose is the

[27] On the relationship between the urban center and the territory of the polis, Martin (1975); Kirsten (1956), 66ff.; Droegemueller (1970); Vernant (1986), 212–34.

[28] Arist. *Pol.* 1252b 27–30; 1280b 39–1281a 2; Arist. *Eth. Nic.* 1097b 14–15; Barker (1946), 7–8; (1959), 5, 233; Lloyd (1968), 249–50. In what follows, however, I bypass philosophical contemplation and its role in the achievement of *eudaimonia*, on which see Mulgan (1977), 3ff.; Hardie (1980), 12–27, 358–65; Lord (1982), 180ff.

encouragement of excellence (*aretē*) among all citizens.[29] That goal is ensured by justice which belongs to and is inseparable from the polis (*Pol.* 1253a 37: *hē de dikaiosynē politikon*).[30]

Justice, then, is an essential condition of the polis. But what does Aristotle mean by justice? Within the *Politics* and *Ethics* (the two works must be read together), various concepts—ultimately interconnected—can be identified. In a "universal" sense, justice is closely related to excellence (*aretē*); in a moral community justice is the quality of the citizen who obeys the law, since the law itself is moral. In a more specialized form, justice is a principle whereby the association distributes honors and rewards to its members, according to each man's due or particular contribution; and at the same time, it is a principle that guarantees that in all transactions and dealings among members, no individual gives (in a general sense of the word) more than he receives, or suffers loss to the advantage of someone else.[31] In sum, justice provides for the protection and definition of each member within the whole, and rests on the assumption that the whole—the community of the polis— aims at *aretē* and a "life lived for noble actions" (*Pol.* 1281a 2–4).

Aristotle's view of justice therefore depends vitally on the arrangement and structure of the community. "Justice— which is the determination of what is just—is the ordering of the political association" (*Pol.* 1253a 37–39). It is clear, however, that behind the obvious institutions to order the community—a constitution, laws, and courts—there must be a spiritual commitment of the citizens, a shared belief that the form and processes of the institutions will lead to goodness.[32]

By this axiom, Aristotle's conception of the polis differs

---

[29] Arist. *Eth. Nic.* 1160a 8ff.; 1172a 3ff.; Arist. *Pol.* 1280b 6–8; Newman (1887–1902), 1:40–44; Barker (1959), 337–45; cf. Hardie (1980), 182–210. Lord (1984) translates *koinōnia* as a "partnership."

[30] Cf. Bourriot (1984), 201–2.

[31] Arist. *Eth. Nic.* 1129a 1–1130b 7; 1131a 10–1131b 24. For additional references and discussion, Barker (1959), 337–45; cf. Hardie (1980), 182–210.

[32] Barker (1959), 323–25.

from modern conceptions of a state. For the philosopher, the polis is (in a general sense) educational, directed to a positive end for its citizens.[33] At the same time it is a community enterprise; citizens are not taxpayers but rather shareholders in a corporation whose profits are moral excellence. Unlike the modern state, the polis does not limit man's natural rights, but rather nurtures his sense of moral responsibility. Man is a *zōon politikon*, said Aristotle (*Pol.* 1253a 1–3), a creature intended to live in a polis; and the polis enunciates what is just, thereby allowing man's best qualities to flourish.[34]

But can a definition tinted by moral purpose actually apply to the historical Athenian polis, or to any real Greek polis for that matter? Contemporary historians have shied away from such criteria, in the belief that any notion of "goodness" is irrelevant to objective and scientific investigation. Accordingly, they have limited their descriptions of the polis to its political characteristics or physical attributes in the archaeological record.[35] In doing so, they have neglected an essential quality of the Greek city-state.

Morality is a tricky issue, but that does not mean that it can be ignored in the search for the historical polis. Because "men make the polis," it is reasonable to ask not only when but why men first came together to make a city-state. And, in discovering "why" the question arises whether they indeed intended this kind of city-state to promote the moral behavior of its members. Such questions are crucial to understanding the development of the Greek state, and membership in it. They are, however, easier asked than answered. The sources for the early history of Greek culture are too fragmentary to provide

[33] Cf. Lord (1982), 36ff.

[34] Newman (1887–1902), 32–33; Burnet (1900), 202; Barker (1918), 7–9; (1946), l–li; (1959), 281–92; Kagan (1965), 207–9. Cf. Arist. *Pol.* 1253a 25ff.; Mulgan (1977), 16–17. For some related comments on the contrast between modern states and the Greek polis, Holmes (1979); Maio (1983); Meier (1984).

[35] See, e.g., Snodgrass (1977); Duthoy (1986). For a more favorable treatment, Finley (1983), 122–26. Morris (1987), 6ff. stresses "the citizen estate" and *koinōnia* of the polis, but his archaeological approach focuses more on the date and process of formation than the nature or causes of the association.

evidence for why men took steps to build a state or what they thought while they were doing it. Nonetheless, a few basic observations can be made. First, any concept of the polis must include a self-conscious sense on the part of the members that they belong to a formal community within definable boundaries; they must similarly understand that within those boundaries they share (as Aristotle held for every kind of *koinōnia*) certain common aims and activities. Expressed more simply, if only approximately, the polis to be a polis had to be composed of citizens with some kind of "civic spirit."[36]

Second, it seems fair to say that the "civic spirit" had to be, at least in principle, based on the citizens' belief that membership in the city-state would enhance rather than detract from their life in society. That belief was based in turn on the axiom that Aristotle ultimately made famous: "Justice belongs to the polis."

Can such assumptions be sustained for the historical polis? Yes—with certain qualifications. Of course the "justice" discussed by Aristotle and other fourth-century philosophers was a more subtle and sophisticated concept than was ever articulated by the founders of early Greek poleis. And, as many scholars have argued, the classical concept of justice grew out of older, less-abstract notions of what was "good" or "correct" or "appropriate."[37] Yet it would be wrong to believe that a fundamental human understanding of fairness and equal

---

[36] Starr (1961), 325 and (1986), 35. Cf. Coldstream (1984), 9 who speaks of "corporate effort for the common good"; see also Finley (1983), 122–41; Bourriot (1984), 201ff.; cf. Goldhill (1986), 57ff.

A civic spirit of the population is not to be misunderstood as denying the possibility of a simultaneous strong competitive ethic among citizens. As many commentators have noted, the historical polis (especially Athens) was marked by a tension between group cooperation and individual desire for excellence, and indeed that tension was a striking feature of the polis' existence. On this point, see, e.g., Adkins (1972); Garner (1987), 11–18; Farrar (1988); Ober (1989). On the concept of *philotimia*, as a "social channel" for the translation of individual honor to the good of the community, see chapter 1, and Whitehead (1983).

[37] Gagarin (1973), (1974), (1986); Ostwald (1973); Havelock (1978); all with references to earlier work. On moral values and their development, Jaeger (1946); Dodds (1951); Adkins (1960) and (1972); Pearson (1962); Dover (1974); Dickie (1978); Lloyd-Jones (1985); Garner (1987).

treatment and their role in the possible betterment of man was unknown before the classical period. Despite the gradual development of the concept, justice (in some general sense) was historically connected to the polis from very early times. Aristotle's basic tenet had a long tradition behind it.

The evidence for this is incomplete but persuasive. First, Aristotle's association of justice with the polis must be seen in its historical context, for it was in part a response to the earlier denials of many of the so-called sophists.[38] In fact, in the *Politics* Aristotle directly challenges the belief of a certain Lykophron that law (*nomos*) did not make citizens good and just but was merely an agreement among citizens to prevent wrongdoing (1280b 10). This essentially negative view of the state first developed during the fifth century, one aspect of the many-faceted debate about the relationship between man's "conventions" (*nomoi*) and "nature" (*physis*).[39] The sophist Hippias of Elis is credited with saying that law (*nomos*), a mere covenant among men, could be a "tyrant over human beings" (Pl. *Prt.* 337 c 6–e 2; cf. Xen. *Mem.* 4.4.14). Antiphon, in a similar spirit, advised his students to ignore the laws whenever it was possible and naturally advantageous.[40] Kallikles and Thrasymachos, portrayed by Plato, advanced theories of justice rooted in a fundamental distrust of the human contracts of the polis.[41]

The teachings of these and other sophists caused a sensation as they spread among young intellectuals eager for new ideas; the sophistic movement was a revolution, and excitement arose around it because basic principles of society were being shaken mightily.[42] But just as Aristotle in the fourth century

[38] Kagan (1965), 201ff.

[39] Cf. Guthrie (1969), 139 who also assigns the idea to the fifth-century city planner Hippodamos, on the basis of Arist. *Pol.* 1267b 37ff. The interpretation of both texts, as well as the "minimalist" theory of the state are challenged by Mulgan (1979). See the reply of Guthrie (1979), and generally Farrar (1988).

[40] DK 87A 44; for identification and interpretation of the fragment, Kerferd (1981), 49–51, 114–17.

[41] Pl. *Grg.* 482c 4–486d 1, cf. Dodds (1959), 266–67. Pl. *Resp.* 338c 1ff.; cf. Kerferd (1981), 120–23.

[42] Guthrie (1969), 14–26; Kerferd (1981), 15–23; cf. Ar. *Nub.* passim.

challenged the earlier ideas of such men as Antiphon, Hippias, and Lykophron, so such sophists themselves were attacking older views already established in their own day. In all likelihood, the established views represented the same basic belief that Aristotle later articulated anew: that the polis was not a simple or convenient convention, nor was it something invented to force men into slavish obedience, but rather it was a special kind of community in which citizens benefited by their membership. And the chief benefit, to be specific, was some kind of justice, providing the potential to make man better.

In fact, a pre-Aristotelian connection between justice and the polis is strongly suggested in many fragments of classical and archaic thinkers.[43] For example, a few fifth-century sophists, in opposition to other sophists' negative view of the state, argued for the positive moral advantage of its laws and institutions. Protagoras of Abdera proposed in his famous myth of society's origins that men's poleis were held together by divinely sent *aidōs* ("a reverent respect for the judgments of others"), and *dikē*, a sense of right or justice. Protagoras links both principles to the "political art" (*politikē technē*) and implies that the polis itself helps provide man's education (Pl. *Prt.* 323 a 3ff.).[44]

The ethical theory of the fifth-century atomist, Democritus, shows a related sensibility. The moral theme of "contentedness" (*euthymia*) is linked in his writings to "what is lawful and just," and he seems to acknowledge the role of the polis' *nomos* as an enhancer of man's condition: "The aim of the law is to benefit human life, but it can only do so when men are willing to accept its benefits; it reveals its excellence to those who obey."[45]

---

[43] I have sidestepped Thucydides in the following discussion, though there is much to be found throughout his reported speeches relevant to the relationship of justice and the polis. See chapter 1 for my treatment of Perikles' funeral oration which of course strongly links the two (e.g., Thuc. 2. 37ff.). For good discussion of Thucydides and the polis and its role in shaping human affairs, see Farrar (1988), esp. 153ff.

[44] Cf. Kerferd (1981), 140–41; Farrar (1988), 81ff.

[45] DK 174; 248; cf. 245 with Guthrie (1965), 495–97 (his translations, adopted here), and (1969), 69. See also Hussey (1972), 125, and (1985), 119–23; Farrar (1988), 253ff.

The late fifth-century theorist, so-called Anonymus Iamblichi, makes a similar if less direct connection between the state, justice, and moral improvement. He suggests that a man achieves *aretē* by helping the largest possible number of people; and that is best accomplished by assisting conventional laws (*nomoi*) and justice (*dikē*). Moreover, the theorist continues, man's communal life depends on his submitting to both. The treatise concludes with a eulogy for the blessings of good government (*eunomia*).[46]

The link between justice, moral improvement, and the polis is even more explicit in the well-known discussion of law that appears in the Demosthenic speech *Against Aristogeiton*. The speaker (probably drawing from a lost fifth-century sophist) explains to his Athenian audience that the *nomoi*

> aim at what is just (*to dikaion*) and honorable (*to kalon*) and beneficial (*to sympheron*) . . . and all men ought to obey them.
> . . . Above all, because every law (*nomos*) is a discovery and gift of the gods, decided on by wise men, a corrector of errors both voluntary and involuntary, and a common agreement of the city-state as that by which every citizen should regulate his life (*kath' hēn pasi prosēkei zēn tois en tēi polei*). (Dem. 25.16)

These reasons for citizens' obedience to the laws are not mutually exclusive but cumulative.[47] A moral aspect of the argument is inescapable. Whatever its date and author, the text must serve as a reminder that traditionally "the distinction between what is legally enforceable and what is morally right was much less clear-cut among the Greeks than it is with us."[48]

Similarly, the several instances in the early poets which associate words such as *dikē* and *dikaios* with the polis demon-

---

[46] Text in Iambl. *Protr.* 20 (= DK 82), esp. 6–7; Guthrie (1969), 71–74. A. Cole (1961) demonstrates the probable debt of Anonymus Iamblichi to Democritus; cf. Kerferd (1981), 149–50.

[47] Kerferd (1981), 128, correctly refuting Pohlenz (1924), 27ff.

[48] Date and authorship: Pohlenz (1924); Gigante (1956), 268ff.; Guthrie (1969), 75 n. 2. The quotation is from Dodds (1959), 266. On the overlap of social, religious, political, and personal codes in early Greek law, Ostwald (1973), 674–77.

strate the same basic notion that within the Greek city-state a
man could expect justice and thereby (even if only indirectly)
could be improved. Recently, some scholars have attempted
to strip all moral qualities from the concepts of "justice"
found in texts before the mid-fifth century, but the arguments
remain unconvincing.[49] When, for example, Pindar calls Corinth the dwelling of the daughters of Themis—including "sure
Justice, the foundation of the polis" (*bathron poliōn asphales
Dika*)—the righteousness of the citizens is surely also at stake;
for these daughters of Themis "are eager to ward off Hubris,
the brash-tongued mother of Satiety."[50] A similar connection
is made by Simonides (writing near the end of the sixth century) in a verse fragment preserved by Plato: "He who knows
justice which brings profit to the polis (*dikan onēsipolin*) is a
healthy man," meaning, in its context, a virtuous individual.[51]

    The intrinsic importance of justice to the polis likewise ap-
pears in the sixth-century poetry of Theognis.[52] He laments

    [49] E.g., Gagarin (1973) and (1974), the latter work at 186 n. 1 summarizing
older scholarship representing the "orthodox" view. I do not question that
the concept of justice in the later classical age was more philosophical and
sophisticated than earlier conceptions; nor do I doubt that *dikē* frequently
implied only a legal procedure or "settlement." But it remains to be seen that
such operations were ever entirely divorced from basic (if archaic) ideas of
moral behavior, and a popular understanding of right and wrong. Akin to
Gagarin, Havelock (1978, cf. 1969) nonetheless acknowledges the "shadow"
of moral justice in preclassical times. Cf. also Claus (1977); Dickie (1978).

    In (1986), Gagarin seems to moderate, or at least qualify his earlier views
(e.g., pp. 47, 99–101); see also his discussion of morality in (1987), 288ff.,
and esp. 303 where he notes various developments in the Archaic age which
"helped make the *polis* and its law the objects of moral concern." I believe
that his definition of justice in (1986), 99 as "the legal process by which disputes are settled and the substantive norms which help determine the context
of these settlements" is not really out of step with the basic form of morality
that I discuss in what follows. For a similar view, and a thoughtful treatment
of the overlapping moral and amoral senses of *dikē* and "justice" in early
Greek society, Garner (1987), 4–10.

    [50] Pind. *Ol.* 13.4–10; cf. Lloyd-Jones (1985), 50. The poem celebrates the
Olympic victory of Xenophon of Corinth in 464.

    [51] Pl. *Prt.* 339a–346d, esp. 346c 1ff. (= Page [ed.] [1962], F 542); cf.
Lloyd-Jones (1985), 48.

    [52] I follow the majority view of Theognis' date and, for the sake of the fol-

(39–46) that his polis is being destroyed not by "well-born good men" (*agathoi*) but by their opposites (*kakoi*) who resort to hubris, corrupt the people, and give over the machinery and workings of justice (*dikas*) to those who are unjust (*adiko-isi*).[53] Elsewhere (131–32) the poet proclaims that the best thing for any man is to have parents who concern themselves with *hosiē dikē*, "sacred justice."[54]

In early sixth-century Athens Solon too saw the value of justice in the polis and the disasters that followed its perversion. One of his poems bewails the public effects of wicked behavior; the verse reports how the polis totters on the verge of destruction, thanks to individuals seduced by greed and lawlessness, unrestrained by the sacred foundations of justice (*dikē*). Solon praises the benefits of lawfulness and good order (*eunomia*), which renders affairs among men appropriate and prudent. And the statesman also implies that all members of the polis suffer under the opposite condition, *dysnomia*.[55]

The benign effects of justice and its place in the polis appear in the *Works and Days* of Hesiod.[56] More than a century before Solon, the Boiotian poet portrays Dikē as a goddess who sits beside her father Zeus, "singing of the unjust hearts of men, until the people pay back for the abominations of their lords who ... pervert judgments (*dikas*) and make crooked pronouncements" (*Op.* 256–62).[57] And like other poets later,

---

lowing discussion, assume Theognid authorship for the poems of the Theognid corpus. For the scholarship on its manifold problems, Young (1961). Citations are from West (1980) whose text I follow for all lyric and elegiac poets unless otherwise indicated.

[53] Gagarin (1974) 193 n. 52 translates *dikas* here as no more than "legal settlements" but cites also Van Groningen (1966) who understands the term more broadly: "les principes, les règles, et les sentences judiciaires sur lesquels se base la vie politique et sociale d'une communauté bien organisée." For the moral qualities of the poem, Lloyd-Jones (1985), 46–48; see also his comments in (1987), 309 on the general relationship between law and morality.

[54] Cf. Van Groningen (1966), 55.

[55] Solon F 4. Compare the same ill result of *dēmosion kakon* in Theog. 49–50. On *eunomia* and justice in Solon's poems, Vlastos (1946). See also chapter 6.

[56] On the polis in Hesiod's poetry, Luce (1978).

[57] Following the text of West (1978) which I use subsequently. The person-

Hesiod warns of the collective punishment that will befall the unjust polis:

> Many times even all of the *polis* shares [the results of actions]
>   of[58] one bad man,
> Whosoever may offend and devise reckless deeds.
> Upon them from heaven the son of Kronos sends suffering,
> Famine and plague together, and the people perish.
> Their women bring forth no children, their households diminish,
> According to the plans of Zeus. Other times
> He destroys a wide army of them, or their wall,
> Or against their ships from the sea does the son of Kronos take
>   vengeance.
>
> (*Op.* 240–47)

At the same time, however, Hesiod demonstrates the advantages for a polis that knows justice:

> But those who give straight judgments (*dikas*) to strangers and
>   *dēmos* alike
> And do not turn aside at all from the path of what is just (*di-
>   kaios*),
> For them the *polis* flourishes, and within it the people blossom.
> Across the land is child-nourishing Peace,
> And Zeus does not mark them out for grievous war.
> Famine and destruction do not accompany straight-judging men
>   but at feasts they eat the fruits of their carefully tended fields.
> For them the earth bears much livelihood. . . .
> Their wives bring forth children who [because they are legiti-
>   mate] resemble their fathers;
> Forever these men flourish with good things.
>
> (*Op.* 225–31, 235–36)

---

ification of *dikē* here and elsewhere (lines 213, 220, 275) causes obvious difficulties for those advancing a nonmoral interpretation of the term in early poetry: cf. Gagarin (1973), 89; Claus (1977). Havelock (1978), 217 sees the beginnings of a moral ideal of justice with this poem.

[58] West (1978), 217–19 defends the suspect *apēura* at line 240 but concedes that the meaning is probably closer to the usual emendation *epaurei*, "enjoys the fruits of."

Hesiod's poem is a moral treatise in that it contrasts the dangers of injustice with the rewards of justice; moreover, Hesiod extends both ideas to the entire membership of the polis. Though he does not directly connect justice with the ethical spirit of the individual (as would later theorists), he nonetheless voices an early belief in its salutary effects on the community of citizens.

In a simple form, then, the polis of Hesiod stands as an ancestor to the Aristotelian concept of the state whose justice enhanced man's life, and which embodied something more than an arbitrary authority to prevent wrongdoing. When Hesiod asserts that unlike wild beasts who eat one another, man received from the gods a most excellent gift—*dikē*—it is significant that he goes on to stress its positive value: "To the man who knows and publicly proclaims just things (*ta dikaia*), far-seeing Zeus grants happy prosperity" (*Op.* 276–81). That such a man, as well as other men, would thus be urged to future just actions follows naturally from Hesiod's didactic verses; the *Works and Days* provides a small but crucial hint of the moral value of justice within the early polis.

The fragments of the earliest poets offer a glimpse of a traditional mentality about the nature of the Greek city-state; they show that the polis, even in its historical incarnations, was identified with the ideal that the members would encounter justice. And through the exercise of justice, it was apparently believed, those members would become better (eventually in a full moral sense) in their day-to-day lives. Though doubtless primitive in its original conception and operation, justice nonetheless represented from very early times a vital condition of the Greek city-state.

We can now summarize the several necessary qualities implied in the idea of a polis. The Greek polis was a politically autonomous community of people living in a defined territory comprising a civic center with surrounding arable countryside. Its society included both agricultural and nonagricultural laborers who were organized by a centrally located authority to defend the state, contribute to its material needs, share in unified worship of the gods, and decide matters of public pol-

icy and personal disputes. Since the polis was in essence its
citizens, clear boundaries between the member and the non-
member existed; within the boundaries of membership, defined by a fixed constitution, the citizens had the right to participate in the community's deliberative and/or judicial
functions whose exercise normally took place in a civic center.
And among the citizens a certain communal spirit could be
identified, based at least partly on the shared belief that as
members of their community they would have access to, and
benefit from, justice.

This definition allows a return to my original questions
about the earliest history of Athens. When did the Athenians
first become a polis? Why did it happen? And when and how
did they first become citizens?

Chapter Three

EARLY SOCIETY

A PURPORTED beginning of the Athenian polis appears in legend with the event known as *synoikismos*, literally "the joining together of family households." During the heroic age, according to tradition, King Theseus unified the many autonomous villages of Attika by bringing them under the political authority of Athens.[1] Though the ancient accounts of the *synoikismos* are colored with anachronistic and romantic elements, commentators today nonetheless accept that some kind of unification must have once occurred which constituted a crucial phase in the development of the Athenian city-state.[2] But when did the *synoikismos* take place? And more important, did it in fact initiate the polis as I have now defined it? Should the origins of Athenian citizenship be assigned to the bold deeds of Theseus?

The date of the *synoikismos* lies beyond real certainty, though not for lack of educated speculation by historians and archaeologists. Estimates have placed the unification anywhere between the thirteenth and sixth centuries, the choice depending partly on whether one considers it to have been a single incorporative event, a lengthy sociopolitical evolution, the manifestation of an economic revolution, or some combination of these and other imperfectly understood phenomena, for example, "urbanization." Each of these possibilities of course implies its own kind of process.

The literary evidence for the *synoikismos* stresses central-

---

[1] Thuc. 2.15; *FGrH* 328 F 94; Isoc. 10.35; Plut. *Thes.* 24–25; etc. For other ancient sources see Padgug (1972), 141 n. 26.

[2] See, for example, Sarkady (1966); Alföldy (1969); Padgug (1972); Andrewes (1982a), 362–63; Snodgrass (1982), 668ff.; Diamant (1982); Simms (1983). For discussion of the romantic elements of the Theseus myth, Connor (1970).

ization of authority: Theseus abolished the individual councils and governments of each Attic village, and established one principal *bouleutērion* and *prytaneion* (implying central deliberative and ceremonial functions) in Athens.[3] In contrast to this "political process," interpretations based on the material record have tended to stress social and economic centralization.[4] Scholarship of this school has variously argued that unification promoted, and at the same time can be inferred from, such phenomena as late tenth-century diffusion of the Protogeometric pottery style in Attika;[5] ninth-century mining of silver in the outlying area of Thorikos;[6] the sudden appearance of wealth in rural Attic burials dating from between 900 and 850;[7] an eighth-century shift from pastoralism to arable farming;[8] a perceived change in burial practices in about 750, representative of greater social cohesiveness between upper- and lower-status groups in the community.[9] Similarly, the unification has been related to the supposed eighth-century institution of the archaic festival known as the *synoikia*[10] and/or the late eighth-century celebration of a common god in the first "public" temple that Athenians ever constructed.[11]

Now, any of these indications might argue for the joining of the villages of the Attic countryside into some kind of a political or social or economic unity, and all of them could be part of the same general process underlying the emergence of the

[3] Thuc. 2.15.2 with Gomme et al. (1945–81), 2:48–49; Plut. *Thes.* 24–25; Andrewes (1982a), 362–63. On the later identity of the *bouleutērion* see Rhodes (1981), 522 and (1972a), 18ff.; on the *prytaneion*, S. Miller (1978), 13ff.; Rhodes (1981), 105.

[4] See the remarks of Musiolek (1981).

[5] Snodgrass (1971), 404.

[6] Coldstream (1977), 70.

[7] Snodgrass (1982), 669.

[8] Snodgrass (1980), 33–37; cf. Lauter (1985), 70ff.

[9] Morris (1987), who argues on the basis of the funerary evidence that this "rise of the *polis*" was temporary, however, and that only at the end of the sixth century did the state fully emerge. See chapter 7, n. 148.

[10] Thuc. 2.15.2; Plut. *Thes.* 24.4 with Parke (1977), 31–33.

[11] Snodgrass (1977), 24–30; cf. Coldstream (1984), 9–11. Polignac (1984) stresses the foundation of a rural sanctuary in opposition to the central cult as the determining factor: see chapter 4, n. 66.

Athenian city-state. For my purposes, however, the evidence is insufficient to distinguish a polis as I have described here. A model based on apparent coalescence around a common festival or around institutions, or a multiplication of social and economic interactions, still lacks key elements of the Aristotelian definition. For example, without a constitution or some formal articulation distinguishing those who could from those who could not participate in its festivals or institutions, the community would not be a polis.[12] Nor would it be so without firm evidence of some "civic spirit" on the part of its members, or their common commitment to the application and value of justice in their daily lives. The stories and other evidence of *synoikismos* hint at some of these things, but they do not decisively identify the polis qua polis.

What did it mean "to belong" to early Attic society? Who were its people? A reasonable chronological starting point is, as mentioned earlier, the end of the Dark Ages, approximately the tenth century. A search for the polis cannot go further back than that because of the clear break between the Mycenaean civilization and the later culture that ultimately developed as "classical." In the Mycenaean period, archaeological data amply attest that Athens and several outlying regions were marked by clusters of settlements. There is some ground for believing that, before the thirteenth century, Attika was a unified kingdom similar to that known at Pylos, ruled by a palace bureaucracy, and the population organized under a rigid system of land tenure and taxation.[13] But even if true, it is clear that this "Mycenaean way of life" had faded away by

[12] *Contra*, e.g., Snodgrass (1982), 668 who talks of ninth-century cultivators of the Attic countryside having a "citizenship of Athens." Starr (1986) distinguishes between the rise of the polis at some early time, and its "crystallization" in the eighth century.

[13] Hooker (1976), 102–3, 223–30 (with references for individual sites), 182–212 (with references to previous scholarship on the "Mycenaean state"); Chadwick (1976), 12ff. For details of Mycenaean organization, Broneer (1956); Finley (1957); Levi (1964); Mylonas (1969). The case for a unified Attika in the Mycenaean period: Stubbings (1975a), 169 and (1975b), 347–48. For an overview on the question of the "state" during this period, Cherry (1984).

the end of the second millennium. Our investigation must begin with a society marked by depopulation, apparent isolation, and a relatively poor level of material culture compared
to what had once been.[14] It was also fundamentally regional-
istic and decentralized: a world of villages, local cults and kinship groupings, and independent neighborhoods.[15]

Any discussion of Dark Ages culture must start with the oikos, the household unit that included not only an extended
family group but even the material possessions that ensured
its livelihood.[16] The oikos, loosely translated as "family," provided the primary principle of classical society, and everything
known about earlier times suggests that this had long been the
case. When, in the fourth century, Aeschines (2.23) boasted
that Athenians had shrines, family tombs, lawful marriages,
and relatives and children in Attika, he appealed to tradition
as old as any member of his audience could imagine. For no-
body knew of a time when membership in the "Athenian community" did not depend on membership in an Athenian oikos.

Nonetheless, the society of Dark Ages Attika was certainly
more complex than randomly distributed Athenian families.
From classical sources we hear of *phylai*, *phratriai*, and *genē*,
larger social units whose membership included several oikoi.[17]

[14] Desborough (1964), 112–16 and (1972), 20–24, 133–39, 263ff.; Snodgrass (1971), 28ff.; Sourvinou-Inwood (1973); Sarkady (1975); Snodgrass
(1980), 33–37; Andrewes (1982a), 362–63. The contrarian view, arguing for
a cultural continuity from Mycenaean through archaic times, and a Mycenaean origin of the polis, has been advanced anew by van Effenterre (1985),
esp. 27ff. See, however, the judicious remarks of Snodgrass (1986b) and Morris (1987), 6ff.

[15] On the regionalism of early Attika, see Sealey (1960); Mossé (1964); Jeffery (1976), 83–84; Walters (1979); Andrewes (1982a), 362; cf. R. Osborne
(1985a), 15ff.

[16] On the oikos see Lacey (1968); Littman (1979), 13ff.; Gernet (1983);
Humphreys (1983d). Compare the identical meaning of a household, as described by Du Boulay (1974), 15ff., in the contemporary Greek village of Ambéli.

[17] For a survey of the evidence and a recent synthesis of the conventional
interpretations of these social units, Littman (1979). For the new school of
skepticism about these social units (and whose views have influenced much of

Though their origins are obscure, all of these corporations can be traced back to preclassical times, and in the case of *phylai* at least as far back as the eleventh century. *Phratriai* and *genē* may be slightly younger, though the date of their emergence is more speculative.[18] Speaking generally of the period between about 1000 and 700 (the evidence allows no greater precision), how did *phylai*, *phratriai*, and *genē* organize and define the Attic community? What did it mean to belong to them?

The *phylai*, usually, if problematically, translated as "tribes,"[19] represented the broadest division of the population. Together they formed the basis of the Athenian "race" and dialect group. Four separate Attic *phylai* are known, their names (Geleontes, Hopletes, Argadeis, Aigikoreis) most likely derived from particular cults that drew together their memberships.[20] However the *phylai* first developed, the families composing them eventually became corporate descent groups in the sense that belonging to one was hereditary. Each tribe was led by a king or *phylobasileus* whose vestigial judicial and sacrificial functions in the classical age suggest the sort of communal activities that from very early times benefited all those who belonged.[21] Solidarity among families of the same *phylē* was further ensured in the face of war; tribes likely served as military divisions.[22]

Some evidence suggests that the phratries were also military divisions, though their functions in times of peace are more

what follows): Bourriot (1976); Roussel (1976); Donlan (1985); cf. R. C. Smith (1985); Finley (1986b); Morris (1987), 8ff.

[18] Andrewes (1982a), 360–61, 366–68; cf. Hignett (1952), 50–55. The date for the creation of the *phylai* depends on the date and nature of the "Ionian migration" which Andrewes places about 1050. The attempt of Donlan (1985), 295ff. to portray the *phylai* as no more than small, Dark Age leader groups ignores the evidence linking the Athenian versions to the migration. On the date of phratries, Andrewes (1961a). *Genē* are discussed later.

[19] E.g., the remarks of Roussel (1976), 9–10.

[20] Busolt and Swoboda (1920–26), 770 n. 3; Hignett (1952), 51.

[21] Latte (1920a), 994–1011 collects and interprets evidence for the nature of the early tribes. For judicial and sacrificial authority of the *phylobasileus* see Plut. *Sol.* 19; Poll. 8.120; and Ferguson (1936), 157.

[22] Hom. *Il.* 2.362–63 with Andrewes (1961a), 129ff.

easily documented. *Phratriai* appear in the classical age as associations of oikoi that shared common cults, performed sacrifices, and publicly recognized the births, marriages, and adoptions of their members.[23] Whether original subdivisions of tribes or (more likely) subsequent social formations, phratries eventually developed into kinship corporations. Their networks of family ties cannot now be reconstructed, but it is clear that fathers introduced their sons and that daughters were also attached (though perhaps more loosely).[24] Individuals of the same family never, except perhaps in certain cases of adoption, joined more than one *phratria*.[25] The names of most phratries imply that their constituents were descended from a common (if mythical) ancestor.[26]

The names of many of the *genē*, like phratries, also suggest that their members were descended from a common ancestor.[27] These too were hereditary corporations whose memberships followed family lines.[28] But beyond that, their identity and role in Attic society are much debated.[29] The apparent privileges of certain *genē*, and the probability that not all

[23] Latte (1920b); Guarducci (1937); Andrewes (1961b); Roussel (1976), 96ff.

[24] On the impossibility of reconstructing family ties within phratries, Finley (1986b), 92. For fathers, sons and the procedures of admission, Wyse (1904), 357–60; Labarbe (1953); S. Cole (1984); Golden (1985). The exact status of daughters in phratries is a vexed question, but it seems clear that even if not "legally" introduced (probably in itself a misleading concept), girls did have a social association with the phratry of their fathers: Golden (1985), 9–11, *contra* Gould (1980), 40–42 who cites previous scholarship on the question.

[25] On admission of adopted sons, Harrison (1968), 82–93. R. Osborne (1985a), 127–28 cites evidence in support of the view that most adoptions involved relatives—and thus typically those from the same phratry.

[26] See the list in Latte (1920b), 755. For worthwhile remarks on the evolution of kinship and para-kinship links in phratries, see Donlan (1985), 298–308.

[27] See Toepffer (1889) for most of the known names.

[28] Bourriot (1976), 95ff. summarizes evidence and traditional arguments with much skepticism; but in his final analysis (1347ff.) he acknowledges familial components in the various types of *genē* that he perceives.

[29] See Bourriot (1976) whose conclusions for the most part I follow. The attempt of Oliver (1980) to interpret *genē* as early military units has little to recommend it.

Athenians belonged to one during classical times, have convinced many scholars that these were exclusively aristocratic
groups.[30] It was long thought that the *genos* represented an
entitled subdivision of a phratry, capable of exercising control
over its affairs and membership. Unfortunately, the evidence
for phratries and *genē* offers no clear and consistent picture of
such a relationship. In the fourth century certain *genē* were
clearly associated with a phratry,[31] the Eteoboutadai even
sharing its altars with one (Aeschin. 2.147). But other *genē*
seem to have had their own shrines.[32] Some phratries auto-
matically admitted members approved by a *genos*, as if the
latter had performed a sort of "prescreening" of candidates.[33]
Yet other times phratries enrolled members without any apparent involvement of a *genos* at all.[34]

The situation is further complicated by undiscriminating
terminology in the sources. Recent scholarship has confirmed
that different types of groups in Attic society were called *genē*;
moreover, the most important of them appear not to have
been exclusively aristocratic. The oldest, known by the names
they shared with particular rural locales (e.g., Kolieis, Kephis-
ieis, Salaminioi) can be traced back to neighborhood unions
in the small hamlets of Attika. Perhaps almost as old was a
second type of *genos*, the sacerdotal families (e.g., Kerykes,
Eumolpidai, Praxiergidai), which performed special functions
in one or more traditional cults.[35]

It is obviously too simple to see *genē* as orderly subdivisions
of the phratries, nor do they fit neatly into any general scheme
of the society of early Attika. Furthermore, even within the
different types of *genē*, variety must have existed. Each sacer-

[30] Andrewes (1961b), 1–10; cf. (1982a), 367.

[31] The best-known example is the *genos* of the Demotionidai and its close
association with the phratry of Dekeleia, following the interpretation of
Wade-Gery (1958), 116ff. with Andrewes (1961b), 3–5.

[32] E.g., the Salaminioi, Ferguson (1938); see also Bourriot (1976), 1043ff.

[33] Andrewes (1982a), 368; cf. Wade-Gery (1958), 119; and *IG* ii² 1237,
lines 13ff.

[34] Isae. 2.14, 3.73–76, 6.22, 8.19; and Dem. 39.4, 39.20, 43.14.

[35] The two types are based on the interpretation of Bourriot (1976), 1347–
66.

dotal *genos* came to have different privileges, and the regional groupings probably had particular and separate customs. In the classical period we hear of individual *nomoi* maintained by *genē*, and a Solonic law of the sixth century attests that corporations of that name had long before had their own internal practices.[36] Apparent inconsistencies in the relationship between phratries and *genē* might simply mean that sometimes their memberships overlapped but sometimes they did not.

In apparent contrast to the complexities of *genē* stand the phratries. The legal function mentioned for members of a phratry in the homicide law promulgated by the lawgiver Drakon implies that at least in the seventh century every Athenian belonged to one.[37] Furthermore, during the classical age all phratries shared certain common gods and a common Ionic festival, the Apatouria.[38] But the often assumed uniformity and standard social role of these corporations may be overstated, particularly for early times. Solon's law records that phratries, like *genē*, had their own individual customs, a conclusion easily supported by the tenor of the procedures seen in the famous phratry in Dekeleia (*IG* ii² 1237).[39] Many phratries maintained shrines of their own gods, and worshipped the deities of Zeus Phratrios and Athena Phratria at separate local *hiera* (sacred precincts).[40] Furthermore, it is not clear that the period of enrollments during the Apatouria had always been celebrated on the same day by all phratries;[41] and as we have already seen, phratries were not uniformly con-

[36] E.g., the *nomoi* of the Demotionidai: Wade-Gery (1958), 119ff.; cf. Bourriot (1976), 1180ff. The Solonic law is preserved in *Dig.* 47.22.4.

[37] *IG* i² 11–20 (= Meiggs and Lewis [1969], no. 86; cf. Stroud [1968], 65–70); Busolt and Swoboda (1920–26), 959.

[38] Parke (1977), 89–92.

[39] *Dig.* 47.22.4; Wade-Gery (1958), 118ff.

[40] Guarducci (1937), 29 and appendix 8–10 collects examples of phratries' individual sanctuaries; cf. the phratry of *IG* ii² 1237: line 52 stipulates that sacrifices be brought to the altar "in Dekeleia." See now also Hedrick (1989).

[41] Parke (1977), 89, 92; see Isae. 7.15–17 for a phratry that allowed presentation of new members at a different time of the year.

nected with the workings of *genē*. In the classical age, not all Athenians necessarily belonged to a phratry.[42]

That there were differing customs among phratries is all the more believable if phratries are understood as organizations originally centered in a specific locale. The evidence, though limited, tells such a story. Whatever the name of the phratry in *IG* ii² 1237 was, there is no doubt that its shrines were situated in Dekeleia. The phratry Dyaleis was rooted in Myrrhinous; the Medontides can be linked with the deme Gargettos; the Therrikleidai worshipped shrines within the precincts of Athens; the deme of Thymaitidai was likely the locale of the phratry Thymaitis.[43] Phratries, like *genē*, probably developed as small neighborhood associations sometime during the Dark Age.[44] Regional variations are to be expected in a world marked by slow communication and difficulty of travel.

If variety among phratries and *genē* made for a certain complexity in Attic society, a few other known associations further complicate the picture. The same law of Solon that concerns private customs for phratries and *genē* also mentions *syssitoi*, *homotaphoi*, *thiasoi*, and *orgeōnes*, each of which had their own *nomoi*.[45] Though all of these groups are poorly understood, they would appear to have established different networks of loyalties among certain segments of the Attic population.[46] Etymology suggests that *syssitoi* were organizations

[42] Roussel (1976), 145; Rhodes (1981), 70; see M. Osborne (1983), 158ff. on grants of citizenship that did not include enrollment in a phratry. Osborne (1983), 175 also notes that certain phratries refused to accept naturalized citizens in the fourth century, perhaps another indication of the corporate autonomy of these bodies. See also the remarks of Sealey (1987), 14.

[43] Wade-Gery (1958), 119ff.; *IG* ii² 1241; Roussel (1976), 141 and nn. 13–18; Hedrick (1983), (1988a), cf. (1988b), 116–17. For a full discussion of Attic phratries, and arguments for their regional distribution, see Hedrick (1984) and (1989).

[44] Andrewes (1961a), (1982a), 367 (though downplaying an exclusively local character); Roussel (1976), 139–42. Donlan (1985), 305–8 proposes a similar model.

[45] *Dig.* 47.22.4; Ferguson (1944), 64 and n. 5.

[46] For the social implications of these kinds of associations, see Murray (1983), 196–97.

whose members ate together, whereas *homotaphoi*, probably yet another kind of regional social unit, may be the name of groups who buried their dead together.[47] *Orgeōnes* are somewhat better attested, as a name for hereditary organizations united in the worship of ancient heroes. They met in specific sacred precincts, their members in some (but not all) cases apparently also belonging to the local phratry.[48] *Thiasoi* were another kind of cult organization whose memberships overlapped, again imperfectly, with the memberships of phratries or *genē*.[49] And from a fifth-century calendar we learn of still another ancient religious unit, the *trittys*, which on select occasions joined in sacrifices with a *phylē*.[50]

If the foregoing sketch seems to lack a rational plan, the anarchy is perhaps not accidental. The data taken as a whole—with all their inconsistencies—provide a useful corrective to the usual schematic portrait of early Attic social organization offered by scholars.[51] True enough, Aristotle can be partly blamed for the "myth of order": a fragment of the *Athēnaiōn Politeia* claims that the multitude of early Athenians was originally divided among four tribes, each of which was divided among three phratries, each of which in turn was

[47] *Syssitoi* may be related to *parasitoi*, "companions of the sacred feasts," a privileged group according to the example of the *genos* Kerykes (Ath. 234 D–F). Spartan *syssitia*, "common messes," were apparently military units: Forrest (1980), 45–46. On the complexities of group kinship burials in Attika: Humphreys (1983e).

[48] Ferguson (1944); Andrewes (1961b), 1–3. The famous law cited by Philochoros (*FGrH* 328 F 35a) that required phratries "to accept into their membership *orgeōnes*" seems to imply that in earlier times *orgeōnes* were not necessarily part of phratries; Andrewes (1961b) plausibly dates the law to the mid-fifth century.

[49] For *thiasoi* within *genē* and phratries, *IG* ii² 2345 with Ferguson (1938), 14, 28 n. 7; and *IG* ii² 1237, 2344, 2723 with Andrewes (1961b), 9–11. For *thiasoi* independent of phratries, Ath. 5.185 C; Isae. 9.30–31; *SEG* 10.330 with Ferguson (1944), 133.

[50] Oliver (1935), 35–37; Ferguson (1936), 151–58; Rhodes (1981), 68.

[51] E.g., Meyer (1892–99), 2:512ff.; De Sanctis (1912), 42ff.; Wade-Gery (1958), 86–115. For an argument similar to what follows, Sealey (1987), 12–16.

divided among thirty *genē*.[52] Although the hierarchy of relative sizes of the bodies may be correct, the mathematical pro-
portions (not to mention, in the same fragment, comparisons
to the seasons, months, and days of the year) are not credible.
Moreover, the testimony of the fragment still leaves one won-
dering how the many other religious and neighborhood corporations fit into the plan; even those mentioned by Aristotle
are neither consistently uniform in their customs nor consistently dependent on one another. Rather than trying to impose
an artificial pattern upon the evidence, it is perhaps best to
accept that early Attic society was marked by inconsistencies
and imperfectly overlapping memberships.

The myth of order underlies a related and misleading scholarly debate. Too often the question is posed whether *phylai*,
phratriai, *genē*, and so on were originally divisions that were
"personal" (based on a given population of individuals) or
"territorial" (based on a geographical area).[53] The debate
flourishes because the evidence preserves indications of qualities seemingly contradictory but which are in fact best seen as
complementary. Most of the ancient Attic corporations display both a personal and territorial identity, and both aspects
of social groupings must be appreciated to understand what it
meant to belong to the community of Attika.[54]

Phratriai, *genē*, and *orgeōnes* did not begin as pure lineages
descended from one common ancestor, but they nonetheless
developed kinship structures over time. Grandfathers, fathers,

[52] F 3 with Rhodes (1981), 67–70 for commentary on sources and historical
problems.

[53] E.g., the debate on the nature of the *trittys:* Hommel (1939), 334–35;
Wüst (1957), 188–89. Such controversies can be traced back to early anthropological theorists (e.g., L. H. Morgan and H. Maine) who explained the rise
of states by the shift from kin-based to territorial-based organizations; cf. Jonathan Haas (1982), 34ff; Finley (1986b), 90–93.

[54] This issue is handled sensitively by R. Osborne (1985a), 127ff.; Donlan
(1985), 302ff. See also Whitehead (1986a), 364–68 who discusses the origins
of the word *dēmos:* "a local community of people living on its own land."
Compare the case of the contemporary Greek village of Ambéli portrayed by
Du Boulay (1974), 15–69 as "a collection of households encompassing people, houses, and the land of their livelihoods."

and sons normally belonged to the same corporations. At the same time, the regional character of many of the social groupings must not be forgotten. In an age of limited mobility and agricultural livelihood, family and land were closely connected. The names and the territories associated with the various social nuclei suggest that they were rooted in a specific area, often around a local cult, and doubtless within reach of family fields. It is easy enough to imagine many of these personal/territorial corporations coming together in small neighborhoods, their members laying claim to the lands left barren after the Mycenaean collapse. Such developments would fit the archaeological traces of the gradually expanding habitation in Attika that began in the ninth century,[55] and which ultimately evolved as a pattern of nucleated settlement—the villages of Attika in later times.[56] The process was neither rational nor even; settlements in primitive societies typically proceed piecemeal, not according to some authorized central plan.[57]

If Attic society was marked by such variations and inconsistencies, how did the individual relate to his community? Presumably he developed a sense of belonging on many levels: broadly to a *phylē*, locally to a *phratria*, perhaps to a *genos*, perhaps also to the *orgeōnes* of his valley or other cult group located a few miles from his village or farm. Worship of common gods, friendship, and kinship would help solidify his sense of place, but regional custom would also affect and shape the meaning of his various memberships.

And even as such memberships extended in many directions, so did they vary according to individual circumstances. Local cults gave prominence to some *genē* where others did not exist; the man of a strong and independent phratry might care less about his ties to a *phylē* than would another *phratōr* elsewhere, perhaps the son or cousin of a *phylobasileus*; the

---

[55] Coldstream (1977), 78, 132–37; Snodgrass (1982), 668ff.; Andrewes (1982a), 363; Lauter (1985), 69ff.

[56] R. Osborne (1985a), 15–63, 192–95.

[57] On settlement patterns generally, see studies collected by Ucko et al. (1972).

farmer who witnessed the sacrifices of his *trittys* felt a certain pride; another man might resent the festival of local *orgeōnes* whose membership excluded him. The inhabitant of Attika enjoyed certain common Ionic traditions with the members of his and neighboring *phylai*, but those traditions provided only a general and distant context for daily actions. His life was based on living in a village and working family land; his kin and religious relationships were both personal and territorial, ancestral and local.

Patterns of membership in this ancient population might be illustrated by comparison to another primitive society without strong central authority. Meyer Fortes's studies of the "stateless" Tallensi of Africa revealed an overlap between personal and territorial identity within the population, perhaps analogous to the Attic society of the first centuries of the first millennium. The Tallensi, "a loose aggregate of clans speaking the same dialect" inhabit the northern regions of the West African Gold Coast.[58] They are an agricultural people who work ancestral land and are organized around *tes* ("settlements"). Fortes had difficulty defining the *tes* because he realized that each one represented a "coalescence of local associations, lineage organizations, common religious cults, political solidarity." The *tes* that Fortes observed were based on territorial but at the same time on nonterritorial relationships. Regional differences among them were common. The sanctity of land varied among settlements, as did the structure of the subunits of settlements (*yizugs*), as did the ancestry and power of the local ruling clans.[59]

The man of early Attika lived in a world not greatly dissimilar. As a dweller in a rural village, his obligations to family, field, and cult drew him into various relationships both inclusive and complementary, differing by locale and his status within that locale. His village and the other settlements that dotted the landscape were not a polis, not only for their lack of any strong central authority, but also for the want of a uni-

[58] On the Tallensi, see Fortes (1940), (1949), (1969); Worsley (1956).
[59] Fortes (1949), 147–66; Worsley (1956), 43–44.

versal sense of shared purpose or spirit among the population. This was a world in which Eleusis had once been its own separate kingdom;[60] in which the Attic demes of Pallene and Hagnous did not allow their inhabitants to intermarry;[61] in which four other villages, Marathon, Oinoe, Trikorythos, and Probalinthos, formed a separate cult unit, the Tetrapolis, which sent its own sacred embassies to Delos and Delphi.[62] The inhabitants of early Attika operated under a veneer of common language and material culture which only partly counteracted stronger loyalties to regional and decentralized groupings.[63]

[60] Thuc. 2.15.1; Padgug (1972).

[61] Plut. *Thes.* 13 implies that the prohibition survived into classical times. On marriage patterns across demes, R. Osborne (1985a), 131ff.; Cox (1988).

[62] *FGrH* 328 F 75 with Jacoby's accompanying discussion. On the Tetrapolis, and other archaic cult organizations that joined together groups of rural demes, D. Lewis (1963a), 30ff.

[63] Cf. Whitley (1988), 176–78 who proposes that the development of herocults in Geometric Attika reflect an intercommunity rivalry between older, established settlements and newer ones.

For some further insight to the nature of tension between regional loyalty and broader cultural affinity, note the remarks of Du Boulay (1974), 48, describing the local pride of the contemporary Greek villagers of Ambéli vis-à-vis other Greeks, even those from closely neighboring villages:

It is found, for instance, in a story which the villagers are fond of telling—of how an Athenian, amazed at the communication between shepherds by means of shouts and whistles, left the area in despair, exclaiming that he would never be able to speak Greek. It is found in the pride with which they admit to a mutual understanding derived from the nature of their life and work, and expressed in the acknowledgement that "we understand one another here." It is expressed too in the instinctive and completely mendacious defence of the reputation of the village with regard to the problem of whether its inhabitants would blacken the reputation of any of its girls who were being sought in a marriage, "no one would give anyone away here." . . . Most significantly of all, it is revealed in the absolute and unquestioning acceptance by any one member of the community of the same values and customs of all, a fact which binds together the whole community in the solidarity of the single unit, "we." This sense of community is, in Ambéli, reinforced rather than undermined by the knowledge that these values do not prevail everywhere [in Greece], and that even in the local market town, the same standards are not demanded by the community as are demanded by the people of Ambéli.

Accordingly, the often-asserted belief that in early times "citizenship was determined by membership in a phratry" is grossly misleading.[64] Such a statement implies that belonging to a phratry provided a uniform and recognized standard, entitling each Attic *phratōr* to a sort of Athenian passport. The phratries, as far as can be known, acted as nothing more than local corporations, self-contained and unconnected, part of a "system" only in the all too orderly reconstructions of modern commentators. It was not until the age of Solon that any kind of public and broadly accepted definition of membership and community existed—one that would embody a formal concept of citizenship for all Athenians.

[64] E.g., Hignett (1952), 55; Patterson (1981), 28; Murray (1983), 198; Hansen (1985b), 73; Starr (1986), 28, 91; and others.

Chapter Four

LAWS, BOUNDARIES, AND CENTRALIZATION

BY THE SEVENTH century the decentralized social mosaic of the earlier Dark Ages began to change. Slowly but perceptibly, the individualistic ways of life within the many regional villages and corporations were overshadowed by the development of an embryonic unity and evolving sense of self-definition across the Attic population. These centralizing trends, as well as the reasons behind them, mark a hastening of the evolution of the city-state. Thus begins the real history of citizenship and the new concept of "Athenian"—a formally defined member of a polis.

The potential for centralization lay in the basic cultural similitude of the Attic people; the Athenians emerged from the Dark Age with all members of their four tribes respecting certain Ionic traditions, worshipping certain common gods, and speaking the same dialect of Greek. Despite their many regional differences and loyalties, the inhabitants of the countryside readily recognized one another's manner of talking and they all taught their children about such mythical ancestors as Ion and Kekrops. They ate olives and wheat raised on neighboring fields and stored their oil in Attic-style pots.[1] But a shared language and heritage did not make inevitable the development of a system of public decision making or coordinated action, or a sensibility about the value of justice—conditions essential to the creation of citizenship. What came to

[1] Andrewes (1982a), 360–61. On the Ionian tribes, festivals, links with the Ionian migration, and the race and dialect of the Attic population, see J. Cook (1975); Chadwick (1975), 818ff.; Parke (1977), 88–92; and cf. Hdt. 1.146–47, 5.66.2, 69.1. On Ionian traditions and the strength of "Ionic feeling," see recently Alty (1982). On the unity and variations of style of Attic pottery, Coldstream (1968); (1977), 25ff., 55ff., 73ff., 109ff.; (1983).

bind Athenians together in common civic institutions, with a shared civic consciousness? An examination of the sources of authority in the community and, more broadly, the nature of authority in the social hierarchy, will help elucidate the process of centralization that lay behind citizenship.

According to various traditions,[2] Athens was originally ruled by a dynasty of kings, the most famous of whom was Theseus, the supposed agent of the *synoikismos*. Thucydides says that in times of danger the independent villages of Attika cooperated with the king, perhaps implying that there was once a council of local chiefs (2.15.1).[3] Independent historical verification of the Athenian kings is not possible, but it is certain that if such leaders once exercised even occasional authority over Attika, that power eventually faded away. The existence of a group of local chiefs is less open to question, and accords with the general picture of the regionalized society thus far described. It also accords with the usual assumption that Attika in the centuries after the Mycenaean collapse came to be controlled by a class of aristocrats; further, that over time this class cooperated among itself sufficiently to form a centralized administration of a primitive state.[4] But these assumptions require scrutiny. Was there in fact a "ruling class" of aristocrats in ancient Attika? If so, what kind of social organization did their authority define?

Plutarch (*Thes.* 25) reports that at the time of the *synoikismos* Theseus created an Attic nobility (Eupatridai or "the well-born") to whom he entrusted the government and religion of Athens. Many scholars have doubted—perhaps rightly—this story; less rightly, some have also doubted the more fundamental idea that in early times a definite status of nobility existed at all.[5] In fact such a status did exist; sources

---

[2] On the tradition (skeptically analyzed), see now Drews (1983); also Rhodes (1981), 65ff.; Carlier (1984), 325ff.

[3] Thus Hignett (1952), 36; and others.

[4] E.g., Wade-Gery (1958), 86–115; Hignett (1952), 47ff.; and others.

[5] Wilamowitz-Möllendorff (1910), 74; see recently Figueira (1984), 454–59.

attest to privileges of nobility in the preclassical age,[6] though we must understand that the boundaries (birth and wealth) which separated this class from the rest of society—and generally, all boundaries within the early social hierarchy—were less sharply drawn than the distinctions embodied in classical law.[7] In their efforts to define, or alternatively to discredit, an ancient social stratum of aristocrats, commentators have wrongly imposed the greater legal clarity of a later age onto a prelegal culture governed by customs rather than statutes.

During the early centuries of the millennium, lines of social status evolved, based broadly on descent and property rights. Although one cannot decisively uncover the history of these apparent demarcations,[8] it is still reasonable to believe in them: the dwellers of Attika clearly understood the concept of privilege; indeed their daily lives were governed by it. Long before Pollux (8.111) wrote that *phylobasileis* were chosen from among Eupatridai, it was surely known among the members of tribes who could and who could not become one. And in the seventh century when, as Aristotle (*Ath. Pol.* 3.1, 3.6) records, the archons were chosen "according to birth and wealth" (*aristinden kai ploutinden*), certain men certainly knew that they could stand for the office and most others knew that they themselves could not. One can only guess about the origins of the early aristocracy, but its existence as an acknowledged elite within the social context is not to be doubted. These were men who wielded economic power and passed it down through their families; exercised its prerogatives publicly, and assumed positions of formal and informal leadership; and emphasized their higher stations symbolically

---

[6] E.g., *Ath. Pol.* 3.1, 3.6, 13.2 with Rhodes (1981), 75–76; *IG* xii 9.296 with Raubitschek (1949), no. 6, 330; Davies (1971), 12–15; and Poll. 8.111.

[7] As per Finley's distinction between a juridically defined "order," a "status," and "class" (1985), 35–61. Cf. Finley (1983), 12. The Eupatridai of the Archaic age are in all respects to be distinguished from the *genos* of that name in the Hellenistic and Roman period: Rhodes (1981), 76; cf. Wade-Gery (1958), 106; Davies (1971), 11–12.

[8] For some attractive speculation: Roebuck (1974); see also Gernet (1968), 335–43; Arnheim (1977), 46–57.

as, for example, the scale, trappings, and structures of their burials would suggest.[9]

Though the aristocrats of early Attika probably exerted most influence in their immediate neighborhoods, after the Dark Ages many of them came to live near Athens,[10] and eventually shared in the governance of the society at large. That seems clear from the appearance of powerful public institutions reserved for members of their status. By the seventh century, Eupatridai performed the duties of archons and served in the Council of the Areopagos; decisions weighing upon the actions of Attic peoples were by then being taken centrally, in Athens, by men preeminent in birth and wealth (*Ath. Pol.* 3.1; 3.6). According to tradition, the rule of archons first developed as an alternative to monarchy. The office passed through stages of decreasing tenures until it became an annual appointment in 682/1.[11]

The nine archons, whose origins Aristotle variously explained, functioned as an executive group in military, civic, and judicial affairs (*Ath. Pol.* 3.2–6). Thucydides (1.126.8) maintained that at the time of the Kylonian affair (discussed later) they "handled most public matters." This assessment seems reasonable given the apparent duties of these office holders. The *basileus*, a legacy from the age of kings, presided over various traditional rituals and probably also over the Areopagos when it sat as a murder court.[12] The eponymous archon gave his name to the year and functioned as the chief

---

[9] Morris (1987), 47ff.

[10] Anecd. Bekk. 1.257; Gomme (1933), 37–39; Sealey (1960), 178–80; Alföldy (1969), 5ff. It is more than likely, however, that many Eupatridai also maintained residences in the rural demes. That would seem to follow from the rich graves found in the countryside as late as the end of the seventh century (Jeffery [1976], 90, 106 n. 4; Snodgrass [1977], 16 and n. 13), and the pattern of settlement in later times. During the classical age, the Athenian elite apparently had holdings both in the country and the city: R. Osborne (1985a), 47–50; cf. W. Thompson (1970); Hansen (1983b), 236ff.

[11] *Ath. Pol.* 3.1, 3.3 with Rhodes (1981), 77–79, 97–101; Cadoux (1948). For an alternative view on the original relationship of archon and *basileus*, Sakellariou (1976–77), 11–21.

[12] *Ath. Pol.* 3.2–3; cf. 57; Rhodes (1981), 99–102; Andrewes (1982a), 364.

executive; the polemarch was the Athenian military leader.[13] The rest of the group were six *thesmothetai*. The original duties of these archons can only be guessed, but it is plausibly surmised that they once had responsibility for recording the judgments of court cases.[14] All of the archons were originally selected by the Areopagos and joined its Eupatrid membership for life after their tenure of office (*Ath. Pol.* 3.6, 8.2).[15] This council thus also wielded considerable power over the lives of early Athenians.

About the origins of the Areopagos little is known.[16] As the preeminant conciliar authority during the Archaic age, it may have developed out of the informal advisory bodies of nobles who served the early kings.[17] Much controversy exists about its exact functions, which were probably not as clearly specified as modern scholars have often maintained.[18] Aristotle (*Ath. Pol.* 3.6, 4.4, 8.4) speaks of the powers of *nomophylakia*, perhaps best translated as "the public guardianship of Athenian customs and canons of social behavior."[19] The Areopagos probably also had the power to punish and fine

---

[13] *Ath. Pol.* 3.2–3; cf. 13.2; Rhodes (1981), 99–101; Andrewes (1982a), 364.

[14] *Ath. Pol.* 3.4. It is generally believed that the *thesmothetai* originated not only before the age of Solon (*Ath. Pol.* 3.5) but even before that of Drakon (c. 620): Rhodes (1981), 102. This assumption causes problems because, first, *Ath. Pol.* 3.5 describes their function as "writing down *thesmia*" but at 41.2 claims that Drakon gave Athens her first written laws. The discrepancy can be explained if *thesmia* were originally either the results of actual court cases or the general rule reflected in a decision, that is, the precursors of regular written laws as instituted by Drakon: Gagarin (1981a); (1986), 51ff.

[15] See also *Ath. Pol.* 60.3; Plut. *Sol.* 19.1; Poll. 8.118; Dem. 24.22; and MacDowell (1963), 40–41.

[16] The fullest recent treatment of the institution is R. Wallace (1989), albeit more skeptical about the earliest period than what follows. See below, n. 20.

[17] Glotz (1930), 46ff.; Rhodes (1981), 106–7.

[18] The point is underscored by Andrewes (1982a), 365; Ostwald (1986), 7.

[19] We must beware of assigning to the seventh-century Areopagos too much of a role for watching over formal "laws" (e.g., the translation of Rhodes [1982], 107) before Drakon first set such down in writing; see Cawkwell (1988), 10–11.

offenders, to serve as a homicide court, and to oversee the magistrates.[20]

In addition to the archons and Areopagos, the main source for the period, the *Athēnaiōn Politeia*, refers to a few other centralized administrative officials, particularly those with financial functions. By the seventh century Athens had "Treasurers of Athena" (*tamiai*);[21] *kōlakretai*, literally "collectors of hams" but during this time probably collectors and dispensers of common funds;[22] and *naukraroi*, in charge of locally based units (*naukrariai*) organized for the raising and maintenance of warships.[23]

---

[20] *Ath. Pol.* 3.6, 8.4, 25.2, 57.3; cf. Isoc. 7; MacDowell (1978), 27–28; Rhodes (1981), 315–17. R. Wallace (1989), 3ff. argues forcefully that, with the exception of *Ath. Pol.*, ancient evidence would have the Areopagos as nothing more than a homicide court until it was made one of two governing councils of Athens by Solon. Wallace acknowledges, however, the likely existence of some aristocratic council before Solon (which met in the *prytaneion*), and if he is right, *Ath. Pol.*'s description of the archaic government may not be so much wrong as misnamed. It is easy enough to believe that during the seventh century some kind of council made up of those "preeminent in birth and wealth" exercised stewardship over Athenian affairs. That leaves open the question of the role of the Areopagos in Solon's reforms. If it were enlarged by Solon to something beyond a homicide court, should we suppose that the council of the *prytaneion* was thereby disbanded? If so, then the historical significance of Solon's creation of a new aristocratic council with certain powers (thus Wallace), as opposed to limiting those of one already in place (so most other scholars), may be substantially the same. A formal role of the Areopagos in overseeing magistrates, including scrutiny (*dokimasia*) and enforcing accountability at the end of their tenure (through *euthynai*), probably does belong to the Solonian reforms: Ostwald (1986), 7–15; Wallace (1989), 66ff. is more skeptical.

[21] Though not certainly attested before Solon (*Ath. Pol.* 7.3; 47.1), the *tamiai* probably date from an earlier period: Andrewes (1982a), 366. For a brief summary of the history of the office, Rhodes (1981), 391–92.

[22] *Ath. Pol.* 7.3 with Rhodes (1981), 139. Their function is assumed on the basis of later duties (see *FGrH* 324 F 36), and the apparent antiquity of the name suggests a pre-Solonian origin. Payments during this time were probably in the form of uncoined silver: Rhodes (1981), 152–53.

[23] The origins and functions of the *naukraroi* are hotly debated, but consensus has evolved that they had something to do with "ships," as the root word *naus* (*pace* Billigmeier and Dusing [1981]) and the evidence of later commentaries suggest. That, combined with *Ath. Pol.*'s linkage of *naukraroi* and *nau-*

The centralized governance of the archons and the Areopagos and the duties of other administrative officials mentioned so far have encouraged many historians to posit the existence of a seventh-century Athenian "state," a characterization that typically strengthens the belief that the *synoikismos* had been completed by the year 700 at the latest.[24] Yet nothing described thus far really allows one to call the Athenian community a polis.[25] For even if the Attic population was by 700 ruled by archons and the Areopagos in Athens, and some of its people were somehow contributing to a central treasury, no firm evidence shows that this "state" had developed a formal definition of who was and who was not Athenian—an essential condition of citizenship. In the same spirit, there is no reason to believe that this "state" had yet established for itself clear territorial boundaries. No traces of these survive from very early times, and once again one cannot assume that the recognized frontiers of any later age had existed from time immemorial. Finally, though the Eupatrid elite may have

---

krariai with the collection of levies and expenditures (8.3), makes it likely that the officers were in charge of a kind of liturgical levy, either of (uncoined) silver to pay for ships or ships and crews themselves. Ships raised in this manner were presumably for military purposes, though they would not necessarily have constituted a "state fleet" at this early date: Gabrielsen (1985), who also summarizes evidence for the office; cf. J. Haas (1985); Figueira (1986). Jordan (1979), 56–62 stresses the financial duties of the office.

Our only evidence of a *naukraria* is that of a place name (Phot. s.v. Kolias; Anecd. Bekk. 1.275.20), which, as argued earlier, could have both "territorial" and "personal" implications in defining an administrative/social unit. *Ath. Pol.* dates this institution to Solon, but the testimony of Herodotus (5.71), placing the *naukraroi* at least as early as Kylon, is to be preferred. That testimony has caused its own share of problems because of its apparent discrepancy with Thucydides (1.126.8) about the powers of these officers relative to those of the archons. Attempts to reconcile the two statements (e.g., Jordan [1970] and [1979], 61–62; Lambert [1986]) are probably best subjugated to the belief that in the seventh century *naukraroi* were important officials, even if ultimately less so than the archons; see Andrewes (1982a), 368–69.

[24] E.g., Hignett (1952), 36ff.; Snodgrass (1977); Jeffery (1976), 84.

[25] That is, according to the definition set out in chapter 2. Many scholars, of course, have written about the existence of the polis by about 700, e.g., Starr (1986), and others cited earlier.

shared a sense of group solidarity through their privilege of
public rule, it would be wrong to project upon the entire Attic
population a shared sense of common identity or purpose.
Athenians were not yet a *koinōnia*, imbued with a civic spirit;
and just because *thesmothetai* now recorded certain judgments of a central court, it did not mean that the population
at large generally held the expectation that any man was entitled to the same kind of justice, regardless of where he lived
and who was his overlord. The government of the community
was more centralized than ever before, but the seventh-century Attic society remained a community of villages, and a hierarchy of statuses across the memberships of *phylai*, *phratriai*, *genē*, and other regional corporations. This might be
called a "state," but it was not yet a unity of citizens.

Toward the end of the seventh century, however, the outlines of a polis begin to emerge. One can glimpse citizenship
evolving as the concept of the state itself—and membership in
it—become more clearly defined. Initial indications appear in
the story surrounding "the first certain event of Athenian history"—the attempted coup d'état of the nobleman Kylon.[26]
In about 630[27] Kylon, a recent Olympic victor and powerful
aristocrat, stormed the Athenian Akropolis with the aim of
making himself tyrant. Ultimately, the coup failed for lack of
popular support; Kylon escaped but his followers were killed
(Hdt. 5.71; Thuc. 1.126.3–12; Plut. *Sol.* 12.1–9). In this age,
the story relates, Athenians would not suffer a tyranny.

What is perhaps more interesting about the story is the portrayal of the Athenians themselves, for our sources depict
them now as a political entity. After Kylon's attack, Thucydides tells (1.126.7), they "all (*pandēmei*) rushed from the countryside" and laid siege to the usurper.[28] Thucydides continues
that the Athenians eventually entrusted the campaign to the
archons, empowering them fully to handle the crisis ("making

---

[26] The quotation is from Jameson (1965), 167; for discussion of sources
and events of the coup, see also Forrest (1956), 39–42; Lang (1967), 243–49;
Andrewes (1982a), 368–69.

[27] For discussion of the exact date, Moulinier (1946).

[28] On the phrase, Jameson (1965), 167 n. 2.

them *autokratores*"). The details of the account are significant, for they demonstrate that by this time the Attic population sometimes gathered together in the interest of the general
welfare; further, now aristocratic archons sometimes depended on the advice and consent of the rural—and largely
nonaristocratic—population.[29] The Kylonian affair bears witness to a subtle but noteworthy transformation: the Athenians
were developing from passive members of a social hierarchy
into active shareholders in a political community.

That transformation accelerated with the creation of a new
kind of central authority: the codification of law.[30] A decade
after Kylon failed (and perhaps in response to the murder of
his followers),[31] public ordinances (*thesmoi*) were promulgated in Athens by the lawgiver Drakon, and for the first time
were set down in writing.[32] Fourth-century sources speak of
several laws dating from this early period which, taken together, may have constituted a complete code.[33] The tradition
is too fragmentary to uncover the full extent of procedures
and offenses covered; in addition to the lawgiver's famous
homicide legislation, the "Drakonian code" may have included laws about slavery and tyranny.[34]

[29] Wade-Gery (1958), 144–45.

[30] On the origin and evolution of Athenian law, Wolff (1946); Gernet
(1968), 173–330; Harrison (1971), 69ff.; Humphreys (1983h); Gagarin
(1986); Sealey (1987).

[31] Busolt and Swoboda (1920–26), 816 n. 3.

[32] On *thesmoi*, Ostwald (1969), 12ff. These are to be distinguished from
the earlier *thesmia* ("judgments") recorded by the *thesmothetai* (above, n. 14,
and Gagarin [1981a], 74; [1986], 51–56). On the Drakonian laws generally,
Stroud (1968), 75ff.

[33] Cf. *Ath. Pol.* 7.1; Andrewes (1982a), 370–71; Stroud (1968), 75–83 discusses the evidence for all possible Drakonian laws.

[34] Forrest (1966), 150 suggests that Drakon's code included provisions
about the *hektēmoroi* seen in Solon's reforms (discussed in chapter 5), and
their enslavement for debts (cf. Solon F 36.8–12 West in which Solon mentions men who had been lawfully enslaved before his time). Some traditions
about the Drakonian laws mention the free status of individuals (Aeschin.
1.6–7; Xen. *Oec.* 14.4), and the homicide law preserves the word *eleutheros*
in an otherwise fragmentary line (35), all perhaps in apparent contrast to the
status of slaves; the latter thus may have been treated in other laws. On the

Whatever the extent of the lost code of Drakon, the creation of any fixed public laws signals a symbolic change and the emergence of an important new mentality. Once laws were written down, recorded, and stored permanently,[35] the exclusive prerogative of aristocrats to make and interpret the rules of social behavior faded; the settlement of disputes now depended less on the whim of an archon or the prejudice of powerful men within the regional corporations.[36] The individual disputant could feel that he had a greater share in the distribution of justice, because, if for no other reason, unvarying and impersonal standards for all now existed.

Formally recorded laws, then, advanced decisively the process of centralization. Their reach extended from Athens to affect the daily lives of individual dwellers of Attika, for all were obliged equally under the terms of the code. Consciously or unconsciously, Athenians were brought together by the impersonal master of public statutes. At the same time, moreover, Athenians during this period were being drawn together in other ways. At least one of the Drakonian laws (homicide) suggests that by the end of the seventh century the community was beginning to define itself along spatial and social lines. The polis took shape as its members and space became more bounded, and public law was both a cause and reflection of the growing definition. A closer look at the homicide legislation will illustrate this point.

The wording of the law only partly survives, reconstructed

---

possible Drakonian law against tyranny, see *Ath. Pol.* 16.10; and Ostwald (1955), 106ff.; but cf. the comments of Gagarin (1981a), 72–77.

[35] On the importance of writing for the development of law see C. Thomas (1977); Immerwahr (1986) cautions wisely about imputing too many modern assumptions to the medium. Gagarin (1986), 51ff. offers a balanced and sensible synthesis of most previous positions, and his own persuasive thesis linking the role of written law to the evolution of the polis and a "civic mentality." For the debate about the actual form and placement of the Drakonian laws see N. Robertson (1986); cf. Stroud (1979).

[36] So Forrest (1966), 147. Gagarin (1986) 121–23 doubts that a popular desire to undermine aristocratic power *caused* the invention of written law; but that reduced arbitrary authority of the elite was an *effect* of the "new technology" seems undeniable.

from a fifth-century copy and documents preserved in the Demosthenic corpus.[37] The text prescribes the punishment (exile) and subsequent treatment of a man accused of involuntary murder.[38] According to the measure, if the crime was decided to be unintentional, the victim's relatives could pardon the killer. In the absence of relatives, and assuming pardon was to be granted, "let ten members of [the victim's] phratry admit him [i.e., let the killer return to Attika]" (lines 11–19). Even without pardon, however, the law guaranteed the murderer's safety as long as he remained in exile: "If anyone kills the killer or is responsible for his death, as long as he stays away from the frontier markets (*agoras ephorias*) . . . he [i.e., the avenger] shall be liable to the same treatment as one who kills an Athenian" (lines 26–29).

The cited passage of the law alludes, probably for the first time in Athenian history, to a territorial boundary; it mentions markets at the frontier, and the text suggests that the limits of Attic territory would have been understood both by the killer who went beyond them and by the *phratores* who would have had to readmit him.[39] Probably such boundaries were not carefully surveyed demarcations but primarily natural limits and marginal lands.[40] However imprecise by modern stan-

[37] Text and tradition presented by Stroud (1968), whose edition is used in what follows. Translations of the Greek are mine, with an obvious debt to Stroud's own rendering.

[38] *Contra* the recent interpretation of Gagarin (1981b) that the law treats all kinds of homicide. See the review of Gagarin by Connor (1982).

[39] Note the gloss of the speaker in Dem. 23.39 discussing this segment of the law in the fourth century: ". . . 'frontier markets.' What did [the lawmaker Drakon] mean by that? 'The boundaries of the territory' (*tōn horiōn tēs chōras*)." The speaker goes on to speculate that "frontier markets" were so named (as anyone might guess) because they were open areas where inhabitants of Attika and neighboring lands used to gather.

[40] For description and discussion of the natural Attic boundaries, Chandler (1926). On the contested boundary with Boiotia formed by Oropos and the territory called Graia: Thuc. 2.23.3 with Gomme et al. (1945–81), 2:80–81. On the border territory formed by Eleutherai, Paus. 1.38.8 with Rhodes (1981), 627, 768. On the marginal lands called *eschatiai* (sometimes but not always at the frontier): D. Lewis (1973), 210–12; on the natural boundaries between other states: Langdon (1985), 5 with n. 4 on pp. 13–14. In contrast

dards, such boundaries are significant for their recognition now by public law; central authority formally acknowledged the limits of territorial space. That recognition was crucial to the evolution—and identity—of a polis.[41] The same process of evolution perhaps is discernible in two other signs of territorial awareness in this general period: the boundaries of Attika sworn to be guarded by the *ephēboi*[42] and the decision of the Athenians to cast the bodies of deceased Alkmeonids, the family polluted by their role in the murder of the Kylonians, "beyond the borders" of Attika (*hyper tous horous*: Plut. *Sol.* 12.3, cf. *Ath. Pol.* 1).

The text of the Drakonian homicide law adumbrates another kind of boundary beginning to form: a public distinction between Athenians and non-Athenians. The law says that if the killer is unjustly slain, his slayer is to be punished "as if he [the slayer] had killed an Athenian" (lines 26ff.). Beneath this statement lies the first indication that any Athenian—even one guilty of a crime—had a certain formal identity vis-à-vis other Athenians, and that this identity was something different from that of a stranger.[43] The law does not mark the first time that Athenians recognized that non-Athenians existed. Nor does it, on the other hand, imply a definite legal status of *xenos* or *metoikos*, each with specific rights and disabilities. It does in-

---

to natural boundaries, cf. the tradition of the pillar erected between Attika and the Peloponnese described in Plut. *Thes.* 25.3.

[41] See also the comments of Starr (1961), 338 and (1986), 39; Sealey (1976), 93–94; Sartre (1979); Polignac (1984), 41ff.; Morris (1987), 192ff.

[42] The ancient ephebic oath (Poll. 8.105ff.; Stob. 4.1.8; Tod [1933–48], vol. 2, no. 204; and see chapter 1, n. 34) includes as witnesses "the boundaries of the fatherland, wheat, barley, vines, olive-trees, fig-trees" (lines 19–20). These boundaries have plausibly been associated with the prehoplite training of the light-armed *ephēboi* whose duties included patrol of the frontiers of Attika. Though the legal institution of the *ephēbeia* cannot be placed before the fourth century, such training can be traced back to much earlier times, and many features of the oath suggest a pre-Solonian origin. For this interpretation, text, and discussion of the oath, see Siewert (1977); on the origins of the *ephēbeia*, Vidal-Naquet (1981).

[43] Gagarin (1986), 80, 140, arguing along similar lines. Jordan (1979), 39 notes that in archaic laws the usual distinction was not Athenian versus non-Athenian, but rather *eleutheros* versus *doulos*; cf. Beringer (1982) and (1985).

dicate, however, that by the end of the seventh century, an awareness in the community between "insiders" and "outsiders" was starting to come into legal focus. To be a polis, as specified in our basic definition, a community had to distinguish formally between members and nonmembers. The homicide legislation symbolizes a notable beginning in the development of citizenship that depended on that distinction.

Further definition within the society would come later. Just as Drakon's legislation does not attest to any separate rights and disabilities of "outsiders,"[44] so the privileges and responsibilities of "Athenian status" were known among members of the seventh-century community primarily as a matter of custom. Drakon did not create a constitution, a politeia, but rather a code that simply prescribed certain social norms.[45] Moreover, during this period most social norms were still dictated by the regional and autonomous corporations. The homicide law is significant for its elevation of a formerly family concern to the concern of the entire community; it is the first secure indication of a public process superseding a traditionally private matter among oikoi. Nonetheless, the prominent role of the phratries (and indeed of family members of the victim) in the law's procedures (see esp. lines 18, 23) bears witness that the centralization of society had progressed only so far.[46]

Still, the process had clearly begun and the centralization that is apparent must somehow be explained. Why at the end of the seventh century did Athenians sometimes come from the countryside to meet together in assembly, and what prompted the establishment of written laws? Historians explain both as responses to specific political events, but beyond such events broader issues were at stake. With new boundaries forming, with the polis itself taking shape, what forces were

[44] See the discussion of Grace (1973) who analyzes not only the original Drakonian law, but also the later additions (as she argues) preserved in Dem. 23.

[45] The Drakonian politeia preserved in *Ath. Pol.* 4.2–3 is almost universally agreed to be spurious: Rhodes (1981), 84–87 summarizes previous debate.

[46] Cf. Sealey (1987), 74–77.

moving men to reshape their society? Although the complex interaction of many variables underlies all social and political evolution, it will be instructive to consider at least some of the possible stimuli to the development of the city-state in this era.[47]

One popular explanation of the social change during this period is economic revolution. The rising predominance of Attic pottery abroad and the evidence for overseas ventures have convinced many scholars that, from the eighth century on, the rural economy of Athens (like that of several other Greek societies) was complemented by growth of a nonrural sector: commercial "manufacturing" and overseas trade. Many suppose that the attendant prosperity of this sector created a new class of men who could stand apart from the control of the old, agrarian-based aristocratic order. Further, these scholars maintain that the freedom produced by nonlanded wealth allowed a psychological independence to flourish among a wider stratum of society. By this view, the polis developed as a product of a new kind of thinking and increased social mobility; these changes fostered the urge among men to rebel against the established aristocratic order and ultimately led to new forms of political organization.[48]

This interpretation has its limitations, especially with regard to Athens. First, the degree of economic expansion in Attika, or even in Greece in general, is not easily measured in the eighth and seventh centuries. Moreover, it is particularly difficult to discern the state of affairs in Attika during the latter

[47] See the remarks of Renfrew (1972), 43ff. on the "multiplier effect" of different factors working together in state formation; also Wright and Johnson (1975); R. Cohen (1978c); Starr (1986), 34ff. Snodgrass (1986a) argues for the role of multiple "peer polity interactions" as a stimulus of polis formation in general.

[48] The economic revolution theory goes back to the ideas of nineteenth-century German historians such as Eduard Meyer (on whom, and the related primitivist-modernist controversy with Karl Bücher see Austin and Vidal-Naquet [1977], 3ff., 53ff. and selected papers edited by Finley [1979]). Its more recent application to the birth of new attitudes and the development of the polis (with various modifications) characterizes the views of Forrest (1966), 145ff.; Mele (1979); Murray (1980), 136ff.; and others.

and seemingly critical part of this period.[49] It is true that in the seventh century, Athenian wine and oil ("SOS type") amphorae proliferate overseas, and that after about 600, Athenian black-figure vases are successfully competing in the markets from Spain to Libya to Syria.[50] At about the same time, Athenian activity near the commercially vital Black Sea begins to appear.[51] But it is a great leap to argue on such basis that the psychology of a widening stratum of Attic society thereby decisively changed; more than a few scholars have questioned whether commerce or trade had any socially revolutionary effect during the Archaic age at all.[52] Finally, even if some Athenians were now feeling more economically independent, we need to further explain why their community at large began to coalesce into a new and political body. Certain men may have now been willing to challenge the old aristocratic order, but

[49] See the remarks of Starr (1977), 76–78; Austin and Vidal-Naquet (1977), 54–56.

[50] Johnston and Jones (1978); for a general survey of Athenian pottery distribution overseas from the seventh century on, Boardman (1979).

[51] At Elaious and Sigeion, probably in the last years of the seventh century; cf. Hdt. 5.94ff.; Strab. 599–600. For discussion of the controversial dates of these colonial foundations and the commercial aspects of the region in general, Meritt et al. (1939–53), 3:89 n. 75; Page (1959a), 152ff.; Jeffery (1976), 89–90, 238–39; Boardman (1980), 264–65; Graham (1982), 121; Andrewes (1982a), 374.

[52] The starting point for such objections is the classic monograph of Hasebroek (1933) whose arguments and its implications are eloquently summarized and analyzed by Cartledge (1983a). Cartledge himself (1983a) and Snodgrass (1983a) provide representative views of the school that stresses noncommercial means and motives for the circulation of goods during this time, and the irrelevance of commercial processes to the politics of archaic society. A different but highly speculative attack on the theories of the "new commercial class" can be found in Bravo (1977), who argues that mercantile trade was significant in the archaic period, but that it was controlled ultimately by the aristocratic landowners themselves. By his view, the transport of merchandise was handled almost always by agent-traders who stood in a relation of personal dependence to society's nobles, i.e., were not a separate class of "revolutionary thinkers." An interesting counterpoint to the Hasebroekians may be found in W. Thompson (1982) who makes a case for the existence of a commercial psychology among ancient "entrepreneurs," at least in the fourth century.

that tendency could not single-handedly determine a citizenship across the many villages of Attika. For our purposes, the "economic independence" theory can only partly explain the emergence of the polis.

Some historians seek the source of social and political developments of the period in the Greeks' adoption of a new military tactic in the seventh century—the hoplite phalanx.[53] It is held that this mode of fighting brought men together in ranks for the first time in Hellenic history; battles fought with phalanxes pitted lines of heavily armed soldiers against one another, each side thrusting and pushing in unison. The tactic put a premium on training a large number of soldiers to do battle as a coordinated unit of "equals." Proponents of this theory argue that social distinctions would have been leveled within the phalanx formation; in battle no man could stand preeminent in the tightly packed rank, for success or failure hung on the solidarity of the unit marching toward its foe. Aristocrat or not, every man had to depend on the cooperation and courage of the soldier on either side of him. Wars fought in this new way would require the Eupatridai to share their traditional military responsibility—and ultimately, some of their nonmilitary prerogatives—with a broader stratum of society than before. Lesser men who now participated in the fighting might expect to participate more in public life, and would accordingly develop the kind of civic spirit crucial to citizenship in a polis.[54]

This interpretation is attractive but again problems intrude. The date, nature, and process of adoption of the tactic in Greece remain controversial and the Athenian case is particularly obscure.[55] The first appearance of hoplites in Attika

---

[53] Recent proponents of this view (to varying degrees): Andrewes (1956), 34ff.; Forrest (1966), 88ff.; Greenhalgh (1973); Cartledge (1977), 22ff.

[54] For a discussion of the social and civic ethos of the hoplite-citizen, see Detienne (1968); Mossé (1968); Vidal-Naquet (1968); Ridley (1979).

[55] Those who stress a gradual and/or nonpolitical evolution of the tactic include Snodgrass (1965); Salmon (1977); and Krentz (1985). The most extreme attack on the thesis of hoplite reform as a turning point in archaic Greece is Latacz (1977, now followed by Pritchett [1971–85], 4:7–93 and

might be assigned to the end of the seventh century,[56] in fact coinciding with the supposed Drakonian politeia (*Ath. Pol.* 4) whose membership was drawn from those men in the community who could provide arms and armor (*ta hopla*). But this "constitution" is of dubious authenticity, as noted earlier, and other indications for the existence of a hoplite army at Athens are indirect, based only on knowledge of various military undertakings during that time. More important, even assuming that the tactic had been adopted in Attika before 600, no firm evidence points to its social or political consequences in creating an institution or sense of citizenship.[57]

In any event, an organization of hoplites in seventh-century Attika would not in itself have embodied a polis. The Drakonian politeia preserved in Aristotle's *Ath. Pol.* is spurious, but its assumptions about arms and armor in this age are not. Hoplites did have to provide their own equipment, a costly requirement that only some men could have afforded. Although this kind of army may have been more broadly based than before, it would not have included all able-bodied Athenian sons (as it also did not during the classical age). The hoplite phalanx could have defined a new and larger status group in society, but not a community of citizens.

Of more consequence than the hoplite phalanx itself was the raison d'être of the new tactic—interstate warfare—which probably contributed more to the development of a broad-based citizenship and the polis than any particular mode of fighting. For however Athenians actually did battle during this

---

Morris [1987], 196ff.) who argues that mass formations of infantry were already central to tactics in battles depicted in the *Iliad*, i.e., there was no sudden emergence of the hoplite phalanx in the seventh century. For some doubts about early Athenian hoplites in general, Hopper (1976), 184. Krentz (1985); Holladay (1982); J. Anderson (1984); Pritchett (1971–85), 4:54ff.; and others have also debated the degree to which hoplite battle was in fact a confrontation of ranks pushing against one another, as opposed to a series of individual, face-to-face fights between soldiers in formation.

[56] Siewert (1977), 111; Murray (1980), 178; Andrewes (1982b), 397; and cf. Starr (1982), 424.

[57] Cf. Salmon's arguments ([1977], 100–101) that hoplite fighting provided in fact the means, and not the cause, of a new political consciousness.

age, their struggles with several rival peoples must have helped foster the kind of civic spirit vital to the establishment of a city-state. Against the Aiginetans in the first part of the seventh century,[58] against the Megarians and Mytilenians toward the end of it,[59] against the Kirrhaians who controlled Delphi in about 595,[60] Athenians waged wars, by land and by sea. Not only the men who fought but also those who contributed their food, or ships, or labor began to realize a sort of unity among themselves in opposition to their foes. Though it is probably still too early to talk about a formal "state" navy or a well-organized army,[61] the Athenians who went on campaign, or otherwise assisted in military causes, increasingly thought of themselves as belonging to a community that stretched beyond the limits of their individual Attic villages or phratries.

The role of warfare in unifying and centralizing loosely organized societies has long been noted by anthropologists. A century ago Herbert Spencer wrote that "wars between societies originate governmental structures, and are causes of all such improvements in those structures as increasing the efficiency of corporate action against environing societies."[62] Since then modern studies of "stateless" or regionalized societies have often demonstrated links between military action and sociopolitical centralization.[63] Anthropologists are quick

[58] Hdt. 5.82–88; on the date, Dunbabin (1936–37). See also Figueira (1981), 203ff.

[59] On the date and nature of the Athenian conflict with Megara over Salamis, see Plut. *Sol.* 8–10; *Ath. Pol.* 14.1; and chapter 5, n. 90. On the wars with Mytilene over Sigeion, see above, n. 51.

[60] Forrest (1956).

[61] Frost (1984); J. Haas (1985); *contra* Coldstream (1968), 361 n. 10; and Andrewes (1982a), 372 who posit an Athenian navy primarily on the basis of maritime scenes on seventh-century pottery.

[62] Spencer (1896), 520.

[63] E.g., Vansina (1966) who explains the rise of several central African states on the basis of war and conflict; and Netting (1972), 241 who notes the organizing effects of aggressive or defensive warfare among the Tiv, Ibo, and Mmembe peoples of Nigeria. For general discussion of this model and related theories, Fried (1967), 213ff.; Carneiro (1970), 734ff.; R. Cohen (1978b), 43ff.

to point out, however, that warfare does not always or completely cause increased state complexity.[64] Similarly, though seventh-century battles and fighting may partly explain the origins of the Athenian polis, other factors deserve consideration as well.

One such factor may be religion, that is, the unifying force of common beliefs in certain things sacred and divine. Of course, from their earliest origins, the Athenian people had shared Ionic rituals and gods, and they continued to do so (and to share many other cults and festivals) throughout their history. It can hardly be doubted that religion was always a primary bonding element of the community, both before and after it became a polis. But did some religious phenomenon play a decisive role in that transition? Some commentators have so suggested, specifically linking the temple building of the eighth century to the rise of the polis throughout Greece: "The building of a monumental temple to a patron deity . . . may be our clearest indication that the emergence of the polis has arrived, or is at hand."[65] Some argue that the construction of a temple formalized a "community of cult" and that in turn helped formalize the polis itself.[66]

Unfortunately, the evidence for the first "monumental temple" in Athens (the remains of a "building of peculiar form" on the Akropolis, dated to about 700) is less clear-cut than at many other sites.[67] Even supposing that the construction of

[64] Carneiro (1970), 734; Fried (1967), 204ff.; R. Cohen (1978a), 8ff.; (1978b).

[65] Snodgrass (1977), 24.

[66] Snodgrass (1977), 24ff.; (1980), 33ff.; Coldstream (1984), 13–14. Polignac (1984) advances the novel thesis that the rise of the polis should be linked not to a centralized place of worship, but to the establishment of a rural, nonurban sanctuary in polar opposition to the monumental urban cult; the interplay between center and periphery was a fundamental tension that characterized the polis' union of town and country. The problem with this otherwise interesting idea is that it fits less well with the Athenian case than most of the other poleis discussed by Polignac (cf. pp. 45ff.). See the comments of Snodgrass (1986b), 262–63.

[67] Quotation from Snodgrass (1977), 26 who cites several more obvious cases such as Perachora, Argos, Samos, etc.; references in Drerup (1969). On

such a temple was an essential criterion of a polis, its existence was not, according to our Aristotelian framework, sufficient to define one. But more to the point, *why* did Athenians come together during this time to build the shrine? And is it even fair to assume that the earliest temple to Athena was necessarily a common effort of and shrine for all or even most Athenians? Did the building reflect a new "community of cult"? Evidence for religious beliefs is notoriously difficult to evaluate, and this case is certainly no exception. It is possible to speculate about a sudden rise in shared religious values throughout the society (if indeed that is what any temple represents), and to attribute that rise to the development of the polis; but such inferences, though plausible, remain a priori.

In recent years historians have given new emphasis to another element of social change long familiar to anthropologists: population growth.[68] Like warfare, demographic increase has been shown in studies of contemporary tribal societies to contribute to centralization and "state formation."[69] According to the thesis of a study that applies this model to the society of early Athens, an apparent "boom" in the number of Attic inhabitants during the eighth century advanced decisively the rise of the polis. A sudden and rapid increase in the population stimulated the spread of fresh political ideas, facilitated the division of labor, and forced a "tighter and more compact social organization" to deal with new shortages of resources.[70]

This argument (by Anthony Snodgrass) is provocative but unfortunately flawed. In the first place, the supposed population boom of the eighth century is based on a perceived sev-

---

the remains on the Akropolis attributed to the early Athena temple, see also Wycherley (1978), 143.

[68] See the summary in Spooner (1972b), xvff.; and generally Glass and Eversley (1965); Wrigley (1969); Hollingsworth (1969); Grigg (1980).

[69] Dummond (1965) and (1972); Fried (1967), 200ff.; Stevenson (1968); Carneiro (1967).

[70] Snodgrass (1980), 15ff. Quotation from p. 25; see also (1977), 10ff.; (1982), 676–77; (1983b).

enfold increase in Attic burials between 780 and 720.[71] The number of burials available for this comparison is small (a total of about 300) and the case rests on the tenuous assumption that the surge in countable graves over the period echoes a corresponding surge in the birth rate.[72] A surge in burials could also reflect an increase in the death rate,[73] and other scholars argue that Attika during this period actually suffered not growth but decimation from drought.[74] In fact, rapid rises in mortality are by far the more common phenomenon in subsistence-level societies.[75]

Second, even assuming that in this case burials are a representative indication of an accelerated birth rate, the numbers indicate improbably steep growth. The implied annual increase—almost 4 percent—is well in excess of normal rates, and even exceeds high growth rates, for preindustrial soci-

[71] Adopted by Murray (1980), 65–66; Gallant (1982), 115; Welwei (1983), 36; R. Osborne (1985a), 225 n. 91; and others. Starr (1982), 420–21 is justifiably skeptical.

[72] Snodgrass (1980), 23–24; cf. (1977), 13–16. On the pitfalls and ambiguity of this kind of evidence for historical reconstructions, O'Connor (1972), 80ff.

Morris (1987) advances the intriguing idea that the rise in the number of graves actually relates more to a structural social change, whereby the practice of making formal burials was widened to include status groups beyond the exclusive ruling elite. He argues that about 750, the practice of "exclusion" from burial gave way to some greater "inclusion" of *kakoi* with *agathoi* in cemeteries; further, that this greater integration of status groups was representative of a new social structure, i.e., citizenship and the polis (see chapter 3). The major difficulty with this notion, at least in the eighth century (Morris portrays the integration as fading away, only to be reborn in the age of Kleisthenes), is the elusiveness of the evidence for the "excluded burials" before the period of integration. As Morris himself points out, the Geometric age evidence for "informal disposal" of the dead—especially in Attika—is faulty and incomplete at best (see pp. 104ff.).

[73] O'Connor (1972), 94–95 offers some interesting examples of this; see also the comments of Hollingsworth (1969), 273–74.

[74] Camp (1979). One of Camp's important objections (pp. 400ff.) to the eighth-century "population boom" theory is the absence of any substantial archaeological evidence for the increase during the following century. Snodgrass (1983b) candidly admits the problem.

[75] Wrigley (1969), 62–69.

eties.[76] A final objection relates directly to the explained rise of the polis. In linking the expanded birth rate to the development of a new kind of social organization, the author of the hypothesis must assume that the sevenfold increase implies not merely population growth but in fact overpopulation. This assumption requires a closer look.

The rise in the amount of material in the archaeological record after about 900 clearly suggests that the number of settlements and people in Attika was expanding after the depopulation of the Dark Ages.[77] Such growth might have fostered a more rapid spread of ideas as well as new divisions of labor, each in its own way conducive to the rise of the polis. But the proposed evolution of a "tighter and more compact social organization" to deal with new shortages in resources only makes sense if the absolute size of the population had outstripped its means to obtain food. The point deserves empha-

---

[76] See the examples collected by D. Engels (1984), 386–87 with n. 5. Hansen (1982a), 175 notes that a 4 percent growth rate is more than that of Mexico today! In fairness, however, it must be admitted that a steep rate of growth is more likely over a short period of time, particularly as a "rebound" after a period of depopulation; Snodgrass's case focuses on only two thirty-year generations in the aftermath of the demographic decline of the Dark Ages. But even under these conditions, a 4 percent rise is extraordinary. Cf. the classic case of short-term rapid growth after decline in medieval England and France after the Black Plague of A.D. 1347: during the three or four generations of most accelerated recovery, population grew at less than 1 percent. Cf. also two well-known historical benchmarks of "rapid growth": Ireland between 1780 and 1841, and England between 1740 and 1851—both well below 2 percent. For these three cases see Grigg (1980), 2ff.; 55ff. See also, more generally, the sensible remarks of Hansen (1985b), 9ff.; (1988), 8–9. (In the latter article, Hansen notes Snodgrass's concession, via personal correspondence, that a growth rate lower than 4 percent is probably likely.)

Snodgrass's argument in (1980) also takes no account of another possible negative variable on growth, female infanticide, which some scholars believe to have been normal practice in Greece: see Patterson (1985) who summarizes the many controversies of earlier scholarship on this subject.

[77] Snodgrass (1982), 668ff.; Andrewes (1982a), 363. Coldstream (1984), 9–10 proposes "the rather more credible figure" of a threefold increase in the population on the successive increase, throughout the Geometric period, in the number of wells dug in and near the Athenian agora; cf. Coldstream (1968), 360 n. 1, and Camp (1979), 400 with n. 12.

sis because studies of many other societies have shown that the "demographic variable" in political development has less to do with a population's actual magnitude than its size relative to the yield of available lands. It is in cases of *shortage*—when the land is strained by excess population—that anthropologists have been able to see the most direct effects of demographic change on the social and political order.[78]

To understand the impact of population on Attic society, then, one can pass over rates of growth and absolute numbers, both of which are all but impossible to determine accurately in this early period. Instead, it is the relationship of the population to the land itself that is crucial. In fact, no good evidence exists to show that agrarian yields of Attika were under pressure during the eighth century. The seventh century, however, seems to tell a different story. By about 600 the region was suffering from overpopulation, and the strain on resources was an important stimulus to the evolution of the polis, and of citizenship. This will become more clear in the next chapter, which examines real property and its social role in early Attika.

[78] E.g., Carneiro (1961), 314ff.; Fried (1967), 200ff.; Harner (1970); Netting (1972), 235ff. Cf. Boserup (1965), 86ff.; and Grigg (1980), 21ff. for a precise definition and attendant symptoms of "overpopulation." Garnsey (1988), xff., approaching the question from the supply rather than demand side, distinguishes between "famine" and "food shortages."

Chapter Five

LAND, SOCIETY, AND POPULATION AT THE BEGINNING OF THE SIXTH CENTURY

A CRUCIAL part of any polis was the territory that surrounded its civic center. That component was indeed vital to the Athenian polis which, as a primarily agrarian community, depended mightily on cultivable Attic land. Athenians farmed it, lived on it, survived by it—by tradition their ancestors were even born from it—and the importance of the soil to their society is undeniable. But who owned the land and who used it? Was land something sacred? How did the customs surrounding Attic land develop in early times? And how did customs contribute to the concept of citizenship that ultimately emerged?

To many scholars these questions can be reduced to simple formulas. Hignett, for example, asserted that before the sixth-century Solonian reforms "full citizenship was probably limited to those who owned their own land," and he has been followed by others who maintain that ownership of real property originally established an Athenian's rights in his society.[1] But such views underestimate the complexity of the situation and, if judged with the kind of rigor implied by contemporary usage of such legalistic phrases, they are simply wrong. They create an impression that early Attika, like some modern state, had a fixed property standard that determined citizenship; in fact, the concept of land ownership—like the concept of citi-

---

[1] Hignett (1952), 79. See also Woodhouse (1938), 81; Gernet (1968), 410; Ehrenberg (1969), 40; Snodgrass (1980), 40; and others. The same inference is sometimes drawn from the inverse proposition that only citizens could own land (Austin and Vidal-Naquet [1977], 25), which does not imply that land was a condition for citizenship, and is in any event an anachronism for this early period.

zenship—evolved only slowly over time, and at the beginning of the sixth century lacked any clear juridical definition.

To understand why, and with what implications, archaic land tenure was vague and primitive, one can begin by looking at the later, and more legally explicit, classical period. First, what did it mean then to own land? Ownership in itself is a difficult concept, but it is clear that in general ancient ideas of it were a far cry from modern statutory formulations.[2] Aristotle's definition (*Rhet.* 1361 a 21) that ownership represents one's power to sell or transfer something can be applied conveniently to the property relations of the fifth and fourth centuries. Indeed, by that time at least some lands in Attika were being sold or otherwise given up, and people who undertook such transactions can be said to have owned the lands.[3]

It is important to note that during this age land ownership was not a requirement for citizenship. For example, in the year 403 a certain Phormisius proposed (unsuccessfully) that politeia be restricted to holders of Attic land. The ancient source (Dion. Hal. *Lys.* 32) says that the measure would have deprived some 5,000 Athenians of their rights; in other words, 5,000 men who owned no Attic property were considered to be citizens at that time.[4] As far as can be known, this was the first time any such law was ever proposed, and there is no evidence that land ownership in any previous era was a criterion for a legal status of citizenship.

During the classical period, however, real property did provide one chief legal boundary between Athenians and non-Athenians, separating those who were allowed to own it from those who were not. Although citizenship did not require a man to have a plot, it did entitle him to acquire one. This fol-

---

[2] Harrison (1968), 201ff.; cf. Finley (1951), 53ff.; Kränzlein (1963), 13ff.

[3] E.g., the story in Plut. *Them.* 18.8 about Themistokles' sale of an estate. For full discussion of the scope and nature of various kinds of transfers in the classical age, see Finley (1981c) and (1986c); in the fourth century in particular, D. Lewis (1973); Andreyev (1973).

[4] Finley (1981c), 65 supposes this landless group to represent about 20 to 25 percent of the citizen population. On Phormisius' motion, see Krentz (1982), 109–10.

lows from the literary and inscriptional sources that affirm
that non-Athenians had to obtain special permission (*enktēsis*)
to own land in Attika.[5] By implication—though not by any
explicit statute—only Athenians could hold Attic property
without applying for permission. Thus they counted the capacity to hold Attic land as part of their legal status as citizens.

But the dating of the institution of this proprietary privilege
requires care. The earliest grant of *enktēsis* to non-citizens
cannot be placed much before 430,[6] and there is therefore no
good reason to assume that the exclusivity of Attic land originated hundreds of years before. On the strength of the evidence, then, the citizen's legal right to real property dates only
from the fifth century.

Even if the legal link between citizenship and land ownership was a limited and relatively late institution, a traditional
relationship had long existed between a man's place in society
and his rights to the soil that provided his livelihood.[7] Looking
back to the preclassical age, then, the question of "ownership"
remains. From earliest times the majority of Athenians had
farmed Attic land, and by custom understood it as "theirs."
But could land actually belong to an individual during, say,
the seventh century? How did land determine what it meant
to belong to the community?

To date, historians have approached these questions by debating the relevance of the aforementioned Aristotelian definition to land conditions in the preclassical age. They ask
whether property could be sold or given away before the fifth
century. That is, was land alienable or inalienable in early Attic history? Older scholarship argued that land was inalienable, held in common by *genē* or extended families, inhabited
and tilled but not transferable outside the kinship group until

[5] Pečírka (1963) and (1966).

[6] Pečírka (1963), 199–200; (1966), 152ff.

[7] On the traditional relationship between Athenians and their land, see
most recently R. Osborne (1985a), 15ff. Other important treatments include
Asheri (1963); Lacey (1968), 125ff.; Bourriot (1976), 745ff.; Starr (1977),
147ff.; Finley (1981c) and (1986c); Humphreys (1978), 130–35. For a contemporary Greek comparison, Du Boulay (1974), 27–40.

the reforms of Solon.[8] The next generation of historians elaborated the case, insisting that the prohibition of transfer lasted until the end of the fifth century;[9] a few other scholars, in reaction, subsequently claimed that land was always alienable, owned by individual families who could sell it or mortgage it as needed.[10]

All of these views suffer from a certain narrowness of vision. They assume that one custom or law (that is, a *nomos*) governed the status of all land of Attika, or even Greece. In similar fashion, they assume that such law or custom thereby determined the socioeconomic status and behavior of every man who farmed the fields. But the property of early Attika was not administered by any law at all, and the customs that surrounded it were in all likelihood many and varying. To grasp the concept of ownership and its corresponding social implications, these customs, their origins, and the conditions that molded them must be understood. As a background to the Athenian case, it is useful to examine property customs and land usage in some other primitive agrarian societies. Patterns of holding are typically complex and variable, changeable and rarely uniform. Furthermore, most "systems" of land tenure are constantly evolving into new systems over time.

A COMPARATIVE PERSPECTIVE ON LAND TENURE

Land tenure in an agrarian community can be affected by any of several factors.[11] Some variables represent variety in the land itself: the number and distribution of differing qualities

---

[8] E.g., Guiraud (1893), 1–23; N. Lewis (1941), 146–47; French (1964), 10; Woodhouse (1938), 74; Lacey (1968), 333; and others—all indebted, in one way or another, to the views of Fustel de Coulanges; cf. Momigliano and Humphreys (1980).

[9] E.g., Fine (1951), 178ff.; Hammond (1961), 76–98; and others.

[10] Swoboda (1905), 241; Thiel (1950); Forrest (1966), 148–50; Andrewes (1967), 97–98; Finley (1986b). Asheri (1963) assumes that land was alienable *until* the reforms of Solon.

[11] On issues and factors affecting land tenure sytems, Meek (1946), 1–10; Parsons (1956), 3–13; Biebuyck (1963b); Bohannan (1963); Boserup (1965), 77–94.

of soil, amount of cleared versus uncleared areas, access to sources of water, balance between cultivation and grazing—any of these can contribute to tenure customs within an area. The incidence of several such factors can promote a range of different customs within the same society. The Chimbu of New Guinea provide an interesting example. These people possess detailed knowledge of soil and terrain, and classify land into as many as seven types according to its productivity. The hierarchy ranges from "very high use" to "useless" and "purely ceremonial"; the society shows a corresponding hierarchy of individual and communal ownership, the more valuable land tending to foster the greater security of title among those controlling the property.[12] Thus, property in this community is both alienable and inalienable, with several degrees of alienability between the two extremes.[13]

Religious beliefs or political programs can determine a particular pattern of tenure within an agrarian society.[14] They might also transform an old pattern into a new one, as can an alteration in climate, irrigation, or soil fertility.[15] As property becomes more or less productive, or more or less sacred, a community's desire to farm and protect it will change. Customs of ownership evolve accordingly.

Land tenure typically responds to changes in the population density through births, deaths, and migrations.[16] The greater

[12] Brookfield and Brown (1963), 26–42.

[13] For another example of a range of alienable and inalienable tenures in the same society, see the case of the Toucouleur in the valley of the River Senegal: Boutillier (1963). For general discussion of the coexistence of several tenure systems, Boserup (1965), 56ff.

[14] On the role of religion in determining a land tenure system, Meek (1946), 6ff.; Biebuyck (1963c). For examples of effects of political change and legislation on systems, see case studies of British colonization discussed by Meek (1946).

[15] For examples of climate and irrigation as factors, Boutillier (1963). On soil exhaustion (leading to a shift toward more grazing land or cultivation of marginal lands), Meek (1946), 4ff.; Worsley (1956), 46ff.; Boserup (1965), 60ff.

[16] On population and its effects on agricultural systems generally, Boserup (1965). For case studies of population pressure and its role in forcing the development of private property and/or more intense cultivation of scattered

the number of users, the likelier the development of private property across once open fields. Scarcity forces cultivators to compete with one another and to establish the boundaries of their personal plots. It can also promote the development of wills, testaments, and other formal systems of inheritance, as cultivators struggle to keep property within their immediate families. And an inheritance system itself can affect a pattern of tenure: greater division among heirs usually means that individual holdings become fragmented and unprofitable over time.[17]

Commercial trends also play a role in land tenure. In the case of collectively tilled property, a shift among cultivators from subsistence to single crop market farming can lead to land division and the development of private freehold titles. Without sufficient security of ownership, farmers are less apt to take the risk of planting exportable crops (which might require several years to mature), or to make any large investment of capital.[18] This effect has, for example, been observed among the Meru people of Kenya. After the expansion of the coffee industry, farmers pressed for the creation of private plots on land earlier controlled by clans. Individual entrepreneurs demanded this guarantee lest they lose claim to coffee trees that they had planted.[19]

In the same spirit, the introduction of money to a previously

holdings and/or consolidation of holdings and/or excessive subdivision and abandonment, Meek (1946), 289ff.; Dantwala (1956); Taeuber and Taeuber (1956); Köbben (1963); White (1963).

[17] On the mutually determining relationship between inheritance and tenure systems, Meek (1946), 7ff.; Beuscher and von Dietze (1956); White (1963), 366–68; Homan (1963), 231ff.; Biebuyck (1963d); Colson (1963). Du Boulay (1974) notes the land fragmentation in the contemporary Greek village of Ambéli, stemming from equal partition of inheritances among heirs. See, however, Fox (1985), 211–28 who argues against the assumption that partible inheritance necessarily yields land fragmentation, or indeed that such anthropological models can be imposed on ancient Greek society.

[18] For the relationship between private property and the commercial agricultural development, Meek (1946), 2, 57–61, 223–25, 243–48; Boserup (1965), 100ff.

[19] Homan (1963), 226–29.

barter economy has been observed as a stimulus to selling and leasing of property once held in common.[20] Cash facilitates exchange, thus transforming what may have been a sacred trust into a more liquid asset. The tribal lands of Uganda provide a good example: the sudden buying and selling of communal fields after 1900 was a direct consequence of the money economy established by the British in that year.[21]

Any community may include types of property identifiable as common, loaned, rented, or private. In actual practice, lands worked by a population tend to display a range of gradations among these types, with one often blending into the next, and several types simultaneously evolving in response to natural and man-made forces.[22] The same society might exhibit several overlapping systems at once, the relationships among them continuing to change over time. It is usually too simple to describe an agrarian society's pattern of tenure by a choice between "alienable" or "inalienable," and the case of early Attika deserves more subtle treatment than the static, monolithic characterizations used by scholars in the past.[23]

A brief survey of tenure among the Tallensi (see chapter 3) illustrates more concretely the potential complexity of a land system in a primitive agrarian society. The farmland of the Tal settlements is patrimonial, inherited within the society's kinship lineages (genealogical descendants of a known ancestor in a male line) from father to son. The land is "owned" by the head of the lineage in the sense that his nuclear group has indefeasible rights over it. The use of the land is at his discretion, but he is expected to consult his kin in arranging its division and cultivation and to treat them fairly in so doing. Fortes described the social value of inherited farmland as "a sacred trust of ancestors. Their labor won it for human use, hallowed

<hr />

[20] Meek (1946), 289ff.; Boserup (1965), 86–87.

[21] Meek (1946), 366–68; Richards (1963), 267–80.

[22] See the typology presented and discussed by Boserup (1965), 89ff.

[23] Two recent treatments handle the issues of land tenure more appropriately, and in a similar spirit to what follows: Gallant (1982) and Wood (1983; cf. 1988). Previously, Finley (1986c) was a lone voice on the dangers of too schematic an analysis.

it, preserved it for descendants. To pledge it is a slur; to sell it is sacrilege."[24]

Nonetheless, Fortes and subsequent researchers saw that land sales do occur. In times of famine or pressing debt (e.g., to pay a bride price) the head of the lineage might sell his fields. Similarly, despite sanctions against it, pledging of land is not uncommon. Pledged land not redeemed causes great anxiety and mystical fears of ancestors' revenge for the man in financial straits; in fact, Fortes thought that much of the land described by the Tallensi as "bought" may have been only unredeemed pledges. Lending and borrowing of land is common, though renting it out is not. Most, but not all land transactions take place among kinsmen and clansmen.[25]

Inalienable patrimonial land is a respected tradition in this primitive society but the tradition has been qualified according to circumstances and changing agricultural conditions. Because of soil exhaustion, quarrels with siblings, or excess division of fields, many Tallensi fail to take up their patrimonial plots. Some clear and cultivate bush or marginal areas, others engage in wage labor, working for somebody else. Thus land is occasionally abandoned, or passes into the realm of a neighboring clan. Ancestral shrines on such lands decay, sometimes replaced by new ones of migrating foreigners. In times of great need, poor men sell their sons into slavery before the sons can take up their inheritance of property. About 95 percent of the Tallensi are entirely dependent on agriculture; the remaining 5 percent are part-time farmers, practicing trade and crafts in the off-season.[26]

To generalize, we might say that the Tallensi are an agrarian, patrilineal society that farms inalienable, ancestral land. Yet this generalization would obscure the nuances and dynamics of this people's property system. The example of the Tallensi warns us against hastily accepting generalizations about land tenure in Athenian history. Working in scholarly

[24] Fortes (1949), 178–91.
[25] Fortes (1940), 249–50; (1949), 179; Worsley (1956), 45.
[26] Worsley (1956), 43–55.

isolation, many historians have too readily characterized early Attika as an agrarian, patrilineal society whose people farmed inalienable, ancestral land. Of course the conditions and variations of Tal customs do not necessarily parallel those of Attic inhabitants during the Archaic age. But the organic complexity of the anthropological case does offer insight to a range of possible land practices among Athenians of the seventh and sixth centuries.

Before turning to the Athenian evidence, however, I want to consider an additional aspect of tenure systems in general: the distribution within the social and economic hierarchy of "insiders" and "outsiders." If one day a stranger appears in a rural neighborhood, where and under what conditions can he begin to dig with his spade, and raise crops for himself? Where and under what conditions can he not? In most agrarian communities, the distinction between "insiders" and "outsiders," critical to the concept of citizenship, depends on rights and access to land.[27] The status of those without privileges inevitably clarifies the status of those with them. An examination of this distinction helps illuminate what it meant "to belong" to a society whose livelihood was based on the soil.

In the same way that land tenure responds to many possible variables, the cultivation rights of outsiders in a rural economy develop according to different conditions. First, the density of population determines the willingness of the "natives" to share their lands with "strangers"; generally the more land available, the less reluctantly it is shared. Anthropological studies of agrarian societies again offer a useful perspective. For example, among the Valley Tonga of Zimbabwe, where property was originally controlled by lineages, rights of cultivation once belonged to any man who cleared and tilled a plot. Until about 1900 strangers could work unused areas without permission, and were even encouraged to do so, as long as land was plentiful.[28] The Bete and Dida peoples of the African Ivory Coast offer a similar example of the effects of

[27] Meek (1946), 1–31; Boserup (1965), 79; Gluckman (1965), 36–46.
[28] Colson (1963), 141.

population. In their sparsely inhabited villages, strangers are readily granted usufruct of common land, sometimes even becoming full members of the community. But in more densely settled areas, land is more precious, and natives extract rent for the same cultivation privileges.[29]

In addition to population, the quality of a locale's land can affect the community's acceptance or rejection of would-be cultivators. For example, among the Xhosa people (eastern Cape Province of South Africa), squatters on the society's most fertile territory must pay its freeholders for use. Over time many have migrated to less valuable communal lands which, by tacit consent of the Xhosa, is available to them without charge.[30] But in such cases, it is important to remember that changing conditions can change the "rules." Generally speaking, the relative "openness" of any rural community to outsiders is affected by fluctuations in population density, climate, or soil fertility.

In agrarian societies where lands are not freely shared, different kinds of contracts between native and stranger may be struck. Among the Shona of southern Zimbabwe, villagers cultivate land held in common by the "wards" of the region. Strangers can settle and work it only with permission of the ward chiefs, but, once accepted, the newcomers traditionally present the chiefs with beer and goats as tokens of goodwill.[31] In other societies, more costly payments in the form of rents or tribute are demanded, and in some cases landholders will even require newcomers to purchase property outright.[32] Of

---

[29] Köbben (1963), 253. For some other examples of population density determining the hierarchy of rights of cultivation, Soret (1963); Levine (1964).

[30] Wilson (1963), 381.

[31] Garbett (1963), 188.

[32] Both kinds of arrangement evolved after the introduction of freehold in Uganda. Large landowners sold parcels of property to strangers to raise capital; on lands that they maintained they replaced the older form of clientage with immigrant labor to whom they paid wages. But smaller landowners encouraged the settlement of newcomers on their land from whom they drew tribute payments. See Richards (1963), 270–74.

course, various less-formal agreements among insiders and outsiders are possible. Among the Shona, for example, a man's duty to support his divorced sister or deceased brother's family may encourage him to invite squatters to work his land. With their help in the fields, he can raise enough crops to fulfill his kinship obligations.[33]

Amid this discussion of "natives" and "strangers" or "insiders" and "outsiders," note that between the two theoretical extremes there exists a practical range of intermediate statuses. Every "indigenous" population stands in relation to both its predecessors and its successors, and "newcomer" is always a relative concept.[34] Foreigners or squatters or strangers do not remain "outsiders" forever as long as a society condones, explicitly or implicitly, cultural assimilation. Although the Athenians claimed that they were all sprung autochthonously from the Attic soil, the population probably was never so homogeneous as legend would have it. Many kinds of processes may have effected the integration of outsiders over time. Once again, examples drawn from anthropological studies can provide valuable comparisons.

Cultural assimilation can occur in a given society to varying degrees and for different reasons. In some cases, particularly when a community has a low density of population, natives simply accept outsiders and allow their full and rapid integration. This was already noted in the example of the Bete and Dida where newcomers easily gained insider status in villages that were sparsely inhabited.[35] The services or benefits outsiders can provide to a local population will also affect the willingness of natives to allow assimilation. Among the Mandari of southern Sudan, foreigners gain membership in society through clientage; by performing duties for a prominent man in the village, they are eventually introduced to local kinship groups.[36]

[33] Garbett (1963), 196.
[34] R. Cohen and Middleton (1970), 12.
[35] Köbben (1963), 253ff.
[36] Buxton (1966), 93.

Power, in fact, is an important factor in cultural assimilation. Among the Tonga of Zambia, for example, eminent men compete with one another to co-opt "guests" into their kinship groups; desire for prestige among the tribal leaders reinforces the society's incorporation of outsiders.[37] In the case of the Nilotic-speaking Alur of Uganda, the process is less voluntary for the foreigners. Captives taken in war are joined to individual households as "chiefship" is extended over new subjects.[38] Elsewhere and at other times the process of assimilation is slower and more friendly; in many societies, it is achieved through intermarriage, particularly when social barriers are broken down by a regional imbalance in the male–female ratio or when a mixed union can confer benefits that outweigh the censure of custom.[39]

Moreover, whatever the method of cultural assimilation, time plays another substantial role in the process. The passage of years inevitably blurs distinctions between insiders and the outsiders who have joined the native population. Fortes, for example, observed that some Tallensi with full property rights within their community were originally descended from captured slaves, and this kind of "eventual integration" is well attested in other societies.[40]

The foregoing discussion of land tenure and rural social relations demonstrates that a static, one-dimensional picture of the Athenian land system can only be misleading. It also serves as a reminder that social and economic analysis must consider the behavior of human beings rather than abstract symmetrical structures; that a community is made up of people whose customs extend only as far as each man's fears or needs or desires will allow. With this in mind, and the perspective

---

[37] Colson (1970), 36–41.

[38] Southall (1970), 76.

[39] See discussion of Goody (1970) on the case of immigrant families living among the Gonja of northern Ghana; also his comments on the marriage process in (1976). For a modern Greek village case, Du Boulay (1974), 46–47.

[40] Fortes (1949), 25–26; cf. Soret (1963); Goody (1970), 130.

gained from these observations of other agrarian societies, let us now turn to Attika.

THE CASE OF ATTIKA

We begin with the land itself. Today, the nonindustrialized portions of the Attic landscape span a variety of regions, each with its own physical characteristics and corresponding modes of agricultural production. The plains of Attika and Eleusis are distinguished by market and dairy farming. The Mesogeia and the area of Laureion, drier in climate, are regions of olive and vine plantations, and livestock and bee raising. The mountainous areas around Parnassos and Pentelikos are suited to livestock and cereals. Marathon, well supplied with water, is farmed for many different fruits, vegetables, and grains.[41]

Only about one-quarter of Attika's total area is cultivated. Pressure on the available usable land has led to increasing fragmentation of plot sizes, today an urgent problem. Besides political and economic obstacles to halting such fragmentation, the great variation among soil qualities in the cultivable land represents the chief barrier against consolidation. Property is almost entirely privately owned, and farmers are loath to sell or trade a rich tract for a poorer one, even if the exchange would mean gaining adjacent acreage.[42]

Previously, the qualities of the cultivable soil determined some variations in the patterns of ownership across the countryside. During the Turkish occupation of Greece, for example, different tenure systems within Attika existed, depending partly on the grade of arable land in each region.[43] As one

[41] For this description of the agrarian conditions and production of different areas of Attika; see Iliopoulos (1951), 105ff.

[42] On the pattern of cultivation, fragmentation, and the obstacles to consolidating land holdings, Sanders (1962), 70ff.; K. Thompson (1963), 116ff.; Damaskenides (1965); Du Boulay (1974), 265–70; Garnsey (1988), 48–49.

[43] Sanders (1962), 64ff.

looks back into the classical and preclassical eras, there are various indications that the ancient Athenians also appreciated the difference between more and less productive areas in their countryside.[44] It is reasonable, therefore, to suppose that they too developed more than one tenure system within their society and that over time the relationship between those systems changed according to at least some of the same kinds of transformative influences noted in other agrarian societies.

Such influences are known in early Attic society: commercialization (albeit primitive), migrations, overpopulation. Moreover, the apparently contradictory evidence about ancient Attic land tenure which has until now divided scholars into "alienable" or "inalienable" camps might best be interpreted to mean that at least two kinds of property then existed. By the beginning of the sixth century, land in Attika had evolved to a mixture of "public" (that is, held in common) and

[44] Andreyev (1973); see also the discussion of D. Lewis (1973), 194ff. on different values of Attic land. R. Osborne (1985a), 21 notes that the Attic vocabulary is "rich in terms with which to describe land . . . according to size, situation, and quality of land described" (e.g., *phelleus*, evidently a kind of poor soil [*SEG* 24.152.2; Poll. 1.227]; and for some other types of infertile soil, Xen. *Oec.* 20.12, Theophr. *Caus. Pl.* 3.6.3). See also ibid., 21ff. for discussion of Attic soil types. Though Osborne 41ff. argues that human choice rather than geography determined the pattern of settlement (in villages rather than on isolated homestead farms), certainly the Attic farmers of antiquity understood the difference between better and poorer soil, and would have worked better plots whenever they had a choice. Note the anecdote of the farmer who complained to Peisistratos that he harvested nothing but evil and pain from the rocky site he was digging (*Ath. Pol.* 16.6).

For a survey of the geography, climate, and agricultural areas of Attika in this century, see Iliopoulos (1951), 13ff. Snodgrass (1982), 659 warns against drawing inferences about ancient Greek agriculture from the modern landscape because of the apparent "younger fill" found in alluvial deposits throughout the Mediterranean. He argues accordingly that the agricultural potential of the ancient land was probably less than it would seem today. Even if so, however, it does not undermine the almost certain existence of differences in relative fertility across areas.

For more sympathetic treatments linking ancient and modern agrarian conditions in Attika: Starr (1986), 4–8; Garnsey (1988), 8ff.

"private," with Athenians working the soil under a variety of different statuses.

THE VARIETY OF THE ATTIC LAND TENURE PATTERN

During the classical period Athenians strongly believed that property ought to remain in the family. In the fourth century, when land mortgages and sales are well attested, speeches in the courts suggest that most men still preferred to leave their land to sons and that sons still preferred to inherit land from their fathers;[45] the classical laws of inheritance show strong bias toward keeping land within the *anchisteia* (relatives of the deceased as far as second cousins).[46] For the same reason, when an oikos lacked legitimate heirs to inherit its property, typically a relative—rather than any other Athenian—was adopted to continue the family line.[47] Reverence for family land is also echoed in an Athenian law against squandering one's patrimonial inheritance (*ta patrōia*)[48] and the cherished sacredness of family shrines and tombs.[49] Such evidence gives the impression that land was a traditional concern of every Attic oikos. But there are signs that land was also a concern of the groupings of oikoi, the regional corporations of Attika,

[45] E.g., Isae. 2, 6; Dem. 43. Andreyev (1973), 20 notes that inscriptional and literary sources of the period show little indication of land sales by peasants forced into penury. Poll. 8.104 records that when an Athenian was enrolled in his deme's *lēxiarchikon grammateion*, he took up his *patrōia:* see however, the comments of Whitehead (1986a), 35–36 n. 130.

[46] On inheritance laws, and their bias toward the oikos maintaining its patrimonial land, Gernet (1920); Harrison (1968), 122–62; Asheri (1966); Lacey (1968), 125–50; H. L. Levy (1972). De Ste. Croix (1970) sees a peculiarly democratic element in this bias, toward preventing landed property from becoming concentrated in the hands of the well-to-do.

[47] See references in note 46 above, and esp. the discussion of R. Osborne (1985a), 127ff.

[48] Aeschin. 1.30, regarding the *dokimasia* of *rhētores* which Rhodes (1972a), 2 argues extended to membership in the *boulē*.

[49] Cf. Dem. 57.54, 67; Xen. *Mem.* 2.2.13; Din. 2.17; and the oath taken by candidates for the archonship (*Ath. Pol.* 55.3 with Rhodes [1981], 617–18; Andrewes [1967], 97–98). Also see chapter 1, n. 82.

and of various rural settlements. Though a significant amount of property in the classical age was held by individual families, various inscriptions and literary sources attest to land sales, rental, and hypothecation (a form of mortgaging) in the "public" sector. Much Attic land in the fifth through third centuries belonged to demes, to religious and cult organizations, and to other regional associations, that is, *phylai, phratriai, genē,* and *kōmai* (villages).[50]

Judging from this classical evidence, many of the "public" holdings hark back to a more remote age. *Temenē* (sacred precincts associated with cults and shrines) tended to be concentrated in areas of central Attika that were more favorable for agricultural production and thus were probably cultivated from earliest times. Property belonging to phratries and *genē* was located in the most densely populated and fertile regions of Attika, again among the sites of earliest habitation. The distribution of these lands further suggests they were archaic and common holdings: not scattered plots but rather single large estates connected with the place of worship, forming a territorial center of each association. Both large and small properties were owned by classical demes, but it is probable that they too were once contiguous lands controlled by those associations. The majority of the plots fell within each deme's territory.[51]

It has been estimated from the surviving evidence that these "public" lands (that is, those not held by individual families) included at least 10 percent of the agricultural property of classical Athens, and thus played a prominent role in the agrarian system.[52] In previous centuries they must have been

[50] Finley (1951), 88–117; Andreyev (1973); Nemes (1980); Walbank (1983a), (1983b), (1984); Whitehead (1986a), 152ff.

[51] Andreyev (1973), 26–37 with figures 1, 2. "Formal" deme boundaries—when they existed—did not evolve until after the reforms of Kleisthenes (W. Thompson [1971]; Whitehead [1986a], 27ff.; and see chapter 7). Each village drew its membership from the surrounding territory which approximately encompassed that of the deme: R. Osborne (1985a), 41ff.

[52] Andreyev (1973), 43.

similarly (or even more) important, though there is no certain way to calculate a comparable percentage. The use made of public lands during the classical period does indicate a heritage of commonality; they do not seem to have been commercial enterprises but were generally employed to serve the interests of the members of the individual neighborhood communities.

Thus, when lands held in common were hired out, the renters were usually affiliated with the associations that owned them.[53] When particular plots were sold off, buyers were typically local inhabitants. Prices of sales listed in the *rationes centesimarum* tend to be round sums, which may indicate that the transfer of a piece of this kind of property was not based on competitive bidding, but rather on some relationship between the individual buyer and corporate seller.[54]

The overall picture that emerges for the classical age is of an agrarian society in which private and public forms of property mingled, and it is not unreasonable to assume that the two kinds of tenure descended from earlier patterns of holding.[55] In fact, evidence for property relations in the preclassical period suggests just that, with both common ownership by regional corporations and private ownership by individual oikoi complementing one another, and even overlapping. Furthermore, it appears that over time the balance between the two shifted toward more and more private tenure, and that this

[53] Ibid., 43–44; cf. R. Osborne (1985a), 54ff. and tables 3, 4 on demes and religious associations renting to their own members.

[54] Andreyev (1973). See however the comments of D. Lewis (1973), 194ff.

[55] The major limitation in using records of sale, rent, and hypothecation from the classical period to interpret earlier patterns is our ignorance about original "ownership." Though some of the "public" lands must have been acquired through confiscations, purchases, and gifts in classical times, others dating from the previous age could also have been lost through acquisition by private individuals, to foreigners with grants of *enktēsis*, or by appropriations (e.g., *IG* ii² 1035). Given the antiquity of the many landholding associations, and the general sacredness of land in the society, we may safely assume at least some continuity between the property patterns of the classical and preclassical periods.

change was directly related to the development of the community into a polis. To reconstruct how that occurred, one must consider the agrarian crisis of the early sixth century, and the background of the land reforms brought forward by the statesman Solon in 594/3.[56]

In the *Athēnaiōn Politeia*, Aristotle stated that before Solon's time "all land was in the hands of the few" (2.2: *hē de pasa gē di' oligōn ēn*). The context suggests that "the few" were rich and powerful men, though we hear nothing of the way in which they actually controlled Attic property. But the statement, taken together with Aristotle's earlier assertion that "the poor were in servitude to the rich," naturally implies that most men were working land they themselves did not own.[57] A further clue is offered when Aristotle comments on the actual reforms of Solon: "He cancelled debts not only private but public" (6.1: *chreōn apokopas . . . kai tōn idiōn kai tōn dēmosiōn*). In the philosopher's day the Greek word for

---

[56] The enormous bibliography of modern views on Solon's agrarian reforms is surveyed (with references) by Cassola (1964). Since then, important treatments include Finley (1965); Forrest (1966), 147ff.; Asheri (1966), 65ff.; Cataudella (1966); Will (1969); Cassola (1973); Murray (1980), 181ff.; Rhodes (1981), 90–97; Andrewes (1982a), 375ff.; Gallant (1982). Wood (1983) and (1988) treats the related questions of slavery and agrarian labor in the classical period with significant implications for various Solonian problems.

In what follows I accept the traditional date of 594/3 for Solon's archonship and reforms, though that has been occasionally challenged (e.g., M. Miller [1968]). For a recent defense, see R. Wallace (1983).

[57] This point can be strengthened on the basis of two important articles by Beringer (1982), (1985). In his analysis of Homeric and Linear B texts, Beringer argues persuasively that before the classically defined distinction of "free" versus "slave," the words *eleutheros* and *doulos* had connotations of "belonging to the community" versus "not belonging." Thus Aristotle's comment that "the poor were in servitude (*douleuein*) to the rich" should really be read as "the poor were unfree," meaning that they were outside the social stratum and community of those who owned the land. This interpretation would fit nicely with the relationship suggested later in this chapter between social corporations and dependent laborers. For a different view, however, of the relationship between, and meanings of, *eleutheros* and *doulos* in the pre-Solonic age, see Raaflaub (1985), 29–70, 313ff.

"debt" (*chreos*) typically meant payment due for borrowing, but the term could also cover a broader range of possible obligations.[58] Whatever its precise sense here, note that there were two different kinds of obligations—public and private—which, again in the context, seems to have had something to do with the land. In his poetry, Solon speaks of "public lands," mentioning them in the same verse with "sacred lands." He attacks the greed of popular leaders who, unsparing of these properties, steal from one another using force and deception (F 4.12–14: *outh' hierōn kteanōn oute ti demosiōn / pheidomenoi kleptousin apharpagei allothen allos*). The rhetorical style of the poem obscures much here, but the reference to public and sacred lands seems significant.[59] These must have been properties held in common, under the control of "public" and "sacred" organizations. The most obvious candidates for such control were the traditional public and sacred organizations of early society: not the "state," for it was not yet a centralized landowner, but rather the phratries, *genē, orgeōnes*, as well as villages, and demes, and other regional corporations. Such "public" bodies held property in the classical age, as already noted, and it is likely that there was a long tradition behind their doing so.

One can imagine, then, powerful and aristocratic men in each of these landholding associations exercising control over a poorer population somehow obliged to them; and that this poorer multitude enjoyed the cancellation of their "public obligations" when Solon passed his reforms, as Aristotle noted. But what was the nature of the obligation? Aristotle specifies that those in servitude to the rich were *pelatai* ("those who work for someone else"; see later), and *hektēmoroi*. *Hektēmoros* means literally a "sixth-parter," and Aristotle uses the gloss to explain the nature of their obligation: "for at this rent

[58] Discussed most recently by Andrewes (1982a), 377–82; Gallant (1982), 111–12.

[59] Cassola (1964) emphasizes a distinction between "public" and "sacred lands," with a conclusion similar to what follows, i.e., the existence of different kinds of property as a background to Solon's reforms.

(*misthōsis*) they worked the fields of the rich" (2.2). The idea of renting for cash belongs not to Solon's day but to Aristotle's when money was more common as a means of exchange.[60] A sort of tenancy—rather than borrowing, as many have assumed—still seems implied, however. Pollux (7.151), quoting from Solon's laws, clearly connects the *hektēmoroi* with sharecropping, that is, an obligation to pay part (one-sixth) of the yield from the land that was farmed but not owned by the laborer.[61]

In light of the above, the first part of the tenure system can now be described: lands were held in common by kinship and regional associations, controlled by powerful elites in each organization, with poorer men farming plots of the estates in return for giving up a share of their annual harvest. The land was inalienable, not because any law dictated, but because the various corporations naturally wanted to preserve their holdings for the use of their members and dependents; the limits of each man's fields within the corporate land would have been vague and somewhat moveable, depending on changing conditions of soil and population. Ties of religion, kinship, or regional cooperation solidified loyalties within each area of settlement, supplementing each man's contractual relationship to pay the aristocrats their due.

A Range of Land and Labor Relationships

The nature of the sixth-part obligation becomes more clear with a consideration of its possible origins. As the territory of Attika was slowly reclaimed after the depopulation that followed the Mycenaean collapse, many of the regional corpo-

---

[60] This is not to deny that some form of "money" had begun to play a role in the rural economy: see below, n. 78. For an extreme view of *misthōsis* that stresses Homeric-style "gift reciprocity," see Gallant (1982), 111–12.

[61] Thus Forrest (1966), 148–54; Andrewes (1982a), 377–78. The earlier view of *hektēmoros* as borrower is found (*inter alios*) in Woodhouse (1938), 42ff.; N. Lewis (1941); Fine (1951); and Hammond (1961). Most scholars now accept that the *hektēmoros* owed one-sixth, rather than kept one-sixth. For the debate, see Busolt and Swoboda (1920–26), 779 n. 2; for an interesting comparison with another preindustrial society, see Kirk (1977).

rations first came together, settling within the more fertile precincts of Attika.[62] The archaeological record reveals the spread of habitation after the ninth century, and particularly during the eighth century; evidence for this period shows that new cults were established at rural grave sites, a finding that might mean that recently formed neighborhood groups were consecrating local lands.[63] As new areas were claimed and groups consolidated, the expanding population would have clustered around the various social nuclei that formed.

Strangers to neighborhoods—whether Athenians moving from areas of greater to lesser population density, or non-Athenians arriving from other parts of the Greek mainland—traveled across Attika in search of lands and gradually became incorporated into the evolving local organizations.[64] Primitive contracts developed between those who already controlled the land and those who came to farm it.[65] The contracts were ultimately symbolized by the *horoi* mentioned in Solon's poetry (F 36.6); these would have been markers placed on the plots

[62] Andrewes (1982a), 380.

[63] Snodgrass (1971), 196 and (1980), 38–40; cf. Coldstream (1976). See however the remarks of Humphreys (1983e), 106 with n. 22; Whitley (1988), 176–78.

[64] On the possibility of non-Athenians adding to the population of Attika before 600, see below, chapter 6; note also the arguments of Beringer (1982) and (1985), as cited above, n. 57.

Interestingly, my suggestion of migrating strangers matches the interpretation offered for the early history of Lathuresa, the sole Geometric settlement to be excavated in Attika. Lauter (1985), 69ff. proposes that the settlement was originally the gathering place of a seminomadic clan who periodically visited the site before occupying it more permanently in the late eighth century. By Lauter's view, the settlers were soon absorbed into already existing local communities. The evidence, however, is extremely sketchy, and Lauter's interpretation is open to serious challenge: Ober (1987); Morris (1987), 97–98.

[65] Andrewes (1982a), 378; cf. Finley (1965). For similar client-style relationships based on usufruct of inalienable land, Boutillier (1963), 121–22; Richards (1963), 269; Köbben (1963), 257. Wood (1988), 81ff., following Murray (1980), 181–84, supposes that the land and labor relationships that developed after the Dark Ages were remnants of the Mycenaean tenure system.

of cultivators who now owed their sixth share to the regional authorities.[66]

At the same time, other kinds of obligations existed among dependent users of common lands, varying according to each man's relative "newness," his status in a regional corporation, and the population density of the locale. One legacy of the different agreements struck may be the *pelatai* who are distinguished from the *hektēmoroi* in Aristotle's account of the pre-Solonian period, and are elsewhere identified as free laborers who worked a plot in exchange for their keep or pay.[67] Although hektemorage was perhaps the more typical labor relation for common land, and the payment of a "sixth" became customary for most men, others could have worked for a simple, standard wage. This kind of arrangement might have evolved naturally from the deal struck with *hektēmoroi*. In the latter case, one man's sixth could be another man's third, depending on the size of their plots, the quality of those plots' soil, and so on. Accordingly, it would have been only a small step for certain "lessors" to move beyond allowing a *hektēmoros* to keep five-sixths of an "open-ended" relationship, to paying other men a fixed, and less-variable wage in exchange for their working a share of the common fields.[68] The hiring of *pelatai* may have been particularly attractive in areas where there was greater competition for land.

This picture might plausibly describe the property relations of Attic lands held in common, but several clues imply that by about 600 not all farming was necessarily under the control of regional corporations. Private, alienable property made up another part of the tenure system in the archaic Athenian com-

[66] Critics who object to the interpretation of the *horoi* as markers of personal obligation rather than "mortgage stones" (as was more common in the classical age) should note the comments of Finley (1951), 15–16: "The fact of encumbrance . . . and not the details, constituted the essential purpose of the *horoi*."

[67] Pl. *Euthphr.* 4 C 3–5; Dion. Hal. *Ant. Rom.* 2.9.2; Poll. 3.82. See Rhodes (1981), 90–91 for other sources and discussion of the lexicographic tradition.

[68] On the close relationship between *misthos* ("wage") and *misthōsis* ("rent") see Wood (1983), 29; cf. MacDowell (1978), 140–41.

munity. The sources, for example, preserve traditions of land being bought and sold about the time of Solon's reforms; the coexistence of private property with land held in common would also explain the law that Solon later passed limiting the amount of land any man could acquire (Arist. *Pol.* 1266 b 14–18).[69]

That at least two different statuses of land and ownership existed during this time is further implied by the different statuses of obligation seen within the rural society. Recall the distinction between *hektēmoroi* and *pelatai*, the latter of whom, working for wages or their keep, were probably employed on private lands as well as on common. And, as noted, Aristotle (*Ath. Pol.* 6.1) reported that Solon canceled two different kinds of "debts," both "private" and "public." This testimony could mean that some men were obliged as holders of private land while others were obliged as workers of common fields.

But how might someone have been obliged as a holder of private land? Here the institution of debt bondage seems to fit. In addition to hektemorage, the sources for the period refer to a kind of indebtedness whereby a man pledged his own person to gain credit. Many scholars simply equate this with hektemorage, apparently following Aristotle (*Ath. Pol.* 2.2) who claims that during the period "all loans were secured on the person." But Plutarch in his discussion of the agrarian crisis

---

[69] For the tradition of land sales in Solon's day, see the story of speculators who profited from the cancellation of debts with advance notice from the reformer: *Ath. Pol.* 6.2; Plut. *Sol.* 15; Plut. *Mor.* 807 D–E; Suid. s.v. Solon. Many of the details are anachronistic, and Aristotle himself doubted the story. But his doubt (*Ath. Pol.* 6.3) is based on the belief that Solon was too civic-minded to have been partial to any group, and the fundamental idea that land could be bought and sold need not be rejected with the rest of the tale (*contra* Fine [1951], 180 n. 45; Rhodes [1981], 129; and others; for a rationalization of the anecdote, M. Miller [1968], 70–73). Buying and selling of land seems all the more possible in the face of the measure limiting holdings. This too has been challenged as spurious (e.g., Asheri [1966], 69–70; Andrewes [1982a], 384), but without good reason; such legislation would not only have prevented concentration of land in the hands of the elite, but also would have helped curb excessive division of small plots, likely a problem during this time (discussed later). For an example of this kind of law and a similar effect on property holdings in Zimbabwe, see Garbett (1963), 191–93.

(*Sol.* 13.4) clearly separates the payment of a sixth from the custom of personal enslavement. Accepting of this distinction solves many of the problems that have plagued past treatments of the Solonian reforms.[70]

Therefore, during this time some men were neither sharecropping nor working for a wage on the common lands of a regional corporation or rural village, but rather tilling their own plots, and taking on the onus of potential slavery in exchange for a loan of goods or capital. These small property holders would have needed to borrow from richer neighbors to survive over a bad year or even until the next harvest.[71] By the time of Solon's archonship, their indebtedness had grown dangerously, and the reformer's program thus included the cancellation of these "private" debts.

Thus far I have distinguished two kinds of land and three kinds of rural obligations, all of which have been described schematically for the purpose of this discussion. In practice, however, the different kinds of property and obligations blended into one another, each with a variety of intermediate forms.[72] For example, it is very likely that some *hektēmoroi* also risked debt slavery for loans, in addition to the standard one-sixth they were normally expected to offer. It is easy to believe that the hard-pressed would not have been immune to more than one sort of debt, particularly in the gloom of economic distress. Similarly, borrowing against enslavement may have been required by some *pelatai* or other dependent laborers who worked another man's fields; and the same credit security could also have been required of laborers on lands of uncertain status between "private" and "public" land. In general, there must have been more than a little vagueness about

[70] See the comments of Forrest (1966), 148 on such problems.

[71] This element of the story characterizes the interpretations of many past scholars, e.g., N. Lewis (1941); Fine (1951), 167ff.; and others. For discussion of agricultural cooperation among rural neighbors in the classical period, Wood (1983), 31ff.; and (1988), 96–99; R. Osborne (1985a), 16–62.

[72] See the discussions of Gallant (1982), 113–14; and Wood (1983), 30ff.; and (1988), 89ff. for similar views about the complexity of agrarian relationships.

what was "private" and what was common among the inhabitants of Attika, not only because of their less-than-modern concept of ownership, but also to judge from the pattern of settlement and land use in later times. For in the classical period the Attic population was clustered in villages, with farmers usually traveling to work in outlying fields rather than living on their own plots. Moreover, individual holdings were often scattered among different areas within the same general locale.[73]

If the foregoing explanation appears complex, it is worth remembering that the probable evolution of different kinds of property tended to break down the more predictable and simple labor relationships of earlier times; the rural lands and relationships were not static but constantly evolving. When Solon, for example, notes in his verse that men had been enslaved both "justly and unjustly" (F 36.9–10: *allon ekdikōs / allon dikaiōs*), the phrase may not imply so much that some creditors had foreclosed on personal pledges fairly and others unfairly, but rather that customary practices of "indebtedness" were eroding in the face of new attitudes about ownership and obligation. The range and multiple variations of agrarian relationships suggested by the evidence makes sense once one assumes that traditional patterns of common tenure were changing while at the same time new patterns were developing.

Indeed, it was the transformation across the landscape and not just the landscape itself that provided the context for the Solonian reforms. The Attic countryside was a dynamic landscape intermingling "public" and "private" lands, with several different grades of property between these two extremes shading into one another. Overall, however, the trend within the system was gradually toward greater definition of individual holdings: plots were being marked out by farmers, as common lands were broken up and marginal or less fertile areas

[73] R. Osborne (1985a), 16–62; cf. Garnsey (1988), 94. This is precisely the situation that Du Boulay ([1974], 10, 265ff.) described in the Greek mountain village Ambéli in the 1960s.

of Attika were cleared by enterprising families. Though the direct evidence for this trend is slight, the analogy of similar change in other agrarian societies helps fill out the picture.[74] Some of the same forces that have produced such a shift elsewhere in time and place can be perceived in Attika toward the end of the seventh century.

In the first place, it seems that by this time some kind of money must have begun to circulate in Attika. Since the 1950s, Aristotle's testimony about Solon's reform of Athenian coinage (*Ath. Pol.* 10) has been discounted by many numismatists who hold that no coinage of any kind was known on the Greek mainland before 580 (at the earliest).[75] But recent treatments on the origin of coinage have argued persuasively for a date in the early or middle seventh century, thereby renewing some credibility to Aristotle's belief in coins in Attika by about 600.[76] Even if Athenians were not circulating coins by then (and the controversy continues to rage),[77] some form of money was almost certainly being used in Attika during this period. For money does not necessarily imply coins, as Keynes reminds us, and it appears that Athenians at the end of the seventh century were at the very least using fixed weights of precious metals as a medium of exchange.[78] Solon's verse mentions gold and silver as one of the many forms of wealth that a man might have (F 24.1–3), and we know that Athenians had been mining silver at Laureion from as early as the ninth century.[79] Some of Solon's laws (Plut. *Sol.* 23) included

[74] For examples of property rights based on the clearing and cultivation of unused or marginal lands, Bohannan (1963), 106–7; Colson (1963), 151; L. Thomas (1963), 319–21; Gluckman (1965), 36–45.

[75] E.g., Kraay (1968). For a survey of the several numismatic issues and previous scholarship relating to Solon see Rhodes (1975). On the debate about the introduction of coinage in general, Kagan (1982b), 343–46; Kroll and Waggoner (1984); R. Wallace (1987).

[76] Kagan (1982b); cf. Cahn (1975); Weidauer (1975), 70ff.; Hammond (1986), 661.

[77] See the reply to Kagan by Kroll and Waggoner (1984).

[78] See the discussion of Rhodes (1981), 152–53; Andrewes (1982a), 383; cf. Keynes (1930) 1:3ff.

[79] Coldstream (1977), 70.

fines and prices listed in drachmas, which, if not coins, were certainly weights of metal that had become fixed standards by then. Similarly, another Solonic law referred to silver to be spent from the funds held by the officials called *naukraroi* (*Ath. Pol.* 8.3).[80] If the cases of other agrarian societies penetrated by money offer a parallel, we should imagine that silver or coinage in Attika had begun to promote new practices and new attitudes toward property sharing and ownership among those working common lands. Limited buying and selling began to appear, with a corresponding redefinition of certain plots as privately held and alienable.

The seventh century witnessed another form of rudimentary commercialization that further increased the development of private property. By the year 600 at least, some inhabitants of Attika were producing commodities for export, particularly wines and oil.[81] The extent and impact of trade in agricultural products, as already noted, can be difficult to estimate, but trade in certain goods clearly had become significant enough by the year of Solon's reforms to prompt his passing a law regulating them (Plut. *Sol.* 24). Thus, market producers were now investing much more capital to develop their lands than were subsistence farmers. Olives are a low-yield, slow-maturing crop, and vines are prone to disease and pests;[82] the greater risks taken by these entrepreneurial farmers would have made them more eager to secure title to their properties. Among this group private ownership was growing, if other agrarian societies that experience similar changes offer a valid comparison.[83]

The final factor to be considered is the impact of population

[80] See chapter 4, n. 23.

[81] So Forrest (1966), 154ff.; Jeffery (1976), 85; Rhodes (1981), 96ff.; and others, chiefly on strength of the overseas finds of "SOS-type" amphorae (Johnston and Jones [1978]); see also my later discussion of Solon's law against exports. The importance of wine and oil in the economy by this time may find some further proof in the Solonian *telē* which rated a man's wealth in "measures both dry and wet together" (*Ath. Pol.* 7.4).

[82] French (1964), 19–22; Finley (1985), 31.

[83] Cf. the case of the coffee growers among the Meru people in Kenya (above, text and n. 19).

on the rural society of Attika. Although, as already pointed out, the impact of demographic growth in the eighth century is questionable, by the end of the seventh century the population had expanded to the point that shortages of resources were occurring. Overpopulation relative to the land was now affecting the Attic tenure system.

Without absolute numbers we cannot calculate any quantitative changes in density per unit of land and yield, but the indirect signs of population pressure are compelling.[84] Colonization provides the first hint. In the eighth century, Athens had not taken part in the so-called colonial gold rush when many other Greek states sent out overseas ventures in search of new land.[85] By about 600, however, Athens had dispatched colonies of its own, to Sigeion in the Troad and Elaious in the Chersonese.[86] True, both sites flank the Hellespont and have been characterized as settlements aimed primarily at promoting Athenian access to Black Sea trade.[87] But their strategic access to the Hellespont does not discount the settlements' potential agricultural value as well.[88] As Diogenes Laertius reports (1.74; cf. Hdt. 5.94), the war that Athens fought with Mytilene for Sigeion during the late seventh century concerned not only a harbor but actual territory (*chōra*). The Chersonese, site of Elaious, was similarly known for its fertile land.[89]

Closer to home, Athens showed other signs of expansion

---

[84] As is often noted, *direct* evidence for settlement, let alone population, in the seventh century is very elusive. For a valuable discussion of the problem, Morris (1987), 163–65.

[85] Forrest (1966), 154; Brunt (1966), 71; Murray (1980), 177; and others. Coldstream (1977), 135 speaks of the Athenian preference in the eighth century "to colonize their own countryside."

[86] See chapter 4, n. 51 for references.

[87] E.g., Beloch (1912), 2:315; Forrest (1966), 155; Boardman (1980), 264.

[88] Andrewes (1982a), 374. Graham (1971) and (1982), 157ff. summarizes the old debate about the motives behind Greek colonization, and reasserts persuasively the case of Gwynn (1918) that overpopulation and "land hunger" were the normal stimuli to overseas ventures. For the opposite view stressing trade motives, see Lepore (1969).

[89] Jeffery (1976), 90; Meiggs (1972), 160.

during this period, perhaps also reflecting land hunger. The struggle with Megara for Salamis, datable to the late seventh century, has been connected with overseas trade, but the farmland of the island may have been a desirable prize as well.[90] Plots on Salamis were valuable enough to lead the Athenians to prohibit settlers (probably klerouchs) from leasing them outside their families in later times.[91]

The contemporary interest of Athenians in overseas trade, moreover, might further argue that Attika was suffering overpopulation in the late seventh century. During the classical period, cities of the Black Sea and Egypt supplied much grain to feed the Aegean states, and it is not unlikely that Athens began importation from these sources before 600.[92] The earliest remains from the trading port Naukratis in Egypt include Attic pots dating from about 620–600,[93] and the contemporary Athenian colonies near the Black Sea could have been founded to facilitate the food trade from that part of the world.[94] If Athens had begun to import grain during this time, it could

[90] On the Salaminian war, see Plut. *Sol.* 8–10; *Ath. Pol.* 14.1 with Rhodes (1981), 199–200. Hopper (1961), 208–17 plausibly argues for a multiphase war that began under Solon, with the island lost and regained finally by Peisistratos in the 560s. See also Andrewes (1982a), 372–73. For trade-related issues as a cause of the war, see French (1964), 25ff.

[91] Meiggs and Lewis (1969), no. 14, lines 4ff. with commentary pp. 26–27. On klerouchies, see chapter 7.

[92] See the remarks of Austin and Vidal-Naquet (1977), 69; Rhodes (1981), 95–96; and fuller arguments by Hahn (1983) and Bravo (1983). For more skeptical views (dating the trade to the end of the sixth century at the earliest), Noonan (1973); Bloedow (1975); Garnsey (1985) and (1988), 105–19. The latter work of Garnsey represents the fullest attack on the widely held view of grain importation in the archaic period. I remain unconvinced by his arguments, which are often subjective. He discounts, e.g., the Athenian wars with Megara, finding them merely "reducible to the tug of war between neighboring city states that was a regular feature of international relations in Greece," and similarly asserts that "activities in the north [i.e., Black Sea area] smack of adventurism" (p. 118). For an antidote to his related view on the lesser significance of imported grain in the society—which may rest on too low an estimate of Attic population in the classical period—see Hansen (1988), 7–13.

[93] Boardman (1980), 125; cf. Austin (1970), 35.

[94] Jeffery (1976), 89; Graham (1982), 121; and others (e.g., above, n. 87).

only mean that there were now more mouths to feed at home than the land of Attika could support. This situation is suggested by the export law that Solon passed early in the next century: as noted earlier, the reformer restricted the export of agricultural produce outside of Attika, with the exception of olive oil (Plut. *Sol.* 24). Solon may have hoped to alleviate shortages at home with the measure.[95]

In general, the agrarian crisis that prompted Solon's reforms is the best indication of population pressure in Attika. From the reports of the troubles it is obvious that there was no contemporary lack of rural labor.[96] Both Plutarch's account (*Sol.* 13.3, 15.5) and Solon's own poetry (F 36.9–10) note that many men had been sold into slavery abroad or forced to flee because of debt. By implication, those who controlled the land at home had an abundant supply of workers to replace those who were sold or who fled. Moreover, Plutarch (*Sol.* 22) also provides direct testimony that Solon passed laws encouraging Attic dwellers to take up *technai* ("trades") because "the city was becoming filled as people were constantly pouring into Attika from all over, seeking security . . . and because most of the land was infertile and worthless . . . and because it could give mere subsistence to those who cultivated it, and was incapable of supporting an idle and unoccupied populace."

Elsewhere, in another passage (*Sol.* 24) often misread, Plutarch reports that Solon took steps to restrict immigration: "He allowed only those to be citizens who were exiled permanently from their own countries or who moved with their entire families to Athens to practice a trade."[97] Thus transient

---

[95] Starr (1977), 184; Hahn (1983), 33; Bravo (1983), 21ff. Jameson (1983), 11–12; and Garnsey (1988), 74–75 are reluctant to infer continuing shortages from the passage of the law.

[96] French (1964), 15.

[97] The best discussion of this measure to restrict immigration is Whitehead (1977), 141–42. That the law sought to limit rather than encourage immigration is the obvious inference in the context of Plut. *Sol.* 22, quoted earlier; the main clause of the legislation restricts rather than relaxes conditions for joining the community. For representative older scholarship that wrongly interpreted the text, Diller (1937), 101, 115; McGregor (1973), 53–55.

labor was discouraged, and limits were imposed on rural agrarian settlement; both are reasonable remedies in a society where too many people work the land.

In summary, the direct and indirect evidence points toward rising population pressure throughout Attika in the late seventh and early sixth centuries. The condition hastened the development of private property as scarcity made men more eager for definition of their own plots amid increasing competition for land. Older and traditional common lands were slowly broken up; fields became more fragmented as successive generations of fathers divided them among sons who worked smaller and smaller plots more intensively; conflicts arose between powerful men who by custom controlled most Attic property and poor farmers who faced greater and greater burdens. Marginal lands were opened up for cultivation; other plots were abandoned as unproductive; Athenians were sold into slavery for debts owed to other Athenians. The older, regionally based social order had begun to crumble, creating the potential for a leader who could reorganize the population into a new form of community, one in which the vagaries of rights, privileges, obligations, and plots of land would be articulated with new and more formal boundaries. The unifying and centralizing trends seen in the age of Drakon would become the basis for the Solonian solution. Out of crisis, Solon created the polis.

Chapter Six

SOLON AND THE "INVENTION" OF THE ATHENIAN POLIS

IN THE CLASSICAL age, Athenians looked back upon Solon as a statesman, poet, and traveler. Historians today describe him (variously) as a founding father of democracy, a popular leader who broke the Eupatrid monopoly of power, a moderate but visionary politician who brought civic justice to his society.[1] For our purposes, Solon can be identified more simply: he is the man who established the Athenian polis, and thereby created the beginnings of a formal citizenship.

It was not, of course, a single-handed achievement, nor was the true import of what was accomplished fully understood by anyone at the time. This special form of political organization had been evolving for some time, but the reforms that Solon sponsored in the early sixth century marked a turning point in the development of the polis' institutions and all-important

[1] On Solon and his reforms see Gilliard (1907); Linforth (1919); Freeman (1926); Massaracchia (1958); van Effenterre (1977); and references in chapter 5, n. 56. On the myths surrounding his achievements, Mossé (1979b). Ruschenbusch (1966) collects ancient testimony for all supposed Solonian laws. Hereafter references to these, as required, will be indicated as *SN* (*Solonos Nomoi*) plus Ruschenbusch's assigned numbers.

It is not my intent to argue the old and vexed questions of whether and which attributed Solonic laws are in fact authentic. Against the well-known skepticism of such critics as Hignett ([1952], 17–30; cf. Linforth [1919], 278ff; Mossé [1979b]; and others), I count myself among the more credulous historians who believe that Aristotle, Plutarch, and other postclassical scholars did have texts of actual Solonic laws to work from; further that their reports are generally (though not always) valid sources for the legislation of the early sixth century. For the best summary of this view, including references to relevant scholarship, see Stroud (1978), esp. 23–26 (cf. [1979]) whose perspective I endorse herein. For other discussions, see Ruschenbusch (1966), 1–14; Andrewes (1974); N. Robertson (1986). In what follows, I take as genuine all cited Solonic laws, unless otherwise noted.

spirit; at the same time, the success of the reforms depended in no small part on the willingness of a majority of the Attic inhabitants to embrace them. The prospect of a new order that embodied a new kind of justice and a new definition of the individual within society was doubtless attractive to Athenians at the time; for such things promised an end to the conflicts and confusions aggravated by economic change, overpopulation, and the turmoil of the previous several years.

Certainly at the beginning of the sixth century the conflicts had reached a crisis. Rural struggles between small farmers and their powerful creditors threatened to erupt into open civil war. Too many people were working too little productive soil; the former network of benign obligations that defined the agrarian society was collapsing, as fields were alternately competed for or abandoned as infertile, and debtors were enslaved or driven into exile. With each passing harvest, survival became more difficult, both for those working common lands and for those who needed to borrow capital to maintain their own plots—or simply to keep from starving. Rich and powerful men who lorded over vast estates and common property resisted change, while a growing share of the multitude demanded an end to their burdens, and even a redistribution of land.[2]

In other Greek communities, such conditions had promoted the rise of tyrants, popular leaders who seized power and ruled by force at the expense of the traditional aristocratic elites.[3] In Athens, Solon might have done the same. Renowned for military exploits against Megara,[4] he could have taken advantage of the social and economic chaos to transform his celebrity into an oppressive personal reign. Fortunately for the Athenians, he did not. Archon in 594/3, Solon instead chose to mediate the problems of his day through political means. His background was suited to the moderate course that he followed. Of distinguished birth and reputation, he was nonethe-

[2] On the call for land redistribution, *Ath. Pol.* 11.2; cf. Solon F 34.8–9; Plut. *Sol.* 16.1. On the later history of such demands, Asheri (1966), 60ff.

[3] Andrewes (1956); Berve (1967); cf. Arist. *Pol.* 1310 b 15ff.

[4] Plut. *Sol.* 8–10; Solon F 1–3; Hopper (1961), 208ff.

less of only intermediate wealth (*Ath. Pol.* 5.3; Plut. *Sol.* 1). In
his poetry he described himself as "a boundary stone," standing between powerful men and the lowly *dēmos*, separating
the warring parties for the benefit of the whole community (F
37.1-10).[5]

The metaphor of the boundary stone was certainly apt. For
a general theme in all of Solon's reforms was the creation of
boundaries—spatial, legal, and even psychological.[6] The laws
that he introduced affirmed distinctions that had been evolving in Attic society; they also gave greater definition to the
community and the place of the individual within it. Accordingly, Athenians emerged from the age of Solon with a clearer
sense of where each person stood in society, and where together they stood in contrast to the rest of the Greek world.
New boundaries made possible both the spiritual and institutional birth of the polis. And thus was born its earliest citizenship.

The most tangible boundaries created by Solon were those
within the realm most needing regulation, the fields of Attika.
In the face of population pressure and the resulting competition for arable soil, Solon established individual rights of
property, and confirmed for each man the traditional limits of
his plot. Under a program that came to be known as the *seisachtheia* ("shaking off of burdens"),[7] Solon canceled the various forms of rural indebtedness (*chreōn apokopē*) across Attika, and lifted the obligations that had oppressed "the many."
New laws abolished the standing obligations of *hektēmoroi*,

---

[5] In fact the exact translation of these lines is controversial, and Stinton
(1976) prefers to read *ouros* ("guardian") for *horos* ("marker" or "boundary
stone"). The debate is immaterial here; most translations acknowledge the
concept of Solon posting himself between the two factions. Loraux (1984)
makes the interesting suggestion that in this poem Solon is marking out the
concept of "no man's land"—collective civic space. Loraux's article represents an important challenge to the traditional image of Solon as a "moderate," though her perspective on the reforms do not vary seriously from mine,
as will be seen.

[6] Murray (1980), 189–90 also emphasizes the concept of Solonian boundaries.

[7] *Ath. Pol.* 6.1; Plut. *Sol.* 15.2, 16.5; Plut. *Mor.* 343 C.

symbolized by the removal of the *horoi* from the earth (F 36.6); at the same time, men who had borrowed capital at interest, risking debt bondage, were freed from all past liabilities. Thus "public" and "private" debts were abolished (*Ath. Pol.* 6.1). The effect was to entitle every Athenian who had been working an area of land now "to own" and keep it for himself and family; similarly, Athenians who had been enslaved or forced into exile were now allowed to reclaim the Attic fields they had once worked. Solon proudly proclaimed that he brought back to Athens many men who had been sold abroad, even those who had been away so long that they were no longer practiced in the Attic dialect (F 36.8–12).

Solon's attention to the boundaries of private property is obvious in several other measures. For example, the reforms mandated that every Athenian's planting, digging, and bee keeping were to be confined within specific limits of his own land; another statute stipulated under what circumstances wells dug on private land could be kept for exclusive use of the owner (*Dig.* 10.1.3; Plut. *Sol.* 23.5–6).[8] Solon also passed a pioneering inheritance law that created the institution of the formal testament, thereby further affirming the boundaries and rights of property for the individual family. By this legislation, Plutarch reports (*Sol.* 21), "friendship" (*philia*) was raised above "kinship" (*syngeneia*) and "each man's possessions were made his own property" (*ta chrēmata ktēmata tōn echontōn*).[9]

By previous Athenian custom, rights of cultivation passed from father to son(s), and the law institutionalized that tradition.[10] But the new law also provided for the case of a man without heirs; after 594/3, any Athenian was allowed to bequeath his plot to an adopted son, if he had no legitimate sons of his own; if he lacked sons but had a legitimate daughter, he

---

[8] *SN* F 60–63.

[9] On Solon's inheritance laws, Gernet (1920), 123ff.; Harrison (1968), 122–62; Lacey (1968), 125–50; Sealey (1987), 25–29; all with references.

[10] This follows from the several later quotations of Solon's law which imply that adoptions cannot be made when legitimate male children survive to inherit the patrimony. For full references to later quotations, see *SN* F 49–53.

was allowed to bequeath the land to a husband whom he chose for her, that is, to a son-in-law. Quotations of the measure from classical times indicate that Solon thus gave every Athenian the right to pass property "to whomever he should wish."[11] Despite this, some historians have doubted whether the reform really effected any significant change in Attic society. Skeptics argue that before Solon, families had always controlled their own (inalienable) lands, and the law's only innovation was to provide the childless Athenian with a greater choice of heirs within the oikos.[12] In support of this, it is pointed out that known cases of the law's application in classical times typically show an heirless father adopting a close relative—rather than a stranger—to receive his inheritance.[13]

These few classical cases, however, do not disprove the broader scope of individual freedom that the new law intended; in practice, that a man without offspring would want to pass his land to kin whenever possible should not cause surprise. Further, to properly evaluate the significance of the statute, we must ask who benefited from the death of such a man before Solon's reforms. In other words, to whom did the property of an heirless farmer revert, before the legislation? If, as Aristotle (*Ath. Pol.* 2.2) maintains, originally "all lands were in the hands of the few," then originally "the few" must have taken control of any defaulted patrimony. Before 594, *genē, phratriai,* and other regional associations had ultimate (if sometimes distant) control over most plots worked by individual oikoi, and the corporate bodies would have asserted that control all the more forcefully when a family had no sons to assume its cultivation.[14]

Solon changed all this. The new state of affairs can be illu-

---

[11] Except not, of course, to bypass legitimate sons (above, n. 10). *Ath. Pol.* 35.2; Plut. *Sol.* 21.3; Dem. 46.14; and other references in *SN* F 49.

[12] E.g., Freeman (1926), 115–16; Fine (1951), 186–90; and others. For a variation on such skepticism, Fox (1985).

[13] See most recently the discussion of R. Osborne (1985a), 127ff.

[14] For a similar interpretation, see Philippi (1870), 192–97; Asheri (1963), 7ff.; and others, all of whom more narrowly view the law as the defense of the rights of the oikos against the authority of aristocratic *genē.*

minated by observing the motives behind the creation of tes-
tamentary laws in other tribal societies. Elsewhere in time and
place, regulations of inheritance typically evolve to protect the
property farmed by individual families against the claims of a
holding lineage or authority.[15] As a general rule, wills and
other institutions created by laws of succession transform the
individual cultivator's rights of residence and labor on a plot
to a privilege of ownership. In the same way, Solon's law
helped establish a primitive concept of private property in a
tenure system already developing a distinction between lands
"owned" and lands "used."

Though Solon attached the land more closely to individual
oikoi, he understood that his measures opened up the potential for buying, selling, and other kinds of transfers—which
had probably already begun to occur in Attic society. To preserve individual rights without encouraging individual abuses,
and to prevent land from becoming a commercial commodity
in the hands of each family, Solon also passed laws limiting
the amount of property that any man might acquire (Arist.
Pol. 1266 b 13–14).[16] He further provided that any man "who
squandered his patrimony" would be punished (Diog. Laert.
1.55; Aeschin. 1.30).[17] The authenticity of these laws has been
challenged but such legislation fits well with the kinds of
transformation in Attic agrarian society seen so far.[18] In ad-
dressing the rural problems of Attika, Solon had to ensure that
lands now guaranteed to small farmers would not once again
end up "in the hands of the few."

Solonic laws that curbed the transfer of real property might
explain why during the classical age so few cases are known
of men losing their lands through indebtedness or sale. But
probably even more important was the force of custom, for it
would be wrong to assume that the establishment of individual holdings or any of the embryonic "commercial" trends
that we earlier described quickly overturned age-old assump-

[15] See chapter 5, n. 17.
[16] *SN* F 66.
[17] *SN* F 104 a–b.
[18] See chapter 5 text and nn. 75ff.

tions among most Attic people about the sacredness of the land. An alternative explanation is proposed by those skeptical of Solon's innovations; if commercial effects of private property are barely visible in later times, perhaps it was much later than Solon that private property was first established in Attika.[19] This view, of course, returns to the debate already discussed about the alienability of Attic land; as we have seen, the issue is a good deal more complex than deciding between "alienable" or "inalienable" for this or any period of Athenian history.

Nonetheless, the question is worth reopening here, with an eye to the effects of Solon's reforms. Those who reject any concept of "private property" in early times believe that Solon's agrarian laws relieved debt but otherwise affirmed the status quo with respect to the Attic agrarian pattern. Proponents point to Plutarch's testimony (*Sol.* 16) that the reformer accomplished no redistribution of land, and to Solon's own verse (probably Plutarch's source) which seems to say that he did not divide anew the property holdings across Attika (F 34.8–9).[20] A closer look at this text indicates that the reformer-poet was not really denying redistribution, but rather making a different point to his audience. Solon's comments on the system of landholding did not endorse the status quo, but rather expressed his refusal to endorse *isomoiria*, equality of properties throughout the society: "It does not please me . . . that noble men and lowly alike should have equal shares of our rich land." The real focus of the poem are *hoi d' eph' harpageisi*, "those desirous for plunder," people whom—whether rich or poor—Solon strove to restrain through new laws and boundaries.[21]

There is no real doubt that the distribution of land was different in Attic society after Solon's reforms than it had been before. But the new land "ownership"—through force of custom and lack of modern legal rigor—represented less of a

[19] See chapter 5, n. 9.

[20] Hansen (1985a), 56 asserts the alternative view that private ownership long preceded Solon and thus that no redistribution of land occurred.

[21] For a similar interpretation, Andrewes (1982a), 382.

sharp break with the past than contemporary perceptions might lead one to believe.[22] The *seisachtheia* deprived *genē*, *phratriai*, and other corporations of ultimate control over many Attic fields, and in so doing established firmer control for individual cultivators. But for many men that change may not have seemed so very great. In preindustrial societies, property rights are typically based on labor and cultivation of a plot[23] and Solon did nothing to undo that; most men would continue to till the same tract they had before, though the new laws now provided greater definition and more just remedies in cases of dispute. Moreover, the change of land distribution was a change of status—not quantity—in each man's holdings. Though many had demanded it, economic equality was not offered by Solon's reforms. The statesman affirmed the ownership of plots traditionally worked by each small farmer, creating a firmer sense for each of "his" property, but not a redistribution of wealth.

Further, despite the importance of Solon's agrarian reforms, one must not overstate the pace of practical change that they promoted. Implementation of the new laws of property depended on cooperation across the countryside,[24] and even after the reforms "the few" still maintained control over enough land that in later times phratries, *genē*, and other corporations had tracts to lease out.[25] It also seems likely that Solon's program did nothing to break up large private estates; there is no evidence that the measure limiting the holdings that a man might acquire was imposed retroactively on owners of large tracts already under individual control. Similarly, with the passage of the reforms, all Attic inhabitants did not suddenly

[22] Thus many proponents of Solon as the creator of "individual title" of a plot overstate their case, e.g., N. Lewis (1941), 155–56: "So far as [Solon's] own action and regulations went, there was nothing whatever in them to prevent every newly-liberated farm in Attika from being next day mortgaged up to the hilt and falling ultimately once more into the hands of noble capitalists." For more cautious statements, Massaracchia (1958), 146–48; Andrewes (1982a), 382.

[23] See my cross-cultural discussion of land tenure in chapter 5.

[24] French (1956), 23–25.

[25] See chapter 5, n. 50.

become small landowners. Newly arrived settlers, returning exiles, or families of more recent heritage could not lay claim to a plot with the same force as other, older families; many of the "newcomers" must have accepted—with fewer defined boundaries—marginal and newly cleared lands beyond the traditional arable fields of the Attic plains. In practice, different categories of property throughout the countryside continued to exist, even after Solon gave legal definition to the evolving concept of "ownership."

In the same way, some variety of working arrangements between landholders and cultivators endured beyond the reforms. Debts were canceled, but the struggle for survival in a subsistence society remained.[26] Solon's reforms did not create a vast and comfortable landed middle class. Some repatriated exiles, various newcomers, and many other statuses of dependent laborers continued to work for wages or took on new forms of obligations that allowed them to farm land that they could not claim as their own. But among all Athenians one kind of obligation was now forbidden, and the long-term significance of this reform outweighed most of the immediate changes in the land tenure system. Solon's laws prevented creditors from taking any kind of loans on the security of the person, and ended forever the practice of Athenians enslaving other Athenians (*Ath. Pol.* 6.1, 9.1; Plut. *Sol.* 15.2–4).

Thus was created yet another boundary, a legal boundary between slave and free which carried immediate implications for citizenship.[27] Slavery had been a part of earlier Athenian society, and was perhaps mentioned in the laws of Drakon;[28] but now for the first time slaves were legally defined as a separate status group outside the limits of the formal Athenian community.[29] By preventing the Athenian enslavement of

[26] Rhodes (1981), 127.

[27] For the importance of this boundary, Finley (1981d); cf. Austin and Vidal-Naquet (1977), 72.

[28] See chapter 4, n. 34.

[29] It is likely that slaves were now (or shortly after the reforms of Solon) for the first time included as a status category treated by Athenian homicide legislation: Grace (1973), 18; *contra* Morrow (1937).

Athenians, Solon's law recognized the sanctity of their persons, a tangible guarantee of freedom that thereafter non-Athenians explicitly lacked. After Solon, an Athenian could not be sold as property, or sent into exile on the decision of a creditor; his freedom became institutionalized as a public and standard right. The development of such public and standard rights helped to distinguish the citizen from the non-citizen; the privileges now starkly separated an "in-group" from the "out-group."

The new prohibition of Athenian enslavement probably encouraged some landholders in Attika to replace lost domestic labor with foreign slaves; in classical times chattel slavery was common in Athenian society, and its origins plausibly belong to the period of Solon's reforms.[30] But if the Solonian measures promoted the arrival of foreign slaves in Attika, they also put limits on free foreigners who might have voluntarily emigrated to the land of the Athenians in search of a new life. For the reforms imposed another and broader boundary, although closely related to the barrier that distinguished slave from free: namely, a keener separation between Athenians and aliens, and in general a sharper demarcation between members and nonmembers of Athenian society.[31]

---

[30] For chattel slavery beginning after (and as a result of) the Solonian reforms, see Westermann (1955), 4; Andrewes (1967), 109; Finley (1980), 87ff.; and others. The date of introduction of chattel slavery is not very controversial but the extent to which it played a role in Athenian society, and particularly agriculture, is bitterly debated. Details cannot be offered here, but on balance I favor the view that slaves did constitute at least some portion of the Athenian labor force during the classical period, including the work force of the countryside. For evidence and arguments in support: Jameson (1977–78); de Ste. Croix (1981), 505–9; and Finley (1980); contra Starr (1958) and (1977), 90–92. A thorough and damaging review of the "agricultural slavery" case was recently offered by Wood (1983) and (1988) which undermines many arguments of Jameson, de Ste. Croix, and others. Nonetheless, even Wood (1983, 31) acknowledges the likelihood of some rural slavery utilized by small freeholders. In any event, whatever the relative numbers of slaves in Attic society, their presence produced the psychological and legal boundaries between citizen and unfree that are clearly visible during the classical age (see chapter 1).

[31] See the discussion of Whitehead (1984a) who notes (54) the interesting

As we have already seen, the origins of this distinction can be traced to the era of Drakon when one of the community's earliest laws first hinted at an Athenian legal status distinct from that of non-Athenians. Under Solon, the legal identity of Athenians advanced further, thanks to legislation that limited the prerogatives of persons not part (and thereby increasingly defined as not part) of the community. One law of Solon prohibited foreigners (*xenoi*) from working in the agora (Dem. 57.31); subsequently this law probably evolved into the special market tax on aliens (*xenika*) in the classical period.[32] Also, as noted in the last chapter, Solon took steps to restrict the immigration of foreigners to Attika. When "he allowed only those to be citizens who were exiled permanently from their own countries, or who moved with their entire families to Athens to practice a trade" (Plut. *Sol.* 24), it was the first time in Athenian history (as far as can be known) that such a measure had been passed. The clear implication of the law is that in earlier times a much wider range of categories of foreigners had been coming to Attika and had been allowed to "be citizens"; now, under Solon, the community shored up the boundaries of social exclusivity.[33]

The restrictive nature of the immigration law has been overlooked by some scholars who cannot imagine that Attic society was ever much different from what it was in the classical age. By their view, Athenians had always distinguished themselves neatly from non-Athenians who were partitioned among the legally subordinate categories of *xenos* and *metoikos*; similarly, they assume that in early times foreigners who

---

point that Athens was unique among Greek poleis in that it did not distinguish freedmen from immigrants (i.e., *metoikoi*). There is, however, evidence of a few minor legal disabilities of freed slaves in classical Athens not shared by *metoikoi*: Harrison (1968), 184–86.

[32] *SN* F 117. The *xenika* is mentioned in the same passage by Demosthenes, but not included as part of the Solonian law. For the possibility of its evolution from the measure excluding foreigners from the agora, Whitehead (1977), 77–78 and 142 for a defense of the authenticity of the latter law (*contra* Ruschenbusch [1966]).

[33] See chapter 5 text and n. 97.

wanted to settle in Attika would be discouraged by the natural exclusiveness of the "pure" Athenian community.[34]

In fact, there are no grounds for assuming that the early Athenians were a cohesively exclusive community, for the very reason that the community itself was regionalized and loosely defined. *Xenos* and *metoikos* did not exist as legal statuses before the sixth century,[35] and no other signs suggest that

[34] E.g., McGregor (1973), 14 who, interpreting the law as an encouragement of immigration, accuses Solon of "un-Athenian activity." See also the comments of Whitehead (1977), 141–42 on previous interpretations of the law. Hignett (1952), 112 doubts that the law is Solonian.

[35] The origin and date of both statuses are controversial, and inevitably, interrelated. *Metoikia* is easier to isolate for its specific features—registration in a deme under sponsorship of a native Athenian patron (*prostatēs*) and subsequent liability for the *metoikion* tax; the creation of the status is most plausibly dated to about the time of Kleisthenes' reforms, though the *metoikion* and some of its other conditions probably evolved later (Whitehead [1977], 140ff.; Baba [1984]; and see chapter 7). The beginning of the formal *xenos* status is more difficult to pinpoint for the broadness of the concept and the term. From earliest times, the word had denoted "foreigners," including "guest friends," inhabitants of other lands, people who visited Attika, and people who came there to settle. After the institution of the *metoikia*, unfortunately, *xenos* as a term continues to have a variety of meanings (it can sometimes still refer to a metic; see e.g., Meiggs and Lewis [1969], no. 23). It is frequently difficult to identify what is meant in the classical instances of the word.

For this discussion I confine the meaning of *xenos* to (1) before the institution of the *metoikia*, the class of foreigners either visiting or residing in Attika: and (2) after the institution of the *metoikia*, the class of foreign visitors to Attika who were not foreign residents, i.e., *metoikoi*. The status of the second category is defined precisely by the second-century writer Aristophanes of Byzantium who distinguished the *metoikos* from the *xenos* by the length of time the man in question stayed: "A *metoikos* is when a man comes from abroad and resides in a *polis*, paying a tax for certain of its fixed requirements. For so many days he is called a *perepidēmos* ["visitor"] and is free from tax, but if he exceeds the limited period, he becomes a *metoikos* and is liable to the tax" (F 38 Nauck). It is not certain how long the "limited period" was, however, or when it was instituted in law, or even whether Aristophanes was writing about Athens in this passage. Whitehead (1977), 152ff. believes that Aristophanes was referring to Athens, and suggests (on the basis of some other inscriptional evidence) that the "limited period" requirement for the *metoikia* status was instituted some time after 414/13 and certainly by 360. If so, this boundary would have necessarily strengthened the boundaries of the status of

in earlier times Attic society functioned as a coordinated entity
that operated formally to keep non-Athenians out, or even, for
any of those who settled in Attika, from becoming "Athenians." True, there had long existed a basis for drawing distinctions between insiders and outsiders—"real Athenians"
were those descended from the original Attic *phylai* and who
shared the customs and dialect associated with that ancestry—
but how often and how strictly in a decentralized and legally
primitive society was that distinction actually enforced?

The answers are probably "not very often and not very
strictly," though here again such a view grates against most
historians' a priori assumptions that have been built up over

---

the *xenos* qua *xenos* at the same time (cf. the three categories of defendants
spelled out in Dem. 23.23: "*xenos* or *metoikos*, or citizen" [*politēs*]). Nonetheless, that does not imply that the nonresident status of *xenos* was invented
this late; it came into existence when the *metoikia* was instituted, though
probably without any sharp legal definition at first: thereafter, *xenos* was simply any foreigner without the privileges and responsibilities peculiar to metics.
Later, during the fifth century, this category became more refined, in step with
the evolving relationship and treaties (*symbolai*) between citizens and allies of
the Athenian empire (see chapter 8). Originally, however, "*xenos*" represented a wide-ranging class of foreigners visiting or living in Attika, that is,
our first meaning of the word.

That said, what are the legal capabilities/disabilities of *xenoi* in the preclassical age? The answer requires much speculation because of the almost total
lack of evidence. Grace (1973) demonstrated that the Drakonian homicide
law did not encompass any differential treatment for slayers of non-Athenian
victims, whereas homicide law in the fourth century clearly did. With regard
to the procedure of *dikē phonou*, then, the differentiation for killers of *xenoi*
(i.e., their trial before the Palladion rather than the Areopagos or *ephetai*)
must be dated after c. 620, and Grace's suggestion (p. 20) of sometime between 550 and 450 is reasonable enough. Earlier than that, the only indication of foreigners' special (inferior) status in Athenian law is the earlier-noted
Solonic prohibition in the marketplace and subsequent *xenika* tax. MacDowell (1978), 221–22 suggests, on the basis of the polemarch's "special responsibilities in connection with aliens" in the classical period (cf. *Ath. Pol.* 58,
but note that these are only *privileged* aliens), that this magistrate in earlier
time had the duty of bringing to court all cases involving any non-Athenian.
But though the magistracy dates at least to the early seventh century (see chapter 4), it is only a guess when—and if—non-Athenians were first distinguished
by this kind of legal procedure, as MacDowell so admits. On the status of
metoikoi and *xenoi*, see also Harrison (1968), 187ff.; Gauthier (1972), 107ff.

time.[36] To go beyond these assumptions, and further understand the important change that Solon's new policy represented, some perspective can be gained from studies in anthropology. What does it really mean to be an "insider" or an "outsider" in a regionalized and vaguely defined community?

"Insider" and "outsider" are always relative concepts. The foreignness of a "stranger" or "outsider" is not absolute but depends on the ancestry and perceptions of the "natives" or "insiders" into whose locale the stranger enters. In a highly regionalized society, several distinct locales exist, each with its own subculture of customs and practices.[37]

In this sort of social system, people across a wide territory can share a common heritage, but the local relationships of small groupings rooted in individual areas counterbalance or even outweigh the traditional cultural ties among the entire population. In the extreme, an "insider" (i.e., member of the native population) traveling outside his neighborhood may be considered equally as foreign in another neighborhood as a newly arrived "outsider" from a different and distant population. Nonetheless, in general, the stranger—whatever his origins—has a greater chance of being assimilated into this kind of society, because there are no centralized and uniform rules or authority to preserve homogeneity across all social groupings. In each neighborhood the local customs, strength of kinship groupings, and availability of resources determine his chances of being accepted, and acceptance is never inevitable. But, in contrast to a formal and centralized social organization (e.g., a "state"), the regionalized society simply offers more potential opportunities to the stranger "for finding an open door," and becoming assimilated.

The case of the Zambian Tonga can help us to better imag-

[36] E.g., the general skepticism of Wade-Gery (1958), 148–49, especially 149 n. 2 about the possible incorporation of foreigners at the end of the sixth century (see chapter 7). For a recent, less-doubting view, Baba (1984).

[37] For this kind of society and the discussion which follows, Fortes and Evans-Pritchard (1940), 9ff.; Kuper (1969); van den Berghe (1969); R. Cohen and Middleton (1970); Middleton (1970); Anderson et al. (1974), 28ff. For a general treatment of "insiders" and "outsiders" in Greek cities, Vatin (1984).

ine this kind of social system.[38] The Tonga are an extended population who share a common language, but their day-to-day life is focused in regional neighborhoods. At the same time, however, most Tonga also operate within a wider area of social familiarity, the "vicinage," based on ties of kinship and marriage alliances. Colson, who performed the original research on this group, identified several vicinages that represented decentralized spheres of personal relationships within the society as a whole. The investigator reported that

> Once outside his vicinage . . . a man became an alien who travelled [either] at his own risk or guaranteed by formal ties of bond friendships (*bulongwe*), forged with influential men who agreed to offer protection in return for such advantages as the traveller could offer. It did not matter whether he was a fellow Tonga speaker or a man of another linguistic group; in either case he was an alien. . . . Aliens who speak other languages can be distinguished (by the Tonga) from aliens in general. . . . [but] only recently has this distinction been important. . . . In the past, for all practical purposes, all aliens were equally strange and equally acceptable. Any alien might settle and rise to full membership in a new community if he found acceptance among its people.[39]

Now, similarities between the Tonga and the early Athenian population may be limited, but it is not unreasonable to imagine that like the members of a Tonga vicinage, the members of a localized kinship group or village in Attika might have been equally suspicious of—or equally indifferent to—the arrival of an "outsider" to their neighborhood, whether he was descended from Athenian ancestry or not.[40] The real issue in this case, as in the case of the Tonga, is under what circumstances

---

[38] Colson (1970).

[39] Ibid., 36.

[40] For other examples of "relative strangers" in highly regionalized communities in modern Greece, see the discussion of the differing and socially significant customs among Ambéli and its neighboring villages in Du Boulay (1974), 46–49; also Campbell (1964), 38ff., who reports how, among the mountain-dwelling Saraktasani, members of the same community who are not kinspeople are actually considered strangers (*xenoi*).

the "outsider" would have been allowed to settle and eventually become one of the "full members" of the community. There is, of course, no single determinant of a stranger's acceptance into a regionalized agrarian society, but as already seen, a major stimulus can be the relative availability of unused land; natives tend to be less jealous of strangers who take up farming nearby as long as resources are plentiful. Thereafter, once a newcomer has settled for a time, he can become incorporated through a variety of ways, whether marriage, assimilation into kinship groups, clientage, and so on.[41]

This kind of incorporation could apply to the case of the underpopulated, regionalized rural society of early Attika; if so, it could explain why Solon's law of immigration implies that before the legislation many foreigners had been able to settle among the "true Athenians" and "become citizens." But is there any reason to believe, independent of the evidence of this law, that foreigners did come to live in Attika, before about 600?

The land of Attika itself suggests at least the possibility that some did. In the centuries before Solon, in a countryside only slowly reclaimed after the Mycenaean collapse, the relative abundance of arable soil would have offered the potential for a new livelihood for immigrants from elsewhere in the Greek world. In the eighth century, land hunger drove many Greeks to leave their homelands and seek overseas colonies, though not, as noted, Athenians.[42] Could it be that some non-Athenians (especially other Greeks) were tempted to settle closer to home, in the underpopulated acres of Attika? According to Plutarch (*Sol.* 22), that was certainly the case by the beginning of the sixth century, and the influx of would-be farmers from all over was by then making the land crowded and unproductive; it is hard to imagine that in earlier times, when rural property was more abundant, immigrants did not also find ways to come and settle in Attika.

The arrival of new settlers in Attika in the centuries before

---

[41] See discussion of land and labor relationships in chapter 5.

[42] See chapter 5 text and n. 85.

Solon might be confirmed by some additional interesting evidence. Archaeological studies have noted the great diversity of burial customs in Attika throughout the Geometric age.[43] Though it is unlikely that every new form of inhumation and cremation was brought by immigrants, it is worth considering whether at least some of this diversity can be attributed to other Greeks who carried their customs with them in their search for land.[44] Similarities between some Attic burials and those found elsewhere in Greece are in fact known,[45] and perhaps certain "Athenian" practices were not merely the result of impersonal "cultural influences" from elsewhere but were actually carried into Attika by migrating non-Athenian families. It is also well known that by tradition (probably older than the tradition of supposed autochthony)[46] the Athenian

[43] Kurtz and Boardman (1971), 27ff.; Coldstream (1977), esp. 119ff., 350–51. See now also Morris (1987), 125ff. whose detailed analysis of Attic grave sites highlights high "mortuary variability" during the Late Geometric period (c. 760–700), and a "fairly steady increase in variability throughout the sixth century, until the sudden expansion shortly before 500 B.C." (p. 137).

[44] Morris (1987), 138–39 considers (and rejects) several possible explanations for "mortuary variability" but, surprisingly, does not address the influence of outside immigration and importation of customs. His own thesis stresses changes in the society's social structure.

[45] E.g., the inhumation of adults in *pithoi*, typical of Middle and Late Geometric Argos (Coldstream [1977], 36, 83, and 145 with references) but found also in the Athenian Peiraieus, Thorikos, and (from the seventh century) the Kerameikos (Kurtz and Boardman [1971], 55, 71, citing *AM* 18 [1893], 133ff.; *AD* 22 [1967], B 138; *Kerameikos* vi.1, 75); cremations housed in bronze cauldrons after 750 in the Attic cemeteries of Odos Kriezi and Kerameikos (Coldstream [1977], 120 and 126 with references) and the similar ash-bearing cauldrons of the cemetery near the West Gate cemetery in Eretria (Coldstream [1977], 196); the practice of burning the body in the grave which appears in Attika first in the late eighth century ("primary cremation": Kurtz and Boardman [1971], 73, citing *Kerameikos* vi.1, 83ff.; *Hesperia* 20 [1951], 80ff.) and the similar practice also found at the Eretrian West Gate cemetery and in ninth-century Lefkandi (Kurtz and Boardman [1971], 183, citing *Arch. Rep.* [1967/1968], 12; *Ath. Ann. Arch.* 2 [1969], 98ff.; and Coldstream [1977], 196–97). The possibility of burial customs brought from both Argive and Euboian sites is of course strengthened by their relative proximity to Attika.

[46] Note the skepticism of Hellanikos (*FGrH* 323a F 161 with Jacoby's accompanying commentary) about autochthony; cf. Loraux (1981), 35ff. on the

land of Kekrops had in earliest times been a refuge for powerful men driven into exile (Thuc. 1.2).[47] That tradition, combined with the recorded foreign ancestry of some important Athenian families,[48] once again suggests that the Attic community had originally been "open" to outsiders.

Finally, some further corroboration of this "openness" can be found among the nonagricultural population. It is now generally agreed that certain of the Eastern influences in Athenian carving, metal work, and ceramics dating from the ninth to seventh centuries can be ascribed not just to overseas contacts but to transplanted artisans.[49] Similarly, a certain number of foreign names have been found among the signatures on Athenian black-figure pottery, datable to at least a generation before the Solonian reforms.[50]

Thus, if we throw out the unwarranted assumptions of many historians that "strangers" in the archaic period were branded by inferior legal categories, or otherwise prevented from coming to Attika, the background of Solon's law becomes clearer. One can imagine not only that some foreigners did settle in Attika but also how over time they became full members of the community. In the countryside, new families

---

late date and propagandistic purpose of the tradition. Note also the traditions preserved by Hekataios that the early inhabitants of Athens included a non-Greek aboriginal people, "Pelasgians": Hdt. 6.137.

[47] This is a statement that archaeological evidence from LH IIIB generally bears out: Sourvinou-Inwood (1973), 213ff.

[48] The Peisistratidai and Alkmeonidai were reputed to be descended from the Neleids of Pylos (Hdt. 5.65; Paus. 2.18.9; Davies [1971], 369 and 445). The Gephyraioi had origins in Boiotia or Eretria (Hdt. 5.57 and Davies [1971], 472–73). Miltiades by tradition had ancestors in Aigina (Hdt. 6.35), and Herodotus (5.66) implies that the family of Isagoras son of Tisander had Carian roots. For a few other examples see Billheimer (1922), 25–27. Even if some (or all) of these traditions of foreign descent were not true, what matters is that they were perceived to be true—revealing contemporary attitudes about the former "openness" of the society.

[49] Higgins (1969), 145–46; cf. Coldstream (1977), 80 and 103; Boardman (1974), 12; (1980), 58–84.

[50] Dunbabin (1950); Boegehold (1962). For some later foreign black-figure potters, Boegehold (1983); cf. Kretschmer (1894), 74ff.; R. Cook (1972), 271–72; Boardman (1974), 12.

may have formed their own phratries or other corporate groups outside the neighborhoods of already established phratries, and consecrated the land they settled with newly devised (or transplanted) cults.[51] Other immigrants would have settled on lands controlled by an Attic descent group, and, by establishing client relationships with local lords, became *hektēmoroi* or *pelatai* who eventually achieved full social membership. Foreign artisans who supplied a valuable craft to a local village over time could have become accepted by its members, perhaps marrying—or having their sons marry—into the family of "true Athenians" who had more daughters than usable land. As the years passed, their descendants became "true Athenians" too. Marriage and social incorporation in the preclassical age may have been more fluid than many scholars have assumed.[52]

---

[51] For this possibility, see chapter 5, n. 63.

[52] It is normally accepted that prior to Perikles' law of 451/50, "citizenship" belonged to legitimate children born of Athenian fathers (Patterson [1981]; Rhodes [1981], 332; Whitehead [1986b], 109ff.), and that unions between Athenian husbands and alien wives sometimes occurred. There is, of course, a long tradition of Athenian nobles marrying foreign women before that time, in step with aristocratic practices and the forging of political liaisons: Gernet (1968), 344–58. But the practice clearly extended far enough down the social hierarchy to give significance later to Perikles' law which, according to *Ath. Pol.* 26.4, was instituted "on account of the large number of citizens." For a summary of known "mixed marriages," Diller (1937), 91 n. 34; the list includes the famous but non-noble Themistokles, born of an undistinguished father and a Thracian or Carian mother (Davies [1971], 212–13).

No "mixed marriages" of foreign males and Athenian females are attested, but given the bias of our sources toward "eminent men" and the small sample of any such social data for this period, it would be wrong to discount the possibility. Indeed, the laws of the fourth century clearly envisaged mixed marriages of either kind, and thus penalties were prescribed for any alien who married any Athenian (Harrison [1968], 25–26; 62). Doubtless custom had always dictated against such unions, but in this kind of male-dominated society (which may even have practiced female infanticide: see chapter 4, n. 76) daughters of families may have sometimes married outside the native Athenian community.

In fact, studies of other preindustrial societies suggest that social preferences for "in-marriage" (i.e., among members of the same community) are nonetheless subject to modification, according to several other conditions. Proximity of "foreign" but eligible mates, imbalances in local male/female

Without firm evidence, these kinds of assimilative processes require some faith on our part, but they are not seriously out of keeping with those of other regionalized agrarian societies. More important, they can explain the social condition that Solon was apparently seeking to change, and, as will be seen, the later tradition of men of "impure descent" playing a political role in the sixth-century polis (*Ath. Pol.* 13.5; see chapter 7). Of course it is important not to overstate the degree to which Attic society was a heterogeneous mix of "true Athenians" and "outsiders" during this time, particularly since relevant quantitative evidence is lacking, and the total number of immigrants may not have been very large. Whatever the extent of immigration, however, population pressure on Attic land had reached a crisis by 594/3, and the society became less tolerant than before of "newcomers," particularly those seeking

population ratio, and potential rewards of goods or status, can variously promote "out-marriage" between natives and strangers. For some examples of "in" and "out" marriage in such societies, and discussion of factors affecting assimilation through mixed unions, see Yalman (1963); Barth (1969); R. Cohen (1970); Colson (1970); Skinner (1970); Southall (1970); Goody (1970) and (1976), 50ff. For a treatment of Athenian marriage practices suggesting some fluidity in the archaic period, Vernant (1973). See also Baslez (1984), 69ff. Legislation of marriage practices (and the legitimacy of children) is sometimes instituted in response to "out-marriages" in a society; some of Solon's laws in this regard (below, n. 65) may bespeak a contemporary desire toward less social integration through mixed families, in the same spirit of his law restricting immigration (above, nn. 33–34). Note that the latter allowed craftsmen to settle only if they came with their entire households (*panestiois Athēnaze metoikizomenois epi technēi*: Plut. *Sol.* 24).

Many scholars have trouble believing that non-Athenians could eventually become assimilated into kinship corporations such as phratries. In addition to considering the kinds of incorporative processes seen elsewhere (see chapter 5), we should bear in mind that in the fifth century phratries sometimes enrolled members of "dubious" status. Thus Perikles was able to enroll his son who was a *nothos* (born of the foreign mistress Aspasia: Plut. *Per.* 37.5) and in the 430s (?) a law was passed to prosecute anyone born of two foreign parents who joined a phratry (*FGrH* 342 F 4 with accompanying commentary). The clear implication of the latter is that such "non-Athenian infiltration" was becoming all too common, and it is easy enough to imagine the same sometimes happening in the seventh or sixth centuries. The differential customs of phratries and other associations (see chapter 3) offer the possibility that some social groupings may have been more "open" than others.

to work Attic land. Thus Athenians endorsed the measures of Solon, which for the first time discouraged the arrival of rural laborers who endeavored to "become citizens" of the community.

This new demarcation between "outsiders" and "insiders" was a key to the evolution of the polis and a legal citizenship within it. Once foreigners, like slaves, became characterized by specific disabilities, their new status implicitly bestowed definition on Athenians who were entitled to the privileges that foreigners and slaves themselves lacked. Correspondingly, Athenians with privileges now more precisely defined a membership in an entity that existed in contrast to the rest of the known world and its universe of nonmembers. The concept of a legal Athenian status, and a formal Athenian "state," foreshadowed under Drakon, now took on greater clarity. At the same time "Athenian consciousness" was also enhanced. When Solon institutionalized what a Corinthian or Euboian in Athens could do or not do as an alien, he inevitably helped Athenians understand for themselves what it meant to be Athenian.

Moreover, the shape of the polis was clarified by the Solonic property orders or *telē*. With this institution, the statesman assigned the inhabitants of Attika to specific grades of privilege, thereby refining the legal status of every individual. Thus, in addition to boundaries between Athenians and slaves, and between Athenians and *xenoi*, Solon created a new form of boundaries between Athenians and Athenians. This distinction too had tangible significance for the invention of citizenship.

The legislator divided Attika's population according to categories of productive worth, introducing material wealth rather than (noble) birth as the basis for holding office. Men qualified for the placement in the groupings *pentakosiomedimnoi, hippeis, zeugitai*, or *thētes*, depending on whether the annual return from their lands (or equivalent) was 500, 300, 200, or less than 200 "measures" (*Ath. Pol.* 7.3–4).[53] Each of

[53] The vagueness of the concept of "measures" and the likely disparity of worth between a *medimnos* of grain and *metrētēs* of oil or wine underlies a

these groupings or *telē* had been formerly vague and traditional categories in society but were now more sharply defined.[54] Each also was now endowed with particular honors and duties in the centralized government and constitution, composed of the *ekklēsia*, new popular courts, and new probouleutic Council of 400.[55]

To the top order, "the men of five hundred measures," belonged the offices of treasurers and archons; for the bottom order, the *thētes*, participation in the assembly was confirmed and their right to partake in law courts was for the first time established (*Ath. Pol.* 7.3, 8.1).[56] Other offices and privileges

long tradition of scholarly discussion about the actual reckoning of the assessment. Much has also been made of Plut. *Sol.* 23.3 which speaks of equivalences among "a sheep, a drachma, and a *medimnos*" (e.g., Waters [1960]). Most attempts to explain the functioning of the system envision overly sophisticated calculations and land surveys inappropriate to the early sixth century (e.g., Chrimes [1932]; Thiel [1950]). But some kind of overall equivalence of produce must be implied in the scheme, and Rhodes's suggestion ([1981], 143–44) is probably right that it was left to the individual to declare, and was accepted unless challenged by another citizen. Assessments might only be controversial among the relatively small group worth more than 200 measures who were competing for offices. Connor (1987), 47–48 adds the attractive idea that the measures were based on the public tariffs or offerings for agricultural festivals—and thus, perhaps not open to much debate. For some calculations of probable agricultural yields during this period, Starr (1977), 153–56.

[54] Plut. *Sol.* 18 says nothing of the earlier existence of the categories, but I follow *Ath. Pol.* and many scholars (e.g., Andrewes [1982a], 385) that Solon took preexisting names and invested them with new significance; it may be, however, that the *pentakosiomedimnoi*, given the meaning of the name, were first created by the reforms. For an attempt to link this "500 measure" *telos* with some pre-Solonian archaeological evidence, Smithson (1968). For discussion of the origins of the other classes (also much debated), arguing the likely case of their military significance, Jeffery (1976), 93; Whitehead (1981).

[55] On popular courts, see below, n. 75. The establishment of a new council (which Plut. *Sol.* 19 described as a second anchor with the Areopagos to steady the state) was challenged by older scholarship but is now generally accepted: *Ath. Pol.* 8.4 with Rhodes (1981), 153–54; add also the arguments of Hansen (1985a), 53–54. Cf. Wallace (1989), 60ff.; and see chapter 4, n. 20. For discussion of its function to prepare business for the assembly, Rhodes (1972a), 208–9; Jeffery (1976), 93–94; Ostwald (1986), 89.

[56] The role of the *dēmos* seen in the Kylonian affair (see chapter 4) refutes the view sometimes expressed (from an overly literal reading of *Ath. Pol.* 7.3)

were also partitioned among the orders, though the details of the distribution are much debated.[57] What is important, however, and about which Aristotle leaves no doubt, is that all offices of the Athenian government were assigned under the system and that the system in turn included all adult males of the Athenian population. In the past most historians have emphasized the establishment of the *telē* as a revolutionary turning point in the struggle between well-born aristocrats and lesser-born men of wealth for political power; for this discussion its greater significance was the inauguration of an all-inclusive legal hierarchy that embraced the entire community.

With new quantitative exactitude, the *telē* gave formal status to all Athenians, as never before. Even *thētes*—those with worth less than 200 measures—were guaranteed full privileges in the assembly and law courts (*Ath. Pol.* 7.3; cf. Arist. *Pol.* 1274 a 15–21). For Aristotle, that alone would be enough to define citizenship: the association of those who "shared in deliberative or judicial office."[58] Despite the limitations of the philosopher's definition,[59] the reforms of Solon did create an Athenian politeia, which simultaneously defined membership and the distribution of offices in the state.

that *thētes* were given the right to join the assembly for the first time by Solon: *contra* Hignett (1952), 98; cf. also Solon F 5. There is also no support for Hignett's view (1952) that landless *thētes* were excluded from the *ekklēsia*. On the courts instituted by Solon, see below, n. 75.

[57] It is not known, for example, whether *hippeis* were also now eligible for the archonship (see *Ath. Pol.* 26.2), what offices were open to *zeugitai*, and which *telē* comprised the membership of the new Council of 400. See discussions of Hignett (1952), 101ff.; and Andrewes (1982a), 385–87. The selection of archons is also an issue of long-standing controversy because of the apparent contradiction between Aristotle *Pol.* 1273 b 40ff., which says that they were elected both before and after Solon's reforms, and *Ath. Pol.* 8.1, which says that they were chosen by lot from candidates elected by the tribes. Andrewes (1982a), 386 offers an elegant defense of allotment; for a recent attempt to reconcile the traditions, Develin (1979).

[58] Arist. *Pol.* 1275 b 18–20; cf. chapter 2, n. 21.

[59] As many have commented upon: Szanto (1892), 2–4; Pečírka (1967), 23–26; Mossé (1967), 17–21; Paoli (1976), 197–200. Note Aristotle's own frustration about the difficulty in applying the definition to different kinds of constitutions (*Pol.* 1274 b 32ff.).

That Solon created a new and more formal identity for the Athenian—made him a "citizen"—is further reflected in a contemporary refinement in meaning of one of the society's most potent legal penalties. For just as the concept of membership now became codified, so at the same time did the concept of *atimia*, or "being deprived of membership," take on greater legal clarity. As mirror images of one another, "citizenship" and "ex-citizenship" developed in tandem, and it is worth digressing here to fully appreciate the significance of this evolution.[60]

Before the sixth century, Athenians could be punished for certain crimes by being declared an *atimos*, roughly speaking, an "outlaw." The *atimos* was liable to slaying and his property could be plundered by any other man at will. In classical times, *atimia* also had a "milder" or "civic" form whereby the criminal was stripped of certain privileges such as participation in courts, assemblies, and magistracies. At some point in Athenian history the "outlaw" penalty took on these "milder" disabilities, although scholarly discussions have reached no consensus on when and why that occurred.[61] One might conclude that the origins of the newer, "civic" meaning of the penalty arose in the age of Solon, for not until an Athenian had such privileges guaranteed in law could he lose them as a punishment.

In fact, another law passed by Solon confirms that the shift in meaning of *atimia* can be attributed to this age, and it suggests why the transformation occurred. Solon's so-called law against neutrality prescribed that any man who failed to take

[60] For the following discussion and additional evidence and details, see Manville (1980); cf. Hansen (1976a), 55ff.

[61] Hansen (1976a), 81ff. who also discusses earlier views. The "shift" in meaning is in fact not as clear-cut as many have thought, as Hansen himself showed. In the classical period *atimia* still sometimes has aspects of outlawry, for reasons that I endeavor to explain in my 1980 article (215ff.). For the purpose of this discussion, I have overstated the distinction between archaic and classical forms; however, I would stress to the interested reader that after Solon, though the *atimos* could still be an outlaw, he was nevertheless an outlaw of a different kind, i.e., one now deprived of the protection of suit and appeal implied in a formal citizenship (discussed later in this chapter).

up arms or side with a faction in times of civil strife would be made *atimos*. The sense of the penalty is clearly "civic," for in quoting the measure Aristotle goes on to explain that such a man was to "have no share in the polis" (*Ath. Pol.* 8.5). The phrase is decisive, for it signals a new refinement of the concept of rights in the community, and indeed the community itself. Solon's reforms helped shape the polis, and thus now, for the first time, the penalty of *atimia* could formally exclude one from membership in it; the *atimos* became a new kind of outlaw, a man without the protection of suit and appeal (discussed later). Under the program of 594/3, this punishment, like the identity of the Athenian and the city-state itself, became less vague and less subject to the inconsistent practices imposed by individuals or the regional corporations.

The neutrality law is an interesting case among the reforms of Solon because its other provisions seem so odd today. Its authenticity is often challenged since many historians doubt that Solon sought to punish "those who failed to take sides in civil strife," particularly given his role as a mediator.[62] But though some ancient commentators were also puzzled by the terms of the law, none questioned its original existence, and there is no persuasive reason to omit it from the canon of Solonian legislation.[63] In the face of initial opposition to his program, Solon probably passed the law to press reluctant supporters into active service; the reformer needed deeds rather than words from backers of his new constitution.[64] But whatever the original application of the law, it symbolized another dramatic aspect of the Solonian revolution: an appeal to civic spirit. For under Solon, a heightened consciousness about public affairs, vital to a polis, emerged in the Athenian community.

A new civic mentality pervaded the entire Solonian order.

[62] There is also the recurrent cry that Aristotle's testimony about Solon is anachronism from the philosopher's own day: e.g., David (1984); French (1984).

[63] See the arguments of Bers (1975).

[64] Cf. Rhodes (1981), 158: ". . . apathy in a domestic crisis is being treated (by Solon) as equivalent to treachery."

Thus several of his laws transformed formerly private concerns into public concerns of all citizens. Solon instituted measures regulating marriage and legitimacy which standardized the matrimonial contract and discouraged bastardy;[65] the care of orphans became a public responsibility (Diog. Laert. 1.55). Further, certain sacrifices, public feasts, and worship were for the first time authorized for the shared benefit of all Athenians;[66] a new common festival of the dead (the Genesia) added public significance to the formerly private matter of reverence for deceased family members.[67] Measures, weights, and currency were brought onto an Athenian standard.[68] Even

[65] A good case has been made that Solon established the institution of *engyē* or legal "betrothal" required to establish the legitimacy of offspring (Harrison [1968], 5; Vernant [1973], 56; cf. Dem. 46.18). His inheritance law (above, n. 9) shows clear preference for legitimate sons, and it has been plausibly suggested that under his reforms the distinction between *gnēsios* and *nothos* first took legal form (Harrison [1968], 62ff.; but Ar. *Av.* 1660ff. may undermine the supposed clarity of the separation). Solon probably also established regulations about heiresses (*epiklēroi*) that promoted their marriage (through *epidikasia*, and in certain cases the provisioning of a dowry) and bearing of children—and thus the preservation of the oikos and its property: Plut. *Sol.* 20 = *SN* F 51–52; cf. *SN* F 53; *SN* F 126 a–b; Gernet (1921), 337ff.; Harrison (1968), 9–17, 132–49; Lacey (1968), 125–37; MacDowell (1978), 95–98. Solon is also said to have limited "marriage gifts" (*tas phernas:* Plut. *Sol.* 20.4 = *SN* F 71a), a restriction of dowries or trousseaux that may have discouraged the marriage of Athenians to non-Athenians (above, n. 52) but certainly discouraged, in the mind of Plutarch, those marriages sought for "profit or price." On the custom of dowries, Lacey (1968), 109–10; see also Wolff (1944), 58ff.

[66] For hints in Solonic *axones* of newly formalized sacrifices, offerings, and feastings, *SN* F 83–89. There is also evidence that Solon legislated concerning the prizes of athletic competitors in Olympic games: Plut. *Sol.* 23.3, Diog. Laert. 1.55–56.

[67] Jacoby (1944). In the same spirit, it is symbolic that Solon received the first public burial in Athenian history: Plut. *Sol.* 32; Aelian *VH* 8.16; Clairmont (1983), 2.

[68] *Ath. Pol.* 10; cf. Plut. *Sol.* 15.2. Despite the opaque testimony of Aristotle's chapter, and the complexity of ancient weights and measures, the tradition that Solon did legislate some kind of Attic standards is defensible. Supposed older "Pheidonian" measures were still in use in Aristotle's day, and they seem to have been smaller than Attic; thus the story that Solon enlarged current measures and made a new standard can be believed. Weights are more

moral behavior of the individual became a public matter. Solonic laws are attested on subjects of prostitution, homosexuality, slander of the dead, vagrancy, and funerary ostentation.[69] Legislation of this kind was not perceived as oppressive or meddling, for the community did not fear the intervention of the "state." The community was the state, and the state was now established under the broad principle of justice.

The expectation of justice by all Athenians became the most distinctive feature of the new civic spirit, and it was a valuable legacy of Solon.[70] Both the operation and the philosophy of Solonian justice represented the invention of a "public" sensibility counterbalancing the "private" sphere; they also reflect the morally beneficial centralization so essential to a polis. The laws themselves (which replaced and improved upon the Drakonian code) created new and clear-cut boundaries for the settlement of disputes among private individuals. The statutes were publicly displayed in the center of Athens, mounted on revolving axles for any man to see.[71] The public authority of the Solonian laws was ensured by another measure that guaranteed their superior status over the traditional customs of regional corporations (*Dig.* 47.22.4), and every Athenian is said to have sworn to obey the new constitution (*Ath. Pol.* 7.1).[72]

---

difficult, but it also seems that he did at least introduce a new, generically Attic weight for the drachma. See Rhodes (1981), 165–68; Andrewes (1982a), 383–84. For a completely pessimistic view about any such standardization by Solon, Crawford (1972).

The same chapter of *Ath. Pol.* speaks of coinage reforms by Solon, but that is generally dismissed because of recent orthodoxy downdating the appearance of any coins in Attika to the later sixth century. That may be questionable (see chapter 5, nn. 75–77), but it is clear that at the very least some standard weights of uncoined silver were being used as currency during Solon's day (*Ath. Pol.* 8.3; cf. Plut. *Sol.* 23); it is not unreasonable that such standard weights were his doing.

[69] Plut. *Sol.* 21, 23; Lys. 10. 6–12; Diog. Laert. 1.55; Dem. 46.14; Aeschin. 1.183.

[70] Jaeger (1946), 143ff.; Vlastos (1946); cf. Gagarin (1986), 80.

[71] For a possible reconstruction, Stroud (1979), 45ff.; and see above, n. 1, for other references.

[72] Despite the apparent difficulty of having every Athenian take such an

At the same time, new opportunities were born for civic participation in the courts. Major public offenses against the Athenian people (such as an attempt to impose tyranny) could now be brought before the Areopagos by any individual. The procedure, *eisangelia*, was either confirmed or invented by a Solonian law (*Ath. Pol.* 8.4).[73] Other innovations of Solon, cited by Aristotle as "most favorable to the *dēmos*," included the right of any voluntary prosecutor (*ho boulomenos*) to bring suit on behalf of someone personally wronged (*Ath. Pol.* 9.1; cf. Plut. *Sol.* 18);[74] and *ephesis*, the right of appeal of magistrates' judicial decisions to public courts of allotted jurors instituted as part of these reforms (*Ath. Pol.* 9.1; Plut. *Sol.* 18).[75] Previously, the right to initiate proceedings had been

---

oath, it is worth noting that the same requirement was thought feasible in the late fifth century when the population would have been larger: Andoc. 1.90, 1.97.

[73] Rhodes (1979), 103–6 who notes, however, the possibility that Aristotle's use of the term *eisangelia* may be anachronistic even if the kind of procedure is appropriate to Solon's day. Rhodes's view is vigorously opposed by Hansen (1980c), cf. (1975). Despite Hansen's many persuasive arguments, I am still inclined to trust the testimony of *Ath. Pol.*, particularly as *eisangelia* fits well with the traditional *nomophylakia* of the Areopagos in earlier times (a point that Hansen undervalues). See also R. Wallace (1989), 64–66; cf. Ostwald (1986), 9 who links *eisangelia* (again, anachronistically labeled) to the institution of *ho boulomenos* prosecution instituted by Solon (discussed subsequently).

[74] Analysis of cases to which *ho boulomenos* could apply suggests that Solon's innovation was to allow volunteer prosecutors to take the lead in situations where an injured party was for obvious reasons unable to act himself, such as the protection of children against enslavement or dissipation of their estate by their father (Harrison [1968], 72ff., 115ff.). On the other hand, as Harrison (1971), 77 notes: "But if in origin *ho boulomenos* was the champion of wronged citizens who but for him might have remained without effective remedy before the courts, he stood ready as a convenient instrument for championing the state in those cases where no individual had been wronged, but only the community as such." Cf. Gagarin (1986), 69. On the nature of Solon's reform see also Glotz (1904), 369–82; Ruschenbusch (1968), 47–53. For a more cynical view about the social value of *ho boulomenos* and *graphai*, R. Osborne (1985b), 40–41.

[75] The precise meaning of *ephesis* is debated; it has been interpreted to mean either "the appeal of a dissatisfied litigant to a court for a fresh hearing" or "the appeal in cases when a magistrate wanted to exceed the legally pre-

limited to an injured party or his family, and for most men appeal beyond an archon's judgment would have been impossible. Solon endowed all Athenians with a share in the process of justice, whether as jurors, defendants, or prosecutors in the interest of the common good. Private wrongs could now be public wrongs and justice belonged to every member of the community who accepted his moral responsibility as a citizen. And that responsibility also found more vigorous exercise with additional reforms regularizing meetings, voting, and perhaps also the selection of magistrates in the popular assembly.[76]

---

scribed penalty that could be imposed on his own authority." The former is to be preferred, as MacDowell (1978), 30–31 argues, emphasizing the sense of the term in Plut. *Sol.* 18.3. (For an attempt to define *ephesis* even more broadly than "appeal," see Sealey [1987], 62–69; cf. Ostwald [1986], 13–14 who believes that the process may also have included the possibility of challenging the Areopagos-administered *euthynai* of officials before the popular court.)

The nature of the popular court(s) to which litigants appealed under this reform is also hotly contested. The majority view has been that the appellate body was the assembly sitting in judicial capacity, primarily on the strength of an etymological argument connecting the meaning "assembly" with the archaic term for "law-court," *eliaia*: MacDowell (1978), 30; Rhodes (1979), 104–5; (1981), 160; Andrewes (1982a), 388; Humphreys (1983h), 242ff. Hansen, however, over the course of several publications ([1975], [1978], [1981–82], [1985a], [1987a], [1987b], 104–5), has argued powerfully against this view, stressing *Pol.* 1273 b 35, the weakness of the etymological argument, and the plausibility of an annually allotted court system as early as the sixth century. For a similar view, see now also the remarks of Sealey (1987), 67–69, 118–19. Cf. the vigorous opposition to the Hansen perspective of Ostwald (1986), 10 n. 27.

Though such courts were doubtless not called *dikastēria*, I believe that *Ath. Pol.*'s evidence can be otherwise taken at face value, and hereafter follow Hansen's interpretation that Solon created new popular courts, which were constituted of something less than the entire citizen body. There can be no doubt, at the same time, that eligibility was open to any Athenian.

[76] The establishment of the new probouleutic council of 400 (for the purpose of preparing business for the assembly; above, n. 55) suggests the likelihood that meetings of the *ekklēsia* now became regularly scheduled: Rhodes (1981), 154. It is also a reasonable guess (direct evidence is lacking) that the procedure of voting was first instituted during this time: Larsen (1949), 170; Griffith (1966); Forrest (1966), 171; Staveley (1972), 83; but cf. Hansen

The ideals of justice and moral responsibility in civic life appear in Solon's poetry as well as his legislation. He recited his verses among the people of his community, for his poetry was public and didactic, not intended for obscure publication, and one must imagine that many men heard his words and turned them over in their minds. The message was clear: moderation and fair play are the hope and salvation of Athenian society, and every citizen must hearken to their call. In his most famous verses, symbolizing the merging of the public and private spheres, Solon warned how the greed of men who ignore "the solemn foundations of Justice (*dikē*)" will cause revenge to fall upon the whole community, striking into the heart of every oikos:

> For it comes upon the entire *polis* like some relentless wound
> Which quickly turns into evil slavery
> Which in turn rouses civil strife and slumbering war. . . .
> Thus public ruin [*dēmosion kakon*] invades each man's own
>   house [*oikad' hekastōi*]
> Nor can the outer doors keep it out
> But it vaults over the high wall and finds him everywhere
> Even if he should flee into the innermost corner of his chamber.
>
> (F 4.17–19, 26–29)

Like Hesiod, Solon perceived that the injustice of a minority would affect the entire community; unlike Hesiod, however, Solon did not portray such ruin as imposed by divine forces but rather as growing out of, and remaining in, the human realm. The *dēmosion kakon* emanates from the people them-

---

(1977b) for some cautionary words about supposed procedures. Forrest (1966), 171 also argues that as a result of Solonian legislation the *ekklēsia* "now played a real part in the choice of magistrates," in contrast to its previous role of (at most) confirming selections made in the Areopagos. Here again, direct evidence is lacking and the question is further complicated by the old debate about whether Solon did or did not introduce sortition for the selection of archons (*Ath. Pol.* 8.1; Arist. *Pol.* 1273 b 40–1274 a 2 with Rhodes [1981], 146–48; cf. Forrest and Stockton [1987]). Nonetheless, it is a fair guess that the regularized meetings of the *ekklēsia* (rather than separate tribal assemblies) provided a convenient occasion for the choice of magistrates, even if election (or *prokrisis*) was organized according to citizens' *phylai*.

selves and at the same time destroys them, and every individual's private wrongs will bring public misfortune. Men do, however, have the power to avert ruin if they order their community justly, and Solon warned his fellow citizens of the urgent need to do so:

> My spirit bids me to teach these things to the Athenians:
> How many evils violence and Disorder [*Dysnomia*] bring to the
>   polis
> And how Good Order [*Eunomia*] makes everything
>   harmonious and well-fitting
> And how often she puts shackles on the unjust,
> Smooths roughnesses, checks excess, undoes violence,
> Shrivels the flowering of destruction,
> Straightens out crooked judgments, and arrogant deeds
> She makes gentle. Under her influence
> All things among men are fitting and wise.
>
>   (F 4.30–36, 38–39)

The poet-statesman preached to the community the lessons of *Eunomia* and *Dysnomia*, and expected those lessons to be learned by all its members. For Solon the well-ordered society was the just society, an equivalence that Aristotle later postulated as uniquely belonging to the polis. Under Solon, the Athenian community now at last approximated the ideal that the philosopher in the fourth century described in the *Politics*.

After instituting his many reforms, Solon traveled overseas (*Ath. Pol.* 11.1), but he left behind a new order which, by our earlier established definition, must surely be called a polis. Indeed by the time of the statesman's departure, the Athenians comprised a "community of place," inhabiting agricultural land around a civic center. They recognized outer limits of their territory, as seen in the assumptions about frontiers in Drakon's homicide legislation, and in the civic oath which Athenian hoplites now swore in witness of gods and "boundaries of the fatherland," the fields that grew wheat, barley, vines, olive-trees, fig-trees. The civic center itself was formally established by Solon: residences there were banned and the agora was cleared and marked out as the gathering place for all citizens.[77] Athenian society included both agricultural and nonagricultural labor, organized officially under the system of *telē*, and those members of the community were now also distinguished formally from slaves and *xenoi*. *Athēnaioi*, as the word appears in Solon's poetry, now firmly meant the people of all Attika and the society that spanned it.[78]

Furthermore, under Solon's constitution, all Athenians had the minimal right—and duty—to participate in the judicial and deliberative decisions in the agora, and shared with the magistrates and councils the authority to defend their city-state, provide for its material needs, organize unified worship of the gods, and decide matters of public policy and personal disputes. Finally, Athenians who embraced the Solonian order, as many must have done, realized a new civic spirit; the statesman accustomed them, as Plutarch says, "to share feelings and pain as if parts of one body" (Plut. *Sol.* 19). Affairs once private became increasingly public; Solon held out, both in verse and in legislation, the promise of justice, and with it

[77] It is usually believed that an older, smaller agora existed in the seventh century, perhaps northwest of the Akropolis; in about 600 the meetings of the *ekklēsia* were transferred to the area due north of the Akropolis, which, to judge by the cessation of burials, wells, and other traces of habitation, then became the new public space of Athens. Remains of the earliest public buildings in the area also date from about the same time. On the older agora, Wycherley (1966) and a new suggestion by Dontas (1983). On the "Solonian" agora, Boersma (1970), 15–16; H. Thompson and Wycherley (1972), 19–20; Camp (1986), 37ff. On the philosophical and political implications of the central space, Vernant (1986), 212ff.

[78] Before Solon, that was not clearly the case. Though the Drakonian law on homicide implies the shadow of a distinction between Athenians and non-Athenians (see chapter 4), a comparison with the language of the eighth-century Homeric poems is instructive. In the *Iliad*, Athens is mentioned only once (2.546), most likely as a place and not a unified kingdom of Attika. Similarly, the few references to "the Athenians" (4.338; 8.196, 689; 15.337) show nothing to indicate that by then *Athēnaios* represented anything more than an inhabitant of the community immediately surrounding the central citadel. For details, see Page (1959b), 145–47, and esp. n. 72, pp. 171–72. Hignett (1952), 35; and Andrewes (1982a), 360 read the Athenian references in Homer more generously, though the latter not without reservations about the validity of the texts as evidence for the *synoikismos*.

the members of Athenian society could expect a better life than they had known ever before.

Indeed these members were now "citizens," because at last the society had become, as Solon proclaimed in his poetry (F 4.1), *"hēmeterē polis"*—"our polis." He established, as Aristotle said, politeia, which now certainly meant citizenship.

Chapter Seven

TYRANNY, TRIALS, AND THE TRIUMPH OF KLEISTHENES

PLUTARCH tells the story that the Skythian prince Anacharsis laughed at Solon for thinking he could stop the greed and injustice of Athenians with written laws. Such things, he said, are like spiders' webs: sufficient to hold back the frail and weak, but easily smashed by the rich and powerful (*Sol. 5*). In the years following Solon's archonship, rich and powerful men once again dominated political events, but the finely spun web of laws and institutions that defined the polis proved more durable than anyone might have guessed. The foundations of a political community of citizens were now firmly in place.

It would be, however, almost ninety years before the ideals underlying the Solonic politeia could take real practical form. It was not until the revolution of Kleisthenes in 508/7 that citizenship was brought to the local level of every citizen, and not until then that the town and countryside of Attika were wholly unified, making fuller and more tangible what Solon first intended. Whereas Solon had defined a citizenship for all Athenians, it was Kleisthenes who defined it for each individual throughout Attika, and thus provided an even firmer legal identity for both the community and its members. At the same time, new boundaries were added to that identity which distinguished more sharply the Athenian from the non-Athenian, and marked out the citizen's status as more valuable than ever before. Kleisthenes' revolution was a triumph for citizenship, but one that was hardly inevitable. Although, as this chapter will demonstrate, it was promoted by the centralization and social change of the rule of tyrants, and given concrete shape in a complex program of legislation, citizenship was finally realized in the successful response to a crisis of freedom by the Athenians themselves.

The immediate aftermath of Solon's political activity was not promising for the future of the politeia. After his archonship, the statesman left Attika to travel overseas, and soon enough civil strife again tore the Athenian community. The newly found unity of citizenship and the polis were shaken mightily. Troubles first began in 590/89 when internal dissension halted the election of the archon eponymous; four years later it was more of the same when the Athenians again suffered *anarchia*. Four years again brought more disturbances; Damasias, archon in 582/1, seized power illegally and held office for fourteen months beyond his normal term.[1] The political strife was temporarily put aside when quarreling segments of society—Eupatridai and lower classes—agreed to share between them the power of the chief magistracy (*Ath. Pol.* 13.2).[2]

Meanwhile, beyond the political turbulence of the agora, economic problems still plagued the community. Despite the reforms of 594/3, hardships and bitterness persisted across the countryside. Some men were driven to ruin by Solon's cancellation of debts, some were angered by the new politeia, others pursued festering private feuds (*Ath. Pol.* 13.3). Poor farmers who had demanded a redistribution of land found themselves disappointed and frustrated; though now in secure control of their own plots, they still faced heavy burdens. Increasing development of private property, equal division among heirs in

---

[1] *Ath. Pol.* 13.1–2. For the archon dates (following Solon's archonship of 594/3: see chapter 5, n. 56), Cadoux (1948), 93–103.

[2] In addition to the Eupatridai, *Ath. Pol.* (cf. Plut. *Thes.* 25) mentions two other ancient classes, *agroikoi* ("farmers") and *demiourgoi* ("craftsmen"), among whom (probably) the remainder of the eponymous archonship of 580/79 was to be shared on a 5–3–2 proportional basis. None of the many attempts to identify these groups, unknown in later times, is completely satisfying (e.g., Roebuck [1974]; Figueira [1984]). I follow the simpler "noble versus non-noble" interpretation of Mossé (1964), 405–13; cf. Andrewes (1982b), 393. For the interpretation of how (and which) archonship was shared, Rhodes (1981), 182; for an interesting perspective on this period, Lévêque (1978); Stahl (1987).

a population already straining the limits of agrarian yield, the resettlement of freed debtors by Solon: as the years passed, all compounded the pressure on Attic land and must have further promoted its fragmentation. Throughout the sixth century there are persisting signs of agrarian distress and the need for new territory: more colonies are sent out,[3] the battle with Megara for Salamis continues,[4] grain is still imported,[5] and loans for small farmers are established.[6] In 594/3 Solon claimed that he had given the people only as much as they were due (F 5.1) but, as the glow of their initial optimism faded, many saw that had not been enough.

It was especially not enough once Solon, with his just but forceful ways, left the polis that he had helped bring into being. He had forged a shared partnership in public life among Athenians, but what the rallying cries had promised was perhaps something more than the actual reality of the "new community"; this was a society by heritage aristocratic, and in its day-to-day life still rural and largely decentralized. The institutions and ethos of citizenship did not mature overnight. In the absence of the man who had uniquely transcended the familiar sources of local power, politics lapsed into a struggle of older centrifugal loyalties. It was not long before the temporary but centralized compromise of 580 between Eupatrids and non-Eupatrids broke down; regional strife erupted anew, and the Attic population fell into three factions (*staseis*) whose memberships cut deeply into the recent unity that had given rise to the polis. Civil war erupted as each faction struggled to establish its own politeia in Athens (*Ath. Pol.* 13.4). The ori-

[3] Including Peisistratos' foundation of Rhaikelos in the Chalkidike after 556/5 (*Ath. Pol.* 15.2 with Rhodes [1981], 192ff.); Sigeion, resettled in about 530 after the earlier seventh-century foundation was apparently lost (Hdt. 5.94ff. with Page [1959a], 155; and see chapter 4, n. 51); the colonization of the Chersonese by the elder Miltiades, before (?) 546 (Hdt. 6.34–40 with Jeffery [1976], 96 and with Rhodes [1981], 198; cf. Wade-Gery [1958], 155ff.). On Athenian foundations at Lemnos and Imbros at the end of the sixth century, see below, n. 156.

[4] See chapter 5, n. 90.

[5] See chapter 5, n. 92.

[6] *Ath. Pol.* 16.2; and see later.

gins of these groupings—*Paralioi, Pediakoi,* and *Diakrioi,* "men from the coast, plain, and hills"—probably preceded the reforms of Solon, but in the generation thereafter, their essential identity remained the same.[7] The core of each was a local network: Aristotle records that their names were based on the area where each group farmed (*Ath. Pol.* 13.5), and evidence of geographical connections confirms the report.[8]

The aristocratic leaders of the *staseis* raised supporters from the neighborhoods of Attika where they wielded influence, and each group included a variety of statuses in property, wealth, and livelihood among its membership. Over time,

---

[7] Plut. *Sol.* 13.1–3 and the regional basis of the *staseis* (discussed later) both imply that their origins probably lie in the seventh century, though it is fruitless to try to identify any of them with factions involved in the Solonian conflict: Sealey (1960), 163ff.; Hopper (1961), 199–200; cf. Stahl (1987), 56ff. Sources that mention the *staseis* (for a complete listing, Rhodes [1981], 179) agree generally on the "men of the plain" (whether Plut. *Sol.* 29 *Pedieis* or *Ath. Pol.* 13.4 *Pediakoi*) and "men of the coast," but the name and identification of Peisistratos' party are controversial. Hdt. 1.59.3 calls them *Hyperakrioi* but *Ath. Pol.* and almost all other writers speak of *Diakrioi.* The latter probably relates to the hilly region of northeast Attika called Diakria (Traill [1978], 94–96) and the former has been reasonably explained (Wade-Gery [1958], 167 n. 2) as "those beyond the hills," i.e., out of the sight of Athens. Whichever name is to be preferred, the general area is not in doubt: *Hyperakrioi* included men from the Diakria, but the regional base of influence also extended to part of the east coast since Peisistratos' family lived in Brauron (Pl. *Hipparch.* 228 b; Plut. *Sol.* 10.3; Davies [1971], 452–55; Rhodes [1981], 185).

[8] Though the Alkmeonidai (family of Megakles, leader of the *Paralioi*) appear in classical times in demes between the city and the coast (D. Lewis [1963a], 23, 39), a case has been made linking them originally to lands along the coast from Phaleron to Sounion: Rhodes (1981), 186. Lykourgos, the leader of the *Pediakoi,* has been traced to the deme of Boutadai (Davies [1971], 348), just west of Athens, and would have been suitable as a base for followers from the rich "plains" around the city. On the *Diakrioi,* see above, n. 7. Andrewes (1982b), 394–97 adequately dispenses of older and more speculative views (e.g., Busolt [1893–95], 304–5) of the *staseis* representing occupational groups. Hopper (1961), 189ff., in most regards sensible, unconvincingly tries to identify the groups with different "foreign policies" in the war against Megara for Salamis. For interpretations stressing primarily a conflict of classes, Mossé (1964), 403ff.; Figueira (1984), 469ff. A good recent synthesis of the regional case is Sealey (1987), 119–21.

however, shared political goals helped blur boundaries, particularly among the *Diakrioi*. Their leader Peisistratos was first backed by inhabitants of Brauron, the site of his family's lands;[9] later his supporters also included "men impoverished from the loss of debts due to them, and those who feared for themselves because of their impure birth" (*Ath. Pol.* 13.5).[10] As the struggle among the *staseis* intensified, Peisistratos' following gained the reputation as the one "most favoring the people" (*dēmotikōtatos: Ath. Pol.* 13.4; Plut. *Sol.* 29). It attracted struggling small farmers from many areas of Attika[11] and ultimately included not only supporters from country villages but also even from the city (Hdt. 1.62).[12] Soon a majority of the citizens who had once hearkened to Solon were rallying around the military leader from Brauron. It would be he and his family who ultimately inherited the legacy of the Solonic politeia and took on custodianship of the polis.

GUARDIAN TYRANTS

After two failed attempts to establish one-man rule, Peisistratos ended the conflict of *staseis* in 546/5 when, with the aid of foreign mercenaries, he made himself *tyrannos* of the Athenians (Hdt. 1.61–63; *Ath. Pol.* 15.1–3). His reign, together with that of his sons who succeeded him,[13] was a custodianship because during their twenty-five-year dynasty the insti-

[9] Above, n. 7.

[10] Hopper (1961), 195 with n. 73 tried to interpret the first group described as *hoi apheirēmenoi ta chrea* as "those who had been freed from debt" but the translation is (unfortunately) not supportable. Such men (e.g., *hektēmoroi* previously released from debt) undoubtedly joined Peisistratos' following, but it is not impossible that the *stasis* also included former creditors as well, given the wide range of rural obligations that existed before Solon's reforms (see chapter 5). On "men of impure birth," see discussion later in this chapter.

[11] Cf. Holladay (1977).

[12] Herodotos' comment dates from Peisistratos' third coup in 546/5. Here and in what follows for the Peisistratid tyranny, I adhere to the chronological reconstruction laid out in Rhodes (1981), 189–99.

[13] On the old question, based on interpretation of Thuc. 1.20.2 and 6.53.3–59, of the age relationship and ruling status of Peisistratos' sons after his death, see D. Lewis (1988), 287–88.

tutions and spirit of the polis further developed while the polis itself temporarily ceased to be a purely self-governed community of citizens. Indeed, during that time, Athenians' civic responsibilities and participation were sometimes colored by the whims and personal agenda of the one family, and the still embryonic legal distinctions between Athenians and non-Athenians were confused by the influx of a certain number of foreigners of uncertain status. The final years of the tyranny were marked by bloodshed and ruthlessness, but still the overall effect of the long regime was positive. Under the Peisistratids the development of citizenship matured and evolved, though the evolution was not always a direct result of the tyrants' own actions.

Peisistratos' accession, and the subsequent strong rule of his family, once and for all put an end to the regional struggles that had threatened to undermine the newly formed polis and politeia. Likewise, social evolution progressed in step with the stabilizing political order. As Athenian society became more heterogeneous, it also became more centralized; town and countryside drew closer together and Athenians grew more accustomed to thinking of themselves not as regionalized dwellers of individual Attic neighborhoods, but as citizens of an autonomous political entity.[14] Solon's reforms, launched to avert tyranny, matured under tyranny's care.

Despite the later democratic bias against *tyrannoi*,[15] citizenship progressed under the custodianship of the Peisistratids. Peisistratos left intact Solon's code, did not disturb existing institutions, and is said to have governed according to the laws, more like a citizen than a tyrant.[16] He used an armed bodyguard and mercenaries to maintain order, but citizens

[14] It is significant in this regard that Kleisthenes' reforms were passed with the support of the *dēmos* as a whole and did not simply represent the will of any one regional grouping of Attika (Hdt. 5.69.2).

[15] Andrewes (1956), 20–30; Podlecki (1966); Ostwald (1969).

[16] Hdt. 1.59.6; Thuc. 6.54.6; *Ath. Pol.* 14.3, 16.2, 16.8; Plut. *Sol.* 31. The maintenance of the normal political and legal process under Peisistratos is additionally indicated by the story of the tyrant's own appearance before the Areopagos on a homicide charge: *Ath. Pol.* 16.8; Arist. *Pol.* 1315 b 21; Plut. *Sol.* 31.

continued to serve in military and naval operations.[17] And though Peisistratos may have helped his friends and relatives into important offices of the government, Aristotle insists that during his rule, he was supported by the majority of both noble and common people (*Ath. Pol.* 16.9).[18] The philosopher also notes how the reign was later described as a golden age (*Ath. Pol.* 16.7, 16.9; cf. Pl. *Hipparch.* 229 b). After Peisistratos' death in 528/7, his sons conducted affairs in the same manner as their father had (*Ath. Pol.* 17.3); according to the

[17] *Ath. Pol.* 15.4 (cf. Polyaen. 1.21.2) reports that Peisistratos disarmed the Athenian people; it is also likely that the mercenaries first employed by Peisistratos in his rise to power continued to play an important role throughout the dynasty: Berve (1967), 52ff.; Bicknell (1969a), 34–37 and (1972), 18–21. Cf. Arist. *Pol.* 1285 a 25–29 and 1311 a 12–13 pointing out the value of bodyguards and disarming citizens in maintaining a tyranny. Scholars who have ascribed a military component to Kleisthenes' reforms in 508/7 (e.g., French [1961]; van Effenterre [1976]; Siewert [1982]) argue to varying degrees from this evidence that the citizen army was rarely deployed or even disbanded for most of the Peisistratid period (cf. Frost [1984], 291ff.).

Thucydides (6.56.2 and 6.58), however, claims that under the tyranny citizens bore arms in the Panathenaic procession and that it was Hippias not Peisistratos who disarmed the Athenians (*contra Ath. Pol.* 18.4). More important (since it is impossible to choose between these contradictory traditions), there are enough instances of military successes during the tyranny to suggest that citizens and not just mercenaries constituted an Athenian fighting force on both land and sea (cf. Parke [1933], 9 who believes that Peisistratos' mercenaries played no part in overseas campaigns). The Athenians after long struggle had been victorious in capturing Salamis from Megara, probably before Peisistratos' first coup (561/60; cf. Hopper [1961], 208ff.; and see chapter 5, n. 90); but nine years after his death, an apparently citizen army beat soundly a significant force of Thebans (Hdt. 6.108). During Peisistratos' tyranny, Naxos was subdued by force, an undertaking of sufficient magnitude that on a later occasion was thought to require at least 100 ships (Hdt. 1.64.2; 5.31.3). Sigeion was reconquered, after a fight, with the result that Hegesistratos was installed there as governor (Hdt. 5.94.1; and above, n. 3). For further discussion, see Andrewes (1982b), 403ff.

[18] Thuc. 6.54.6 reports that the Peisistratids took care to ensure that there was always someone of their family in office; in fact, evidence from the archon list (Meiggs and Lewis [1969], 9–10) shows that sometimes they relied on the cooperation of leading nobles as well, including the well-to-do [On]et[orides], archon in 527/6 (as restored, Davies [1971], 421); Kleisthenes the Alkmeonid, archon in 525/4; Miltiades son of Kimon, archon in 524/3. Andoc. 2.26 gives further evidence of the tyrants' efforts to seek accommodation with leading aristocrats, including through marriage alliances.

best traditions, Hippias the eldest was in charge, a man described as public-spirited (*politikos: Ath. Pol.* 18.1).[19]

Under the Peisistratid umbrella of peace and relative tranquillity, Athenians became more comfortable with the benefits and operation of Solon's polis, even if a few of its laws withered through disuse (*Ath. Pol.* 22.1). The *ekklēsia* continued to meet; buildings for the Council of 400 were enlarged[20] while the council itself continued to administer the agenda for the assembly's meetings; the law courts dispensed justice for the common man who now appeared more frequently in the agora.[21] In the era of tyranny, the exercise of citizenship in the central and public institutions became a little more familiar for many Athenians.

Rural citizens would have now traveled to Athens more regularly, and others came to settle permanently. The urban center grew as men from the countryside migrated there, seeking new opportunities and abandoning unproductive land.[22] When Peisistratos instituted his program of agrarian loans to small farmers, it was to discourage too many people from spending their time in the city and becoming involved in public affairs (*Ath. Pol.* 16.3).[23] The inference, of course, is that this was now beginning to happen. But public affairs were not the only draw of Athens; the city offered the lure of new com-

[19] For Hippias as the eldest son and successor of Peisistratos see also the polemical assertion of Thuc. 1.20.2, 6.54.2, 6.55; *contra* Pl. *Hipparch.* 228 b 5–6; Ael. *VH* 8.2; and Hellanikos(?); cf. Beloch (1912) i.2, 293–97.

[20] Rhodes (1972a), 18; Boersma (1970), 23; both with references.

[21] For discussion of the workings of the government under the Peisistratid tyranny, Hignett (1952), 115–23; DeLaix (1973), 17–18; Stahl (1987), 140ff. For a more cynical view, Berve (1967), 58.

[22] For some sensible remarks about the nature of Athens' "urban" expansion in this period, Whitehead (1986a), 26–27; D. Lewis (1988), 302 is more skeptical. On the relationship between town and country and its changes, E. Gutkind (1969), 463ff.; Humphreys (1978), 130–35. For general background on urban centralization and functions, Martin (1975). For discussion about definitions and models to describe "urbanism" in preindustrial communities, Layton (1972); M. Smith (1972); Wheatley (1972).

[23] Cf. Arist. *Pol.* 1292 b 25–29; 1318 b 9–16; 1319 a 26–32 on farming and its role in diverting people from the city and politics. Dio Chrys. 7. 107–8; 25. 3 comments on Peisistratos' keeping Athenians in the countryside.

mercial gain.[24] A massive public building program of the Peisistratids provided new jobs,[25] as did the expanding industries in manufacture and overseas trade.[26] By now Attic black- and red-figure wares were being produced for shipment throughout the Mediterranean world;[27] the scenes painted upon them and dedications on the Akropolis attest to the variety of other crafts and trades in Athens by the end of the sixth century.[28] As more Athenians left the countryside, changing their agricultural livelihoods for *technai* (which Solon had earlier encouraged them to do: Plut. *Sol.* 22), the city also needed better services. Thus by about 525 the tyrants had completed a new fountain and pipe system, a functional as well as ceremonial improvement in the Athenian center.[29] Finally, even the center became better defined; Peisistratos is credited with constructing the first structural perimeter around the city.[30]

[24] Here again, I skirt the heated and long-standing controversies over the "primitive" or "modern" interpretation of the Athenian economy and the corresponding question of the nature of "the city" in such a schema (see chapter 4, n. 48). Full discussion is not possible here, but my slight bias toward the "modernists," particularly for this period, will be clear to those readers familiar with the debate. On the growth of Athens and the urban economy I follow mostly the views of Starr (1977), 100ff.; (1982), 419ff.; cf. the original arguments of Busolt (1893–95) 2:335ff. on the Peisistratid encouragement of trade and industry.

[25] Boersma (1970), 8ff. I follow Boersma's view that despite the possible involvement of private individuals in some projects "the tyrants became deeply involved with the building program of their time and . . . left their stamp on it."

[26] See generally French (1964), 42ff.; Starr (1977), 70–89; Hopper (1979), 43ff.

[27] Starr (1977), 69 with n. 49; Boardman (1979). Hopper (1979), 97–98 summarizes the debate (going back to Beloch and Hasebroek) over the volume and economic significance of pottery remains.

[28] Scenes depicted on pottery reflect the manufacture and trade of textiles, furniture, armaments: Andrewes (1982b), 408; cf. Boardman (1974), 212. For dedicatory inscriptions of potters and other kinds of craftsmen during this period, Raubitschek (1949), 457, 465.

[29] Thuc. 2.15.5; Paus. 1.14.1; Boersma (1970), 23. The identification of the archaeological remains of the southeast fountainhouse in the agora with the Enneakrounos attributed to the tyrants is, however, problematical: Thompson and Wycherley (1972), 197–200; Shear (1978), 10–11; Camp (1986), 42–43.

[30] Vanderpool (1974), 156–60; cf. Boardman (1982), 442–43.

Meanwhile, for the majority of Athenians who continued to live in the countryside, the city itself reached out—in the form of more centralized administration that influenced their daily lives. A system of traveling dikasts was established. These judges journeyed to the rural demes, bringing the process of justice to farmers unable to come to Athens; Peisistratos himself rode through Attika to settle disputes and survey the state (*Ath. Pol.* 16.5).[31] Other administrators were probably sent out from the city too. Peisistratos had levied a 5 percent agricultural tax[32] to support his program of loans, and this would have been assessed where produce was harvested, in the rural demes.[33] Travel to and from the center was facilitated by Peisistratos' sons who improved Attic roads, and marked them with new milestones indicating distance measured from the central agora.[34] And during the tyranny (at the latest) one other aspect of urban life began to touch the outlying regions of the polis. A state coinage circulated in Attika and the silver images of Athena and her owl found their way into the hands of the Athenian population, symbolizing the progress and pride of centralization.[35]

---

[31] Hignett (1952), 115 reasonably argues that the institution of traveling dikasts limited the authority of local nobles who had previously settled minor disputes in the countryside.

[32] *Ath. Pol.* 16.4 speaks of a *dekatē* ("one-tenth") levied by Peisistratos whereas Thuc. 6.54.5 of *eikostē* ("one-twentieth") collected by Peisistratos' sons. Either we have to imagine that the rate was reduced over the course of the tyranny (e.g., Berve [1967], 53, 65–66) or (preferably) that *dekatē* in *Ath. Pol.* is a generic term for "tithe" and that Thucydides' testimony is the more precise (and quantitative) description of the tax: Rhodes (1981), 215; cf. (1984b), 58.

[33] Hignett (1952), 115 suggests that the tax was collected through the naukraric system (see chapter 4, n. 23) which was remodeled to provide a centralized administration for all of Attika.

[34] The hub of the road system was the Altar of the Twelve Gods established in 521 in the agora (Thuc. 6.54), and from which distances in Attika to the heart of the polis were measured: Hdt. 2.7.1, cf. *IG* i² 2640; Wycherley (1978), 33. Distances were recorded on inscribed herms erected along the roads: Pl. *Hipparch.* 228 b–e; *IG* i² 837; Crome (1935–36); Kirchner and Dow (1937); Camp (1986), 42. For the tradition and popular role of the herms, R. Osborne (1985c).

[35] For the vexed question of the dating of Attic coinage, see discussion in

As town and countryside merged, so merged further public and private affairs, continuing the process begun by Solon. Under the tyrants, the polis sponsored and enhanced more religious activity, adding a civic component to cults and worship once only regional. The Eleusinian Mysteries were embraced by the ruling family.[36] In the early part of the tyranny Peisistratos constructed a city sanctuary to the goddesses Demeter and Korē; later, in Eleusis, his sons extended both the sacred Telestērion ("House of Mysteries") and the precinct of the female divinities.[37]

Emblematic of the new public consciousness, the religious focus in the city shifted from the Akropolis to the civic space, the agora. Building activity and votive dedications on the citadel declined as more attention was paid to the open area below.[38] The tyrants established public shrines of Zeus Agoraios and Apollo Patroos in the western agora, where, symbolically,

---

chapter 5, with nn. 75–78. Whatever the date of introduction of the first Attic coins (so-called *Wappenmünzen*), it is not seriously doubted that Attic "owls" began to be minted at the latest sometime during the tyranny (I am not concerned with distinguishing between Peisistratos and his sons in this matter). See Kraay (1956) and (1976), 60ff., and his (1962) response to W. Wallace (1962) who attempted to downdate them to Kleisthenes' era; cf. Bicknell (1969b). Francis and Vickers (1983) propose a radical new chronology for the period with important implications for Kraay's case; see however the objections of Boardman (1984), 163.

[36] R. Osborne (1985a), 154ff. has seriously challenged the common view (e.g., Solders [1931]) that regional cults such as the Eleusinian Mysteries and Artemis Brauronia were "annexed by the state" during the Peisistratid tyranny, and argues instead for a continuing centrifugal tension between rural and central religion (cf. Polignac [1984]). His case is particularly persuasive for the Brauronia whose sanctuary in Athens cannot be securely dated to this period. On the other hand, though it is probably wrong to speak of "annexation," there can be little doubt that the Peisistratid interest in the Eleusinian Mysteries at least reflected a centralizing affirmation of the cult.

[37] Mylonas (1961), 77ff.; Boersma (1970), 35, 162–63, 185; Boardman (1975), 3–5.

[38] Raubitschek (1949), 456; Boersma (1970), 14–15; Vernant (1982), 47ff.; Stahl (1987), 233ff. There is no proof, as is sometimes suggested (e.g., Cornelius [1929], 24) that Peisistratos lived on the Akropolis. Boersma (1970), 16–17; Shear (1978), 6–7; and others have proposed that a building in the southwest corner of the agora may have been the tyrants' residence, but that too is uncertain.

these household gods now joined the new national hero Theseus, celebrated as the founder of the polis.[39] During the same period Dionysos was also honored in the agora, and Peisistratos instituted the festival of the City Dionysia. Though modest at first, this festival ultimately became the sacred occasion of Greek tragedy, the dramatic art form that was itself initiated in Peisistratos' reign by the actor Thespis.[40] Reflecting the new interest, painted vases from the period show a marked increase in scenes depicting Dionysos; also in about 520 a small temple to Dionysos Eleuthereus was built in the city.[41]

To be sure, many of the new public programs of the tyrants celebrated their own personal glory. In the most obvious case the Peisistratids sought to identify themselves with the hero Herakles, witnessed, for example, in the iconography of contemporary coins and vase painting and the massive temple they undertook for Herakles' father Zeus.[42] Yet one should not underestimate the appeal that all festivals, building projects, and communal occasions would have had for the citizen population at large. In particular, special patriotic awareness was raised by the steady and generous attention paid to Athena, the goddess of Athens.

Before Peisistratos came to power, Athenians had already built several small shrines to Athena, and in the 560s the first

[39] Boersma (1970), 15–17; cf. Jacoby (1949), 219, 394–95 n. 23. Hedrick (1988c) 206ff. argues that Peisistratos actually created the cult of Apollo Patroos.

[40] Wycherley (1957), 162–63; Pickard-Cambridge (1962), 69–89 and (1968), 58; Boersma (1970); cf. Andrewes (1982b), 412.

Winkler (1985) makes the interesting suggestion that tragedy's origin and the City Dionysia are to be explained partly as a reflection of Peisistratos' desire to celebrate the nontribal loyalties of the ephebic population and to solidify the allegiance of young Athenians to the polis, at the expense of the regional corporations. He goes on to propose that the dithyrambic competition, datable to 508, in turn solidified allegiances to the Kleisthenic tribes (discussed later). The argument is thoughtful and provocative, though Winkler makes too much of the symbolism of the *ephēbeia*—which cannot be dated before the fourth century (see chapter 1, n. 34).

[41] Kolb (1977), 133; Boersma (1970), 26.

[42] Boardman (1972) and (1975); Boersma (1970), 25.

temple of Athena Polias, "Athena of the *polis*," was erected.[43] From about the same time dates the institution of the festival of the Great Panathenaia whose climax was celebrated by a procession and presentation of a sacred robe (*peplos*) to the goddess on the Akropolis. Peisistratos significantly enhanced the festival, adding musical and athletic events to its celebration.[44] He also contructed a ramp for better access to the Akropolis and renovated the Polias temple thereupon.[45] Under his hand a grand and elaborate ceremony now stirred the pride of all Athenians. The civic magnificence of the dynasty helped polish the image of citizenship throughout the polis.

The image was polished further by other successes of the tyrants. Under the Peisistratids, Athens became a formidable power in the Aegean, and the exploits of her citizens abroad helped sow the seeds of the imperialism that became the source of wealth and power of the fifth-century polis. Peisistratos' first victory in foreign affairs, the capture of the port of Nisaia from the old Athenian rival Megara, established his public reputation and a patriotic following (Hdt. 1.59; *Ath. Pol.* 14.1).[46] Later and farther afield, the tyrant again demonstrated Athenian power when he installed his ally Lygdamis as the ruler of the important island of Naxos (Hdt. 1.61.4, 64.2; *Ath. Pol.* 15.2). Still farther afield, sending his son Hegistratos to Sigeion (Hdt. 5.94ff.)[47] and the aristocrat Miltiades to the

[43] Boersma (1970), 13–14 with references and discussion of possible earlier temples to Athena on the Akropolis; Shear (1978), 3–4. On archaic cults of Athena, see Herington (1955); cf. Andrewes (1982b), 410–11.

[44] A Panathenaic festival held in Hekatombaion is probably to be traced back to the seventh century, but the first Great Panathenaia is attributed to the work of Hippokleides, archon in 566/5 (*FGrH* 3 F 2), or of Peisistratos (Schol. Ael. Arist. 13. 189.4–5). Consensus is now that the latter enlarged the celebration rather than originated it. See Davison (1958) and (1962); N. Robertson (1985); for details of its celebration, Parke (1977), 33ff.; on its political significance, Meyer (1921–25), 2:665–66, 785; Andrewes (1982b), 410.

[45] On the ramp up to the Akropolis, Camp (1986), 36; Boersma (1970), 20 and 109 nn. 226–29 for previous scholarship on the debated details of the temple renovation.

[46] On the war with Megara, see chapter 5, n. 90.

[47] For scholarship on the tangled chronology of this event, see above, n. 3.

Chersonese (Hdt. 6.34ff.),[48] Peisistratos at last secured Athenian interests near the entrance of the Black Sea. The tyrant also established Athenian political links with Thrace and with Macedon,[49] and, in a striking symbolic gesture, "purified" the Aegean sanctuary of Delos by removing unholy graves on the island (Hdt. 1.64.2). The act was a deliberate announcement to the Greek world of Athenian primacy among all Ionian lands.[50]

During the Peisistratid tyranny, only a minority of Athenians participated directly in such overseas adventures but the victories and glory would have affected a much larger part of the population. Many Athenians knew only their country demes but, with increased communication and administration between the center and the periphery, more and more citizens

[48] The rationale behind Miltiades the elder's trip to the Chersonese is debated, and has been seen by many to depend on the interpretation of this period's problematical chronology (above, n. 3). Those who place the expedition after 546 and Peisistratos' establishment of rule assume that the foundation was a "state" enterprise undertaken through some agreement between the tyrant and Miltiades. Others who date the trip before 546 suggest that it was an independent undertaking, and stress Herodotos' testimony that Miltiades left in part because he could not endure life under Peisistratos in Athens. In fact 546 may not be a pivotal date, since Peisistratos had two earlier (albeit interrupted) spells of tyranny during which Miltiades could have left "under orders" from the ruler. Moreover, the motives ascribed to Miltiades by Herodotos may derive from a tradition of (unreliable) antityrannical gossip. Peisistratos' sons later dispatched the younger Miltiades (son of Kimon, and nephew of the elder Miltiades) to regain his uncle's dominion that had fallen into Thracian hands. On this basis it is reasonable to assume that the elder Miltiades and Peisistratos may have originally had some understanding, and that the first expedition was done with the advice and support of the tyrant. For this view, Jeffery (1976), 96; for some earlier scholarship and the debate on the "state" versus "individual" expedition, Berve (1937), 9ff.; Ehrenberg (1946), 121–28; Hignett (1952), 326–31; Hammond (1956); Wade-Gery (1958), 166ff.

[49] Peisistratos' relations with Thrace date to his collection of gold, silver, and mercenaries from the Mt. Pangaion area after 556/5: Ath. Pol. 15.2. Connections with Macedon are implied by the Peisistratan settlement of neighboring Rhaikelos in the Chalkidike (Ath. Pol. 15.2), and by the later offer of refuge to the exiled Hippias by the Macedonian king Amyntas (Hdt. 5.94.1): Andrewes (1956), 112; cf. How and Wells (1928), 2:55.

[50] Andrewes (1982b), 403; cf. Solon F 4a; and Thuc. 3.104.1–2.

began to come under the influence of the affairs of the city; and some of these same Athenians now heard and thought about faraway places and the role of Athens—their polis—in a world outside their own immediate experiences. In the city, tales of visiting poets and artists complemented the foreign memories of aliens who now also worked there, and traders returning from the Euxine or Italy too had their stories to tell.[51] For most Athenians, events and places abroad seemed remote, even exotic, but reports of far-flung successes made such things seem less distant every day. Against a widening international backdrop, the nature and value of the domestic Athenian polis grew with the esteem of its citizens.

As Athenian interests expanded abroad, civic affairs at home took on new and patriotic significance. Public festivals, worship, buildings, coinage: all became symbols of an Athenian identity, of a polis with its own self-conscious image. The identity of each individual citizen began to be drawn into the centripetal whole, and each man's social membership matured as a share of a public, all-embracing corporation. Society became more centralized, and broader values emerged which transcended the plurality of regional and ethnic loyalties. Older, and traditional differences across the population became less important as the more vigorous and universal civic spirit that briefly bloomed under Solon now spread across the community.[52]

That widening spirit, however, did not totally eclipse the

[51] Hipparchos brought the poets Anakreon, Simonides, and perhaps Lasos of Hermione (the teacher of Pindar) to Athens: *Ath. Pol.* 18.1; Hdt. 7.6.3; Pl. *Hipparch.* 228 c; cf. Ar. *Vesp.* 1410–11. For foreign artisans, see chapter 6, nn. 49–50. For some evidence of sixth-century foreign sculptors, Jeffery (1962), 151–52; Raubitschek (1949), 484, 491–95, 502–3; M. Robertson (1975), 78 nn. 15–16; 87 with n. 37; 89 n. 40; 101 with n. 62. For the possibility of foreign architects working in Athens: Boersma (1970), 3–10; Burford (1972), 57–67; Coulton (1977), 15–29. Boersma (1970), 24 also suggests that the Peisistratidan water system may have been built by the Megarian engineer Eupalinos who constructed the similar system in Samos. For foreign merchants and traders in Athens, see Johnston (1972) and (1979), 49–52; Hopper (1979), 43ff.; Cartledge (1983a), 11–12.

[52] For a similar line of argument, Stahl (1987), 229ff.

persistent ambitions of many aristocrats to once more assume leadership of the state. Their ambitions were ultimately realized by the beginning of the last decade of the sixth century, but, significantly, it was not personal power but rather the concept of citizenship that became the center of political controversy once the tyrants were gone. As we shall see, Kleisthenes rode to power by resolving this controversy when he redefined the Athenian polis and membership in it.

The apparent harmony of Peisistratid rule was destroyed by the murder of Hipparchos in 514/3; his surviving brother Hippias reigned for another four years in a regime that turned brutal and fearsome (Thuc. 6.59; Hdt. 5.55, 62; *Ath. Pol.* 18.4–19.1). There is little doubt that the chief instigators— and initially, the chief victims of retaliation—were members of noble Athenian families.[53] Harmodios and Aristogeiton, the slayers of Hipparchos, were young men who traveled in aristocratic circles;[54] they were apprehended, and under torture Aristogeiton implicated other accomplices, "men illustrious by birth" (Thuc. 6.57; *Ath. Pol.* 18.4). Thereafter, other aristocrats continued the struggle, including a certain Kedon who failed in an attack against Hippias,[55] and the Alkmeoni-

[53] On the aristocratic character of politics in this period, Hignett (1952), 124–26; Forrest (1966), 191; Ostwald (1969), 137–43; Stahl (1987). I leave aside the old debate about whether the murder of Hipparchos was prompted by personal or political motives; that it ultimately led to a political uprising is obvious. For sources and judicious remarks on these issues, see D. Lewis (1988), 299–300.

[54] Both were members of the Gephyraioi (Hdt. 5.55) but Harmodios appears to have been of a more upper-class branch of the *genos*; cf. Thuc. 6.54.2. For evidence and discussion, Davies (1971), 473–74.

[55] Kedon's background is obscure, but a contemporary drinking song honors his effort and raises a toast *tois agathois andrasin* ("to noble men"). But, depending on one's translation of the passage, the case might be even firmer: Rhodes (1981), 248 (following Wilamowitz and others) reads the reference to this man in *Ath. Pol.* 20.5 as "Kedon *of* the Alkmeonids," rather than "Before the Alkmeonids, Kedon. . . ." For discussion of the drinking song and the event it celebrates, Bowra (1961), 383–84; *contra* Bowra, however, the dates of both Kedon's attack and the attack of the Alkmeonidai from Leipsydrion belong after Hipparchos' death. For this view, Ostwald (1969), 127 n. 5, and

dai family who, after several unsuccessful tries, ultimately succeeded in driving the *tyrannos* into exile (*Ath. Pol.* 19.3–6, 20.4–5; Thuc. 6.59.4; Hdt. 6.123). The final victory was achieved with help from the Spartan king Kleomenes (Hdt. 5.64–65; *Ath. Pol.* 19.4–6). Thus, in 511/10 foreign soldiers and Attic aristocrats ended the tyranny in Athens.

ARISTOCRATIC BACKLASH AND THE CIVIC SCRUTINY OF 510/9

When the Spartans withdrew from Athens, public affairs predictably shifted to the control of aristocratic families, and the political climate turned against the Peisistratids and their popular following. A Drakonian law prohibiting anyone from aiding or abetting a tyrant was reenacted.[56] Commemorative statues of Hipparchos' slayers were erected, probably the propaganda of a proud faction of nobles.[57] In memory of the unlucky Aristogeiton, a law against torture of Athenians was instituted (Andoc. 1.43).[58] Finally, the Peisistratids themselves were officially banned from Attika, their names marked on a stele on the Akropolis.[59] Against such a background the *dēmos* who had largely supported the tyrants began to get, in Herodotus' words, "the worst of things" (5.69.2).

The bad situation for the *dēmos* was underscored in a bitter fight about citizenship, and thus the identity of the polis itself. Who would and who would not be considered a member of

see pp. 120–60 for the chronological reconstruction of the period 514–507, which I follow hereafter.

[56] *Ath. Pol.* 16.10. For the date and discussion of the law, and the date of its reenactment, Ostwald (1955), 108–9.

[57] The statues of Harmodios and Aristogeiton done by Antenor are dated to 509 by Pliny *NH* 34.17, and are not to be confused with the later, "democratic" statues by Kritios and Nesiotes erected in 477/6 (*Marm. Par.* ep. 54 with Paus. 1.8.5). On these, see Podlecki (1966); and Brunnsåker (1955), the latter of whom objects to the Pliny date of the Antenor group. His arguments are met by Ostwald (1969), 131–33, cf. Jacoby (1949), 339 n. 2. I do not follow Ostwald's attempt (1969), 133ff., however, to link the Antenor statues with the contemporary (?) drinking songs crediting the tyrannicides with making Athens *isonomos* (Page [ed.] [1962], nos. 893–96).

[58] MacDowell (1962), 93.

[59] Thuc. 6.55.1 with Ostwald (1955), 109.

the formal Athenian community? And what would that community be? In 510/9 the Athenian population was subjected to a civic scrutiny or *diapsēphismos*.[60] The reason, according to Aristotle, was that "there were many sharing in the politeia for whom it was not appropriate" (*Ath. Pol.* 13.5). The enormous significance of the *diapsēphismos* for the development of citizenship demands a close look at the details and implications of this event.[61]

Typically, scholars address two questions about the *diapsēphismos*. First, who was behind it? Second, who were its victims? But in addition to these, two further, and for our purposes, more pressing, questions need be asked. How did the *diapsēphismos* actually work? And what happened to those who "failed the test"?

Aristotle connects the *diapsēphismos* to the "impure birth" of some of Peisistratos' followers (*Ath. Pol.* 13.5). The fairest conclusion to be drawn from that connection (and even more, from the anti-Peisistratid climate after 511/10) is that the prime targets of the scrutiny were members of the *dēmos* who had supported the tyrants. (I will return shortly to the issue of "impure birth" among the group.) The answer to the question of who pushed for the scrutiny is more difficult; it is often assumed that the instigators of the *diapsēphismos* were simply "the aristocrats," eager to undo the popular following that had kept the Peisistratids in power.[62] But the struggles among different aristocratic families in earlier times, and the similar struggle for power between the nobles Kleisthenes and Isagoras that followed the *diapsēphismos*, make it unlikely that the scrutiny was the unified effort of a Eupatrid class working in

[60] Hignett (1952), 132–33 effectively disposes of various skeptical views including the notion that the *diapsēphismos* is in conflict with the tradition of the "Kleisthenic enfranchisements" (Arist. *Pol.* 1275 b 34–37; and see discussion later in this chapter) or that it belongs to a period after the reforms of 508/7. For additional defense of the date see Ostwald (1969), 141–42; Rhodes (1981), 188.

[61] Important treatments include Welwei (1967); Murray (1980), 255–56; Luzzi (1980); Rhodes (1981), 188, 255–56; David (1986), 8ff.

[62] Hignett (1952), 133, e.g., proposes that it was an effort of "the Alkmeonidai as well as the oligarchs."

harmony against the *dēmos*. With Hippias gone, different factions of aristocrats now vied for leadership of the polis, and the *diapsēphismos* was inevitably part of that fight. This will become clearer as we consider the question of how the *diapsēphismos* actually functioned.

This *diapsēphismos* was (as far as is known) the first in the history of the Athenian polis. There is no precedent and there is almost no evidence for its operations or results. There were, however, two other scrutinies attested subsequently in Athenian history, in the years 445/4 and 346/5. We know the most about the procedure of 346/5 (described by the slightly different term *diapsēphisis*) which required that every Athenian's citizen status be put to a vote before the fellow members of his deme.[63] Sources inform us that those rejected became *metoikoi*, but appeal to a jury court was possible. Winners of appeals were vindicated as citizens; losers were sold as slaves.[64] The defense of the rejected Euxitheos in Demosthenes 57 suggests that the process in his deme Halimous had its fair share of improprieties and factional infighting. In addition to claims of bribery and coercion among the membership, the defendant notes that the demarch had actually lost the deme's citizen register (9–14, 26, 60–62).

The scrutiny of 445/4 is more poorly attested,[65] but may also have taken place in the demes; those struck from the list (some 5,000, according to the sources) are described by Philochoros as *xenoi parengegrammenoi* ("strangers registered"), perhaps a reference to men who had been illegally entered on *lēxiarchika grammateia*.[66] The fate of these *xenoi* is

---

[63] Dem. 57, with Libanius' hypothesis; Aeschin. 1.77–78 (with schol. *ad* 77), 86, 114; 2.182; Isae. 12 with Dion. Hal. *Isae.* 17; Dion. Hal. *Deinarchos* 11; Harpoc. s.v. *diapsēphisis*. For a convenient summary of scholarship on the event, Whitehead (1986a), 106 n. 103.

[64] Isae. 12, hypothesis (= Dion. Hal. *Isae.* 16); Dem. 57, hypothesis. Cf. Rhodes (1981), 502; and *contra* Gomme (1934), 130–40 who argues that rejected appellants were sold into slavery only if they had been slaves before.

[65] Plut. *Per.* 37.4; *FGrH* 328 F 119.

[66] Hignett (1952), 345. Diller (1937), 93 with n. 42, followed by Whitehead (1986a), 100, proposes the alternative possibility that illegal claimants were prosecuted in a series of *graphai xenias* (see chapter 8, n. 8). Patterson (1981),

uncertain, other than that they were denied a share in the gift of Egyptian grain which had occasioned the review in the first place.[67]

Now, despite the sparse information about the *diapsēphismos* of 510/9, we do know that it differed from these other scrutinies of the classical period in one important way. In 445/4 and 346/5 a clear definition of the requirements for citizenship existed. Though members in individual demes might vote unfairly in a review, the basis for every man's membership in the polis was by then at least known and recognized: enrollment in the deme upon verification of his age and legitimate free birth from two Athenian parents. Before the establishment of that standard by Kleisthenes' reforms of 508/7 (and modified by Perikles' measure of 451/50), there is no proof that any such legal criteria existed.[68] On the eve of the sixth-century *diapsēphismos*, citizenship extended to all Athenians who came under the wide umbrella of the Solonian *telē*; centralization had still not progressed to the point where the polis had any law determining precise qualifications for its corporate membership. The system of deme registration was not yet invented, and there was no legal machinery in place for the review or appeal of a citizen's "official" status. There was also

122–23 n. 63 takes a view midway between the two, and suggests all citizens applying for the handout were scrutinized by tribal and deme officials in Athens at the time of the distribution. Patterson (p. 123) believes this scrutiny to have been "the first major test of the state citizenship [sc. Perikles'] law," though she rightly dispenses of earlier scholarship that tries to link the events of 445/4 with the implementation of Perikles' measure; cf. Hignett (1952).

[67] Plut. *Per.* 37.4 says they were enslaved, but Jacoby *ad FGrH* 328 F 119 (Suppl. IIIb, p. 463) argues that slavery was the penalty only for those who unsuccessfully appealed their case in court. The issue is complicated by the implausibly high number of those supposedly rejected, on which see Whitehead (1977), 169 n. 51.

[68] On Kleisthenes' definition of citizenship, see later discussion; on Perikles' law of 451/50, see chapter 6, n. 52 and chapter 8. Stroud (1978), 29–30 believes that the scrutiny of 510/9 occasioned the issuance of a decree in permanent form that included a definition of the qualification for citizenship; in the absence of any definite proof, this remains only speculation. For a similar (unsubstantiated) view, Murray (1980), 255.

yet no status of *metoikos* by which rejected members could be neatly categorized.[69]

In contrast to these classical examples, the absence of any centralized standard in the year 510/9 is not appreciated by many scholars who assume (as seen before) that "before Kleisthenes, citizenship was determined by membership in an Attic phratry." By their view, the *diapsēphismos* was conducted methodically in the *phratriai*, according to well-established rules. There is no evidence that phratries conducted this scrutiny; given the rallying cry later heard during Kleisthenes' reforms—*mē phylokrinein* ("no more investigation by tribes": *Ath. Pol.* 21.2)—it might just as well have been done in the *phylai*, though that cannot be proven either.[70] But wherever and however the scrutiny was conducted, I stress again that there were no centrally agreed-upon rules for its implementation. Regional corporations and kinship groupings had their own practices; if the case of the deme of Halimous in 346/5 was marked by its own peculiar circumstances in an era when law was more fixed, a fortiori there would have been a variety of possible practices and circumstances in the sixth-century community now judging—for the first time ever—the status of its many members.

The review of 510/9 was further clouded by the range of non-"native" inhabitants that made up some part of the population during this time. Though it is important not to overstate the size of this group of people, it seems undeniable that the tradition of "impure birth" (admittedly a propagandistic kind of phrase) did apply to some inhabitants of Attika. To express the point more neutrally, in 510/9 some men who had come to share in the life of the polis under the tyranny would not have been able to trace their descent back to the remotest

[69] On the *metoikia*, see later discussion. No evidence exists for the *graphē xenias* procedure before the fifth century (Patterson [1981], 108ff., *contra*, e.g., Bonner and Smith [1930–38], 1:319; see chapter 8, n. 8), so we cannot imagine that to have been the means by which the *diapsēphismos* was conducted in 510/9.

[70] Cf. Poll. 8.110 and Hesych. s.v. *phylokrinein* with David (1986), 9.

ancestors of Attic society. This group's composition and social situation can help explain the nature of the *diapsēphismos*.

The preceding chapter described how Solon had passed laws to limit the settlement of foreigners in Attika, and I argued that both the measures themselves and social conditions in earlier times imply that some "outsiders" had been joining and been assimilated into Athenian society. But thereafter, what happened to the new policy of "exclusiveness"? What was its fate after the reformer's departure? Aristotle reports that some of the Solonian laws fell into disuse under the tyranny (*Ath. Pol.* 22.1). Some evidence suggests that the measures discouraging immigration were indeed among those "forgotten."

In the city the growth of trade and crafts drew not only Athenians from Attika but artisans and workers from abroad, some by this time fleeing the expansion of the Persian empire in Ionia.[71] Recall that whatever their origin, immigrants who came to Athens to practice a *technē* were allowed to "become citizens" under Solon's law.[72] Foreign signatures on black- and red-figure pottery and Attic sculpture indicate the increasingly heterogeneous culture in Athens during this time, a trend that already had begun in the seventh century.[73] But in addition to potters and sculptors there were other kinds of workers who did not leave their marks on surviving materials, men who labored in the Peiraieus, helped design new buildings, hauled stones for their construction, sold Pontic grain in the market. The Hasebroekian conception of the classical period that only metics engaged in commerce or trades cannot be imposed on sixth-century society.[74] Once again note that the legal status of *metoikos* had yet to be invented, and the "banau-

[71] M. Robertson (1975), 78 n. 78, noting, e.g., how eastern Greeks abandoned Teos and Phokaia (Hdt. 1.163–68; and see chapter 1). Cf. Andrewes (1982b), 408–9. For the evidence of foreign artisans in Athens, above, n. 51.

[72] See discussion in chapter 5, with n. 97 and chapter 6.

[73] Above, n. 51, and chapter 6, nn. 49–50.

[74] Nor would I necessarily press it too hard, even for the classical period, *pace* Cartledge (1983a); see above, n. 24 and chapter 4, n. 52.

sic prejudice" of later theorists, that artisans were necessarily an inferior and separate population, should not be projected back, anachronistically, on this community.[75] There is no reason to assume that the work force in the city during the sixth century was "pure Athenian."

Another foreign component of the population included mercenaries; Peisistratos' final and successful coup at the Battle of Pallene was achieved with both money and men from outside sources. Argos, the city of his second wife, sent troops, as did the Thebans and Naxian Lygdamis, then in exile. The tyrant had earlier gathered forces in Thrace and probably also received support from Thessaly, a connection suggested by the other name (Thessalos) of his son Hegistratos who supplied him with 1,000 soldiers (Hdt. 1.61, 64; *Ath. Pol.* 15.2–3).[76] How many of these troops were "on loan" as a political favor from other rulers and how many were more permanently hired by the tyrant can only be guessed. But the Thracians and Argives are specifically described by the sources as mercenaries, and Herodotos comments how Peisistratos soon after Pallene "firmly rooted the tyranny with bodyguards and money" (*Ath. Pol.* 15.2; Hdt. 1.61.4, 64.1). In any event, at least some of the paid soldiers must have remained in Athens after the victory, to help the tyrant maintain his power. And though their loyalty was inherited by his sons, they did not accompany Hippias into exile in 511/10. It is likely, therefore, that some of these soldiers had settled permanently around and in the city (Hdt. 5.65; *Ath. Pol.* 19.6).[77]

In the countryside, the continuing agrarian problems probably discouraged much immigration to rural demes. Nonethe-

---

[75] See recently the sensible remarks of Balme (1984) and Wood (1988). For earlier discussion of the social status of, and prejudices against, artisans and traders, Aymard (1945) and (1967); Burford (1972), 28ff.; Whitehead (1977), 116–21; Austin and Vidal-Naquet (1977), 94–109; Hopper (1979), 108–17; Vernant (1986), 187–247; and cf. Hasebroek (1933), passim.

[76] For the suggestion of Thessaly's assistance, Jeffery (1976), 95; cf. *Ath. Pol.* 17.3 (Thessalos) and the support offered Hippias in 511/10, cited in *Ath. Pol.* 19.5.

[77] See Bicknell (1969a), 34–37; Ostwald (1988), 304; and above, n. 17.

less, the increasing security of land ownership, and the successful efforts of some men to produce agricultural surplus for overseas trade, may have provided a few more opportunities for newcomers to find work in the outlying areas of Attika. Meanwhile earlier settlers continued to mingle and marry among the "native" society. Some supporters of the tyrants later considered to be of "impure birth" could have been the descendants of mixed unions between Athenians and foreigners who came to Attika before the age of Solon.[78] And among the rural population one must also consider the possibility of freed slaves, whether those brought to Attika in the aftermath of Solon's reforms, or children of uncertain status born of debtors returned from bondage abroad.[79]

Overall, there is no way to judge the magnitude of this shadowy segment of society. But foreigners and "men of impure birth" cannot have been, as some historians have argued, a totally negligible population. More important than numbers, however, is the degree to which they had become assimilated in the Attic community, and that is worth reflecting upon. How rude a shock would the threat of the *diapsēphismos* have been to the mercenary who had served Peisistratos, or to the Corinthian potter working in the Kerameikos? To what extent had he become "accepted" by society and now felt that he "belonged"? Here again, one can only guess, but the tyranny probably encouraged the process of social incorporation already under way through marriages, clientage, and assimilation by kinship groups. In particular, under the Peisistratids the relative urbanization and centralization hastened the process of strangers becoming "Athenian."

The breakdown of the regional memberships and the blurring of distinctions across the population were fostered by the growth of the city. The expanding urban center with its nonagrarian work force and political institutions lessened differ-

[78] Rhodes (1981), 188 nonetheless doubts they were numerically important.

[79] For this suggestion Welwei (1967), 453–56; Bicknell (1969a), 34–37 (but *contra* Bicknell [1972], 51 n. 9); Whitehead (1977), 144–45; all reflecting an interpretation of Arist. *Pol.* 1275 b 34–39 (discussed later).

ences between Attic groupings and also among newcomers to the society. This general incorporative process is observed in other urbanizing agrarian societies: the city assimilates diverse populations. Studies of African towns, for example, have shown that tribal origins tend to lose their meaning once an individual leaves the countryside. John Paden, who studied the breakdown of ethnic differences between Hausa and Fulani peoples in Kano City (Nigeria), offers some general conclusions about the phenomenon: "If several rural ethnic groups migrate to an urban center, there should be a tendency for new values to emerge, and for minor cultural differences to become archaic. A regrouping may occur in the city, based on urban categories of communal identity. This process tends to reduce the total number of ethnic migrant groups."[80]

In Athens, differences among the people of the city also diminished. Much of Peisistratos' support came from urban dwellers whose political companionship allowed them to transcend ethnic and regional differences; popular participation in the centralized assembly, courts, and council leveled older distinctions based on the hierarchy of status in the regional corporations of Attika.

Needless to say, this kind of comparison should only be taken so far, and the extent of "incorporation" must not be exaggerated. To be sure, a newly arrived Corinthian trader or Thracian mercenary would not suddenly have the opportunity to become an archon or plead before the Areopagos. On the other hand, it is not unlikely that the day-to-day life in the center of the polis included some general political activities of some less-than-ancient inhabitants of Attika, and that those activities tended to deemphasize the "newness" of these relative newcomers. There may also have been a few more recent arrivals who were by now sharing in the Athenian public realm. What would keep the resident sculptor from Argos or the potter from Ionia from sometimes attending the *ekklēsia*? Its meetings were occasional in this period and there is no ev-

[80] Paden (1970), 245.

idence of any formal review of those who chose to join in.[81] It is easy to imagine that such men could be "lost in the crowd."

Meanwhile the centripetal centralization of the tyranny played its own assimilative role. The rule of the tyrant, his administrators, and traveling dikasts could only have undermined the authority of the regional corporations over their local members. Once that process was under way, it became less important for newcomers—or even the children of older families—to join and play an active role in a phratry or other association in their neighborhood. Doubtless the pace of change here was very slow, and by the end of the sixth century most Attic inhabitants still belonged to tribes, phratries, and sometimes *genē*. But now a few perhaps did not belong, while others, even if still members of such bodies, began to gain some independence from the traditional regional influences on their lives.

Again, the overall number of "impurely born" Athenians in sixth-century society may have been small, but clearly there were some. More important, some were being accepted as part

---

[81] Though regular meetings of the *ekklēsia* probably date to Solon's day (see chapter 6, with n. 76), it is doubtful that the assembly normally convened more than ten times a year before Ephialtes' reforms in 462/1: thus Rhodes (1981), 522 who proposes this as the earliest *terminus post quem* for the increase of meetings from one to four per prytany (cf. Griffith [1966], 124; but also Hansen [1985a], 63 for a later date). But the date of the origin of the prytany system in turn raises the question of when even ten meetings became the normal frequency for the assembly. Rhodes (1972a), 17 assigns the innovation again to Ephialtes, though others (e.g., Griffith [1966]) have placed it (at the earliest) at the time of Kleisthenes' reforms. A fortiori, in any case, the assembly probably did not meet very frequently before 508/7.

The only evidence of any control of the membership of the *ekklēsia* are fourth-century references to the *pinakes ekklēsiastikoi* (Dem. 44.35), usually assumed to have been kept by demes as a list of those eligible to attend the assembly (Whitehead [1986a], 104, following, e.g., Busolt and Swoboda [1920–26], 994 n. 5, and 996). The exact purpose of these "lists" is shadowy (cf. Hansen [1987b], 7, and 139 n. 52), however, and in any event, if the normal view is right, they cannot predate the establishment of the deme organization by Kleisthenes. Rhodes (1972a), 173 n. 4 guesses that the *pinakes* were first instituted at the same time that assembly pay was introduced, i.e., after 403.

of the formal Attic community. Under the tyranny the distinctions between "Athenian" and "non-Athenian" had become a little more hazy; Solon's reforms had been most concerned to distinguish free Athenians from slaves, but now the differences among free "Athenians" came to the fore. By the end of the century, the notion that any "outsiders" might be able to become members of the polis threw open to suspicion the origins of almost everyone, particularly in a society lacking a centralized and firm definition of the "right to belong." This kind of suspicion must have been deeply troubling to the Athenian *dēmos* in the face of something strange and unheard of, a membership scrutiny that came to be called *diapsēphismos*.

Perhaps the review was conducted in *phratriai*, perhaps across *phylai*, perhaps only among men now living in Athens. But inevitably, powerful men took the lead in putting citizens to the test, and they would have endeavored to protect the status of their own followings, and to strike out against the followers of their opponents. The shifting factionalism of this turbulent period does not allow us to determine how and which aristocrats took best political advantage of the *diapsēphismos*, though it is a reasonable guess that the leading antagonists of the following year, the Alkmeonidai and Isagoras (and allies) all had an active hand in the process, with varying results depending on local conditions in their individual spheres of influence.

What was the outcome of the scrutiny? Aristotle tells us nothing about that, but another piece of evidence not often connected with the *diapsēphismos* may be relevant. In his speech *On the Mysteries*, Andocides looks back to the defeat of Hippias and comments on the punishment meted out to the followers of the tyrants: "Some they put to death, some they exiled, some they allowed to live in Attika deprived of their rights" (1.106). This latter category of men may have suffered a legal form of *atimia* first distinguished under Solon; deprived of their rights as citizens, they had no recourse to the protection of justice or courts of appeal.[82] The men who were killed

---

[82] See discussion in chapter 6.

or exiled obviously suffered more, though the *atimoi* might have feared that the same fate would soon befall them. All of these victims of revenge in the aftermath of the tyranny were in fact victims of their citizenship undone; and herein lies the story of the *diapsēphismos*. This "scrutiny" was not an orderly or parliamentary review of citizen lists (which did not exist at this time). It was a reign of terror, caught up in the bitter civil war among aristocrats, ruthless leaders striving for political power now that Hippias was gone. And just as large numbers of Athenians were driven out or rendered legally vulnerable by this event, Isagoras and the Spartans would later call for the exile of thousands of Kleisthenes' supporters (Hdt. 5.70.2–71; *Ath. Pol.* 20.2–3).[83] During 510/9, for the many men who were not aristocrats—and many others who were— exile and "disenfranchisement" (and with it uncertainty about one's very life) were to be feared as much as anything they had ever known. The prospect of loss of property, lost status, and even death haunted a multitude of Athenians.

It is against this background of the *diapsēphismos*—a reign of terror in which "true" citizenship was a man's only defense—that the enormous popularity of Kleisthenes' reforms can be appreciated. Indeed, scholars are often puzzled how the reforms, complex and fundamentally concerned with the registration and organization of citizens, had such an appeal, even to the point of being passed "in the teeth of the (opposing) archon in power."[84] The puzzlement is exemplified in

[83] *Ath. Pol.* reports the expulsion of 700 families (*oikiai*, cf. Herodotos' *epistiai*) associated with the pollution of the murder of the Kylonians (see chapter 4) which by any reasonable accounting must have run into the thousands.

Wilamowitz-Moellendorff (1893), 1:31–32 rejected the number as too high, but Wade-Gery (1958), 150 n. 1 defended it on the basis that the curse had been passed down on both the male and female side of all who had originally accepted the surrender of Kylon and his followers (cf. Thuc. 1.126.11). Wade-Gery also rightly stressed that those expelled represented Kleisthenes' supporters and not just the Alkmeonidai, which is quite clear in Herodotos' account.

[84] Ostwald (1969), 143; cf. Wade-Gery (1958), 136, 142–43. For useful

modern attempts to translate—inevitably too narrowly—Aristotle's statement about Kleisthenes' program. Before proceeding, we should examine Aristotle's comment, since its translation and interpretation have shaped most scholarly thinking about the reforms of 508/7.

KLEISTHENES AND CITIZENSHIP

After the *diapsēphismos*, strife broke out between Kleisthenes and Isagoras, and the latter soon gained the upper hand. Though his family had played a role in the scrutiny, Kleisthenes in desperation now turned to the *dēmos* in a daring new tack. Aristotle says that "as Kleisthenes was getting the worse of the party struggle, he attached the people to his following, *apodidous tōi plēthei tēn politeian*" (*Ath. Pol.* 20.1; cf. Hdt. 5.66, 69). How is this latter part of the sentence best construed?[85] Previous translations usually fall into one of two camps.[86] The first emphasizes the democratic element of Kleisthenes' reforms: "He attached the people to his following, by proposing to give political power to all the people" (or "the masses").[87] The second camp takes *politeia* to mean "citizen-

---

discussion of the question of "Kleisthenes' appeal," D. Lewis (1963a); Andrewes (1977); David (1986).

[85] The first part of the sentence, "As Kleisthenes was getting the worst part of the party struggle" (*ēttomenos de tais hetaireiais*), has generated its own share of controversy since it has been held to be proof of the sixth-century existence of the aristocratic political clubs, *hetaireiai* (cf. Herodotos' verb *prosetairizetai*). See Rhodes (1981), 243 for the debate and whose more conservative interpretation (and translation [1984], 63) I have instead adopted. I have not followed his translation for the rest of the sentence, as discussed later.

[86] See David (1986), 8–9 for discussion of past views and whose conclusions are similar (though to different effect in his argument) to mine.

[87] Wade-Gery (1958), 139 n. 2; 147–48 who glossed the phrase *universo populo tribuens rempublicam*. Rhodes (1981), 245, in basic support of the view, nonetheless prefers *plebi* "common people" (or "masses" in his [1984] translation) as the recipients of the "political power"; see also the comments of Ostwald (1986) who follows Rhodes.

The question here is whether *plēthos* is intended as merely a stylistic synonym for *dēmos* in the first part of the sentence or represents a deliberate dis-

ship," in the narrow sense of restoring rights to those who lost them in the *diapsēphismos:* "giving back the citizenship to those who had lost it."[88] Proponents of the second interpretation support their view with the evidence of Aristotle's *Politics* (1275 b 34–37) that after the fall of the tyranny, Kleisthenes "enrolled in tribes foreigners and freedmen (*ephyleteuse xenous kai doulous metoikous*)."[89]

Wade-Gery (a chief proponent of the first view) rightly objected that the second translation impossibly reads "*tōi plethōi*" (literally "the mass") as "those who had lost (their citizenship)." He then went on to argue as unlikely that "smuggling in a few borderline Athenians" could have been the foundations of Kleisthenes' popularity. After all, he insisted, "to get his majority in the *ekklēsia* (not to mention the *boulē*) Kleisthenes wanted people with votes, not the voteless."[90]

Indeed, politeia was of vital concern to those with the votes—but why do we need to exclude the sense of "citizenship" in translating this word when Aristotle himself did not?[91] Ever since the reforms of Solon, "citizenship" was not a passive category but rather an active identity; a man's place in the polis was one and the same with his "political power"—both its duties and its prerogatives. And in particular, citizenship now represented freedom from the terror of another *diapsēphismos*. As noted earlier, Athenian civic status was insepa-

---

tinction between lower classes and the whole of the Athenian people. On this point, Wade-Gery's translation is the more straightforward (cf. Ruzé [1984], 262ff.), and Rhodes's seems to be overly subtle.

[88] See the discussion of David (1986), 8 with references; cf. Wade-Gery (1958), 149.

[89] On the significance (and interpretation) of this phrase, see below, n. 103.

[90] Wade-Gery (1958), 149 with n. 1.

[91] Despite his insistence about the translation of the phrase, Wade-Gery (1958), 147 n. 1 does acknowledge the dual meaning of the word *politeia*. David (1986), 9 also acknowledges the richness of the term, but supposes that Kleisthenes was deliberately manipulating its ambiguity to appeal to the greatest number of supporters. But the ambiguity was not manipulated; it was embedded in the very culture of the polis, and for that reason Kleisthenes' program generated such enthusiasm.

rable from the exercise of the citizen's rights in the polis, and those rights included privileges in the assembly and institutions of justice. Without such rights, as the recent scrutiny had shown, any man was not merely "out of touch with politics" but ultimately vulnerable for his homeland and life. Scholars err when they translate politeia in too limited a way; on the eve of Kleisthenes' reforms, "citizenship," in the fullest sense of the word, was of central concern to all Athenians, both those of "impure birth" and those who knew that they too might someday be accused.[92]

The promise of a new legal definition of membership in the polis thus had very great appeal; we may translate the important sentence as "Kleisthenes took the *dēmos* into partnership by rendering to all Athenians what was their due: citizenship."[93] To do so, Kleisthenes newly established and at the same time reaffirmed the meaning of belonging to the polis. The program that emerged from his contest with Isagoras in 508/7 guaranteed and formulated citizenship as never before. The legislation he passed created a clearer and standardized basis for defining Athenian membership, organized according to a new system of local demes.[94] These units encompassed all areas of Attika,[95] but the ultimate authority over the citizen

[92] Cf. Meier (1973) and (1980), esp. 91ff.; *contra* Ostwald (1988), 312.

[93] For this sense of *apodidous*, s.v. LSJ. The point is not the return of civic status to those specifically deprived under the *diapsēphismos*, but rather to reestablish, on the soundest possible basis, the privilege for all Athenians of sharing in their polis—which had been thrown into question by the scrutiny.

[94] See Whitehead (1986a), for complete discussion of the demes, their history, and significance in Athenian society.

[95] The purely territorial basis of the demes (as argued by Eliot [1962]; cf. Traill [1975], 73 n. 6) has been adequately refuted by the important article of W. Thompson (1971). Cf. D. Lewis (1963b), 724; and Whitehead (1986a), 27–30, 364–68 who stress both the "personal" and "territorial" aspects of the unit. (Cf. chapter 3, with nn. 53–54.) The demes were thus simultaneously villages, their inhabitants, and the land around them, or a comparable part of the city of Athens (since there were also demes alloted to the "city" *trittyes*, i.e., *peri to asty*).

Interestingly, three liminal areas now under Athenian influence were not included in the Kleisthenic system of demes: Salamis (cf. Meiggs and Lewis [1969], no. 14), Oropos (see chapter 4, n. 40), and Eleutherai (chapter 4, n.

population was central and not regional. Under the reforms, Athenians were to be registered and enrolled on a regular basis, and according to set procedures, in their own neighborhoods. But this registration was subject to appeal and review by the courts and council in Athens.[96] That is, for the first time in Athenian history, there existed a uniform system of membership in the city-state. The identity and relationship between the polis and every one of its members thus became stronger and more tangible. Solon had created the corporation; Kleisthenes now more precisely defined its shareholders. In so doing, he also established the basis for a more formal sense of "belonging." Kleisthenes' reforms thus renewed the self-esteem of a polis community which had been thrown into question by the scrutiny.

The legacy of the *diapsēphismos* can explain the emphasis that Kleisthenes and his supporters gave to establishing a completely new system of civic organization. For the Kleisthenic

---

40, and Meiggs and Lewis [1969], no. 48, line 96). See Rhodes (1981), 253, 768 who supposes Athenian citizens in at least the latter two territories must have registered elsewhere; in Salamis, Athenian klerouchs are attested, following the interpretation of Meiggs and Lewis.

[96] For the process of deme registration, see discussion in chapter 1, with nn. 18–20. Here and in what follows I support Whitehead (1986a), 34–35, 98 (and others before) in the important point that Kleisthenes' measures either "embodied or swiftly called into being" the procedures for all demes to enroll and register their members. Patterson (1981), 13–14, 25–28 argues that "it is not justifiable to assume that the system of deme scrutiny, registration, review by the *boulē* and possible appeal to a *dikastērion* emerged full-blown from the head of Cleisthenes" (p. 27). That may be right, although the time to work such things out may have been only months rather than decades, as she supposes. As with Whitehead, I find it difficult to believe that the main outlines of the registration process were not part of the Kleisthenic reform, given the enormous role the demes played in that reform, and the firm tradition (*Ath. Pol.* 21.4) about their importance in providing a new nomenclature for all Athenians (discussed later). If, as Patterson supposes (1981), 28, "through the early fifth century citizenship was determined by one's neighbors and kin on a traditional and family basis," it remains to be seen how the Kleisthenic politeia could have engendered the rallying cry of "*mē phylokrinein*" (*Ath. Pol.* 20.2). The clear implication of Aristotle here is a break with the past, and one wonders how sharp that break would have been if demes merely decided upon their memberships with the same variable criteria of other traditional bodies in the society.

politeia not only provided a standardized basis for citizenship, but also one distinct from the abuses of past tradition. Thus the new politeia bypassed all earlier groupings that had previously determined, or passed judgment on, "membership" in the community. We are told that Kleisthenes left the *genē, phratriai,* and priesthoods with their traditional privileges (*Ath. Pol.* 21.6); but he did replace the traditional Ionic *phylai* with ten new (i.e., artificial) "tribes" to which the population was allotted in an ingenious and revolutionary fashion (*Ath. Pol.* 21.2; Hdt. 5.66.2, 5.69).[97] The demes, new administrative centers for each group of local inhabitants, were assigned among thirty new *trittyes* based on tripartite division of Attika: city, coast, and inland. Thereafter the *trittyes* were assigned by lot—randomly—to the ten tribes so that each had members from all three areas of Attika (*Ath. Pol.* 21.3–4).[98] The Kleisthenic tribes became the basis for membership in a new probouleutic *boulē* of 500 and the military divisions of the Athenian army (*Ath. Pol.* 21.3, 22.2, 61). In exercise of these and (eventually) other civic functions, men from different parts of the polis were therefore intermingled.[99]

[97] On the significance of the new tribes in creating shared religious feelings—not at odds with older cultic associations—see Kearns (1985).

[98] The problem with *Ath. Pol.*'s statement about allotment of *trittyes* is how such a process could have created even roughly equal tribes, given the apparent disparities in sizes of both *trittyes* and demes (inferred from their bouleutic quotas) that composed them; yet equality would seem to have been required by the tribal structures later seen in the army, *boulē*, and other aspects of public life. It may be that equality in the number of hoplites rather than total citizens was the desired goal of the distribution (thus W. Thompson [1964], 400–401; Bicknell [1972], 19–21) but that still does not explain how sortition could have guaranteed a balanced division among all the tribes. Rhodes (1981), 253 (cf. Eliot [1962], 138ff.) doubts that allotment was actually employed. Andrewes (1977), 245–46, however, puts forward the interesting thesis that *trittyes* were named and allotted to tribes before their composition was worked out in detail. This suggestion (followed by Whitehead [1986a], 17ff.) not only solves this apparent dilemma, but could also explain the origin of the few but significant cases of "political gerrymandering" of demes that some scholars have made so much of (below, n. 101). For a different, and more radical point of view, Kinzl (1987).

[99] For other (later) examples of the tribal framework in public life, see *Ath. Pol.* 47.1–2; 48.1; 55.1.; 63–69.

It is not coincidental that Aristotle cites "mixing" as the goal of the Kleisthenes' reforms: "He wished to mix them up so that more would share in the citizenship" (*anameixai boulomenous hopōs metaschōsi pleious tēs politeias*: *Ath. Pol.* 21.2; cf. 21.3 and *Pol.* 1319 b 19–27).[100] Though some scholars have interpreted the new organization as reflective of subtle regional maneuvering among different aristocratic factions, there can be no doubt that the ultimate effect was indeed a "mixture."[101] The population of Attika had already been "mixing" for many years; Kleisthenes' system now confirmed the social evolution of the polis,[102] and ended the va-

[100] As with the aforementioned phrase in *Ath. Pol.* 20.1, scholars have labored to distinguish between different meanings of politeia here: either Kleisthenes was mixing them up "so that more [existing] citizens should have a share in running the state," or "so that more men should be members of the citizen body," i.e., be enfranchised. Thus the view of Rhodes (1981), 250 who prefers the former interpretation (following Wade-Gery [1958], 148 n. 1; Welwei [1967], 423 n. 4; and others). Here again, I believe the richness of the word "politeia" must be preserved, with both its senses, and I thus translate with the semantically broad "citizenship." Kleisthenes mixed them up because he wanted more men to be able to exercise the prerogatives of sharing in the polis—both those who had escaped or been unaffected by the *diapsēphismos* and those who had been threatened by it (I discuss this again later in the chapter).

[101] D. Lewis (1963a), 22ff. first noticed that the composition of some of the *trittyes* cut across older divisions, breaking up certain regional cult-centers (and thus the focuses of aristocratic influence?); the division also seemed to particularly strengthen Alkmeonidai interests through the joining of areas of their influence in three tribes together. Since then, he has been followed by many (e.g., Forrest [1966], 197–200; Bicknell [1976]; Stanton [1984]) who emphasize a deliberate, politically manipulative motive behind the reforms, with Kleisthenes aiming to undo the regional power base of his rivals and build up his own family and allies. None of this is impossible, but Kleisthenes' personal intentions (whatever they may have been) must be separated from the overall outcome of the changes instituted.

For some intelligent criticism of the "political manipulation" view, and persuasive suggestions about the importance of the new tribal cults in creating the "mixing" of the population, Kearns (1985); cf. Connor (1987), 41ff. Ostwald (1986), 16ff. takes an intermediate position, interpreting the reforms as a civic-minded "mixture" of aristocratic and popular sovereignty designed to end the chaos of factional strife of the previous decades.

[102] Note the point of Bradeen (1955), 22–30 that the *trittyes* of the *asty*

garies of status which had been so handily exploited during the *diapsēphismos*. If later tradition portrayed the reformer as "enrolling foreigners and freedmen in tribes," it was only because commentators affixed an anachronistically legal label on broad social change.[103] The "enrollment" did not import and enfranchise aliens and slaves in some deliberate parliamentary manner. Rather, in one stroke, the reforms embraced all Athenians of any defensible status, even the many accused of "impure birth," and made them all part of the polis. Kleisthenes' citizenship was the official amnesty that ended the uncertainty provoked by the scrutiny; there would never again be "judgment by tribal descent." Every man was given a new official identity in step with the change. From 508/7 on citizens were to be known by their deme rather than father's name (*Ath. Pol.* 21.4).[104]

---

were distributed through all ten tribes, reflective of the growth of the city during the sixth century.

[103] Specifically, Arist. *Pol.* 1275 b 34–39, cited earlier, and which has drawn much scholarly attention. The meaning of the problematical passage is further obscured by an apparently defective text. Oliver (1960) tried to emend and gloss the passage to mean that Kleisthenes created a separate class of metics, but his forced interpretation was properly refuted by Kagan (1963). Though as argued below (following Whitehead [1977], 143ff.), it is likely that the institution of the *metoikia* belongs to this general period, Aristotle's testimony here cannot be made to mean that. The more natural reading is that Kleisthenes enrolled in tribes foreigners and (freed) slaves who were resident in Athens (taking *xenous* and *doulous* as parallel adjectives qualifying *metoikous*, as Newman [1887–1902] in his commentary on the passage; cf. Welwei [1967], 435–36. Most scholars who accept this tradition assume that Kleisthenes enrolled these "outsiders" as part of his reforms, and speculate about the various kinds of foreigners and "slaves" whom Aristotle was describing (thus Bicknell [1969]; Whitehead [1977], 144–45; Murray [1980], 255–56). Others challenge or deemphasize the story (Wade-Gery [1958], 148ff.), while still others (Kinzl [1977], 200 n. 8) assign it to another period. In general I follow the first group in accepting the tradition, but with the qualification that the "enfranchisements" were not individual and calculated acts but part of an overall reaffirmation of all Athenians' citizenship. See later discussion.

[104] Here again we must distinguish between what Kleisthenes' reforms seem to have intended and how they actually took root. Forrest (1966), 195; Rhodes (1981), 254; and others have doubted the validity of Aristotle's testimony and that any Athenian would ever have been fooled by a man now

Kleisthenes decisively advanced the ideal of the Solonic politeia by establishing a systematic, formal definition of every citizen. At the same time he made more tangible another vital aspect of the polis that in earlier times had existed more in potential than reality. With the creation of the system of demes, the union of town and country became complete. Every citizen, whether or not he was able to travel regularly to the urban center, could now share in "local" public life; simultaneously, the public life of the center now came to every man's own neighborhood.[105] Eventually, citizens in every deme selected an administrative chief (demarch), and gathered in a regional deme assembly.[106] Through this local government deme members participated, directly or indirectly, in the sacred and secular affairs of their villages. From today's perspective, we might say that the deme also acted as "the agent of the state": it enrolled and authorized its members as citizens, selected members for the new Council (*boulē*) of 500 (discussed later), and eventually took on additional military, fiscal, judicial and religious functions on behalf of the centralized Athenian community.[107] The sense of the phrase "agent

---

using a demotic rather than a patronymic. It is true that in later times the new terminology did not totally supplant the old, but the use of the demotic became common enough, even in the early fifth century (e.g., the evidence of ostraka: Vanderpool [1970], 7ff.). It is not unreasonable to imagine that old habits faded away less quickly than Kleisthenes may have wanted, but that indeed the change was something that he had hoped for: Andrewes (1977), 241. Moreover, following the line of argument thus far set out, the establishment of the demotic was probably not so much "to disguise" newly enfranchised immigrants, as symbolically to set all citizens newly defined on an equal but nontraditional footing.

[105] This point is an essential thesis of Haussoullier (1884). More recent treatments include Hopper (1957); R. Osborne (1985a), esp. 184ff.; Whitehead (1986a), 253ff.—all of which I have read with profit.

[106] For details of the deme assembly, Whitehead (1986a), 86–129. The process whereby demarchs were selected, especially at the time of the Kleisthenic reforms, is obscure. I follow Whitehead (1986a), 32, 114–16 in believing that once the deme system was in operation demarchs were either elected and/or (later?) chosen by lot from among, and by, fellow demesmen. For a different view, see R. Osborne (1985a), 77ff. For sources and older scholarship on the question, Whitehead (1986a), 114–16, nn. 114–54.

[107] Whitehead (1986a), 255–90. Humphreys (1983h), 239–42 argues that

of the state" can be misleading, however. The authority of the deme was not so much granted externally as internally, and thus was largely self-defined. It fell to the demes themselves to validate their own constituency and actively contribute to the larger commonality. Demes were not passive administrative units but rather living, self-determining bodies of Athenians. They became the bridge of representative government that linked the individual formally to the polis—and thus translated practically the vision that the "state" was the sum of its citizens.

The very practical aspect of this reform must be stressed. Though the mechanism of the overall Kleisthenic system of "mixing" was deliberately artificial, the creation and functioning of the deme organization were keenly attuned to the Athenians that it served, and to the social changes that pervaded the population.[108] Natural and traditional boundaries between settlements across the Attic countryside were kept in mind when the reform was implemented,[109] but the demes were *not* simple territorial divisions.[110] Their essence was their people—both in the city and villages in which all Athenians lived. The Kleisthenic demes were not "invented" out of thin air but were rather newly defined within the social landscape that reflected their evolution; they embraced nuclei of local and urban populations that now transcended the intercon-

---

the Kleisthenic reforms also instituted the public arbitrators, and that service in the role became an age-class duty linked to deme registration. But the majority view would have them established sometime after 403/2 (cf. *Ath. Pol.* 53.1–2; MacDowell [1978], 207–11). For the local versus central judicial role of the demes, see Whitehead (1986a), 261–64.

[108] For representative scholarship highlighting some of the "continuity" with the past in Kleisthenes' reforms, Forrest (1966), 209ff.; Ostwald (1969), 158ff.; Roussel (1976), 271ff.; Andrewes (1977), 244ff.; Whitehead (1986a), 15ff.; Sealey (1987), 121–26.

[109] For the natural and traditional aspects of the Kleisthenic demes (including many traditional names that were adopted under the reform, Rhodes [1981], 257), Whitehead (1986a), 24–30, and 25 n. 92 for previous scholarship on these issues. In contrast to earlier works cited there, Whitehead argues for the natural aspect of the demes of the *asty* as well as those in the countryside.

[110] Above, n. 95.

nected yet eroding and uneven networks of kinship and religious organizations. The system was ingenious because it was so obvious; the new citizenship emerged naturally from the citizens on which it was based, affirming the changes, migrations, and breakdown of older memberships that had occurred over the previous years. And though the compass of each administrative unit was both revolutionary and evolutionary, its future was firmly rooted in the past. As had always been the case with all memberships in Attika, belonging to a deme became hereditary. Sons were registered in the same deme as their fathers.[111]

But the center was no less important than the periphery in Kleithenes' reforms. Another small reflection of continuing centripetal development was improvement and further delineation of the heart of the polis itself. By the end of the century, citizens who entered the precinct of public life passed by its new markers that proclaimed "I am the boundary of the agora."[112] On the west side of the agora stood a new *bouleutērion* to house the recently created Council of 500.[113] With this important body, and other new public responsibilities and privileges for citizens, the centralization seen under the tyranny increased further.

The Kleisthenic Council of 500 was the successor of the older Solonian *boulē;* its initial functions were similar (the preparation and supervision of business for the assembly), but the membership was now selected by lot, with fifty *bouleutai* drawn from each of the ten tribes.[114] Candidacy was open to

[111] The evidence for this is all indirect, based on the identifiable membership in the same deme by different generations of the same family. As Whitehead (1986a), 67–68 points out, however, this principle could not have been left unstated at the time the new system was established. A man changed his deme membership only by being adopted by a member of another deme (e.g., Dem. 44).

[112] Camp (1986), 48; citing *Agora* I.5510.

[113] Thompson and Wycherley (1972), 25–38; Rhodes (1972a), 30–35. Homer Thompson, however, recently (1982) suggested a date approximately forty years later for this "Old Bouleuterion," but the arguments have not been widely accepted. See the comments of Camp (1983), 113–15.

[114] *Ath. Pol.* 21.3; for details, and discussion of the relationship with the

men above thirty years of age, but probably excluded *thetes*.[115] Nonetheless, the new *boulē* came to represent a wide cross-section of society: later commentators described it as a *mikra polis*, "miniature polis" (Schol. Aesch. 3.4).[116] No man could serve more than twice in his life, thus ensuring that the responsibilities would not be confined to any small group.[117]

The responsibilities were significant, if not at first in Kleisthenes' day, certainly in later years under the full democracy.[118] Each group of fifty comprised a prytany that administered public business for their segment (one-tenth) of the year. These "presidents" convened and presided over the *boulē* and assembly; they received messengers, envoys, and applicants who wished to address the *dēmos;* during their term of service, members were required to live and take meals in the circular public chamber in the agora called the *tholos*.[119] In the year 501/500, the civic and moral duties of citizens who served were formalized by a sacred oath; each *bouleutēs* was required to swear to serve the best interests of the *dēmos* and polis (*Ath. Pol.* 22.2).[120] Eventually members of the council

---

Solonian *boulē*, Rhodes (1972a), 1ff., 208–9. The appointment of *bouleutai* is controversial. For sortition dating from Kleisthenes' age, Griffith (1966), 123. Rhodes (1972a), 7 is more cautious, and acknowledges the possibility of direct election prior to the 450s.

[115] On the age requirement, Xen. *Mem.* 1.2.35 with Rhodes (1972a), 1 n. 7. For the restriction to the three upper Solonian *telē*, *Ath. Pol.* 7.4 with Rhodes (1972a), 2. There is no direct evidence for the latter, and Bicknell (1972), 5 has argued that *thētes* too served in the membership.

[116] Cf. Rhodes (1972a), 4; and see chapter 1, with n. 66.

[117] *Ath. Pol.* 62.3 with Rhodes (1972a), 3, 214–15 for discussion and the argument that in the fifth century service may have been restricted to only once per man's lifetime. The two times per life service in the fourth century and later is the subject of controversy between Rhodes (1984a) and Ruschenbusch (1981) and (1985). See also discussion in chapter 1, and n. 66.

[118] Rhodes (1972a), 16ff. who argues (p. 17) that the original duties of the Kleisthenic *boulē* were only probouleutic; also (pp. 17, 224–25) that the division into prytanies was not effected until the period of Ephialtes' reforms (462/1).

[119] *Ath. Pol.* 43–44 with Rhodes (1972a), 20ff.

[120] On the contents of the oath, Wade-Gery (1932–33); Rhodes (1972a), 194–98 who treats the question of what additions were made over the course of the fifth century to the text preserved in *IG* i³ 105 (= *IG* i² 114). I also

handled many of the most important financial, administrative, and judicial duties of the polis. Participation in the *boulē* educated citizens in the issues and deliberations of public affairs, just as the group as a whole helped the *ekklēsia* be a more responsible sovereign body.[121]

In the *ekklēsia* too the citizen's public role was enhanced by the reforms of Kleisthenes. Under the new politeia the man in the assembly was guaranteed, perhaps even for the first time granted, the right to vote for war and peace, to pass death sentences, to inflict fines, and to choose military officers.[122] From this period as well must date the all-important "freedom of speech" (*isēgoria*) that allowed any man in the *ekklēsia* to address the multitude.[123] After 508/7 the assembled *dēmos* also concerned itself with the welfare of the polis in another, though seemingly curious way—the procedure of ostracism (*Ath. Pol.* 22.1–4). By this law, any Athenian considered to be a serious threat to the polis could be exiled from Attika for ten years if the majority of a quorum of 6,000 of his fellow citizens voted against him.[124] This civic institution, probably pro-

---

follow Rhodes (1972a) in believing that the oath marks the culmination of Kleisthenes' reforms rather than a restriction by which the council swore not to exercise certain powers it had first been given in 508/7 (*contra*, e.g., Larsen [1955], 15–18; Ostwald [1986], 33).

[121] Gomme (1962), 185ff.; Woodhead (1967); Rhodes (1972a), 214.

[122] These powers for the *ekklēsia* are implied by the bouleutic oath, as reconstructed by Wade-Gery (1932–33), following the earlier interpretation (above, n. 120) that it represents the confirmation rather than limitation of powers established by the Kleisthenic constitution. Cf. Ostwald (1986), 31–37; (1988), 329–31 whose interpretation of the text—as a post-Kleisthenic curtailment of the council's powers—also envisions the *boulē* serving both a preliminary role in the assembly's deliberations about war, certain fines, and as a venue for mandatory appeal from the Areopagos for capital crimes against the polis.

[123] Ostwald (1969) 157 n. 2, arguing the probability on the basis of the first attested usage of the word in Hdt. 5.78 which referred to the events of 506 (discussed later). Others have taken a more cautious stance, assigning the institution of *isēgoria* to, e.g., the period of Ephialtes' reforms: Griffith (1966).

[124] On the procedures and details of ostracism, Diod. Sic. 11.55.2; Plut. *Arist.* 7. 5–6; Poll. 8.20; Schol. Ar. *Eq.* 855; *FGrH* 328 F 30 with Thomsen (1972), 61ff.

posed by Kleisthenes with Isagoras in mind, gave the members of the polis a means to keep in check the overweening ambitions of quarreling politicians.[125]

The burden of civic responsibility that Solon placed on each individual was expanded under the Kleisthenic constitution, and in general, the increasing responsibility of citizens is a crucial theme of this period. Under the reforms, the dēmos acquired additional powers and, with those powers, additional obligations; each individual became more accountable for the welfare of his polis. At the same time the polis too became more accountable. First, it was now literally accountable, with standardized procedures laid down in every deme for distinguishing citizens from non-citizens, and (if required, after appeal to a *dikastērion* and/or scrutiny by the *boulē*) for ensuring the registration of those entitled.[126] Second, the polis was now accountable on a broader level. As the sum of its citizens, the polis had no one to blame but itself for the decisions it took, and that was a freedom and responsibility never before fully realized under the single-handed statesmanship of Solon or the rule of the *tyrannoi*.

The actual passage of the reforms of 508/7 marked a turning point in that accountability. Though they are commonly referred to (here, as by other scholars) as "Kleisthenic," they were not brought forward by Kleisthenes in the same way that

---

[125] Though *Ath. Pol.* and several other sources ascribe ostracism to Kleisthenes, the testimony of Androtion (*FGrH* 324 F 6) seems to date the institution closer to the time (488/7) of its first victim, Hipparchos. There have been some attempts to reconcile the accounts (Keaney [1970]; Walters [1984]), and many others in support of Aristotle, the latter requiring explanation of why the institution was not utilized until some twenty years after its origin (e.g., Kagan [1960]). Still others have argued in favor of accepting the testimony of Androtion (e.g., Hignett [1952], 159ff.). For a succinct summary of the controversy, Jeffery (1976), 247–48, who upholds the Kleisthenic date (which I follow). For the purpose and motives behind the law, Rhodes (1981), 270; cf. Moore (1983), 243; Ostwald (1988), 334–46 who notes the symbolic fit between ostracism and the spirit of *isonomia*. See also Rhodes (1981), 268 for discussion of the (dubious) account of ostracism originally conducted in the *boulē*, preserved in MS Vat. Gr. 1144, 222 r–v.

[126] As above, n. 96, dating the provision for appeal and *dokimasia* to the same general period of, rather than much after, Kleisthenes' reforms.

Solon had unilaterally legislated his measures in 594/3. Solon's laws had been *thesmoi*, imposed by his authority on the community; in 508/7 Kleisthenes sponsored his laws but they were proposed and ratified by the Council of 400 and assembly—that is, by the Athenians themselves.[127] These were *nomoi*, that word for the first time denoting norms and regulations that a people accepted as valid and binding on their own behalf.[128]

In the same spirit there emerged during this time a related term, and very likely a rallying cry of Kleisthenes and his followers: *isonomia*. This "equality of *nomos*" meant that what was valid and binding for any man in the polis would be valid and binding for all.[129] The community and its members were now mutually accountable to one another, and all citizens among themselves; laws and justice were to be applied equally and fairly, determined by the consensus of all the people who now set the standards. Solon's "good order" (*eunomia*) had evolved to "equal order,"[130] and that in turn depended on the orderly and standardized definition of all shareholders in the community.

This newly defined politeia now represented a fully developed citizenship. Once again, however, why did Athenians embrace so widely the changes that made citizenship possible? I have argued that the reforms were (in the immediate context) a response to the aristocratically motivated *diapsēphismos* of 510/9. But once the laws were firmly in place and the threat of another unfair scrutiny was removed, what made the reform

[127] This was argued by Wade-Gery (1958), 135ff. and has never been convincingly refuted.

[128] For the distinction between *thesmoi*, and the meaning and significance of *nomoi* during this period, Ostwald (1969), 158ff.; (1986), 85–89.

[129] Ostwald (1969), 137–60; cf. Frei (1981); and Ostwald (1986), 27 who describes *isonomia* as "political equality between the ruling magistrates, who formulate political decisions, and the Council and Assembly which approve or disapprove them." Though clearly *isonomia* was a vital precursor to *dēmokratia*, I am not convinced by the arguments of Vlastos ([1953] and [1964]) who defines the term much more broadly and associates it with democracy.

[130] Murray (1980), 258.

take root so quickly and strongly? Thus far I have described the legal origins of citizenship under Kleisthenes, but whence came its supralegal, intangible qualities—its civic spirit?

As before, it would be wrong to search for one and only one factor. One common answer to the question is the self-discovered democratic consciousness of the Athenian people: once the *dēmos* saw the power of its own judgments, its desire to take on more and more authority and to implement changes that promoted its rule grew stronger. By this view, of course, Kleisthenes was the "father of fifth-century democracy" and set in motion a revolution that gathered momentum over the next hundred years.[131] Another answer sometimes offered (especially by Marxist scholars) is socioeconomic: the Kleisthenic reforms undid at last the landed influence of the Eupatridai, and thus allowed the true political tendencies of a poor agricultural and nonagricultural proletariat to flourish.[132]

The first explanation is almost certainly part of the story, and the second, if sometimes overstated, cannot be excluded, given what we know about the growth of the city during the sixth and following century and the increasing significance of the *prostatēs tou dēmou* (the "leader of the demos") in Athenian politics.[133] But there is a third explanation, one largely ignored in treatments of citizenship, and particularly relevant to the years surrounding the Kleisthenic revolution. It will also explain the apparent anomaly of the new politeia that provided for the "official" incorporation of at least some number of men of "impure birth." For if the reconstruction I have offered is valid, Kleisthenes' reforms bestowed citizen status on some Attic inhabitants who might very well have been excluded from the community once most Athenians put the *diapsēphismos* behind them, and secured their own status. Why did the *dēmos* accept the new heterogeneity among itself?

---

[131] E.g., Forrest (1966), 191ff. For an elaborate argument stressing the self-conscious identity of the *dēmos*, citizenship, and its role in the creation of fifth-century democracy, Meier (1977), (1978), and (1980).

[132] E.g., de Ste. Croix (1981), 283–93.

[133] Connor (1971), 87ff.

The answer to this question, and a partial answer to the related question about the intangible qualities of the new citizenship, is "a crisis of freedom." In brief, Athens in the last years of the sixth century faced severe threats to its independence, and powerful enemies came very close to overwhelming the polis militarily. In this climate, Athenians let fall their internecine struggles, and the more democratic politeia—one that blurred past differences among Attic inhabitants of varying "nativeness" and class—was quickly endorsed throughout the population. At the same time, a new spirit emerged, born ultimately from the success in meeting the challenge of a major external threat. A closer look at the jeopardy Athenians found themselves in will point up the severity of this crisis and the pride that developed out of their eventual victory.[134]

With the departure of Hippias in 510 and the ensuing factional strife among aristocrats, Athens laid itself open to the aggressions of ambitious enemies. One such foe was Sparta who during the last decades of the century maneuvered to build up a powerful league of allies under Lacedaimonian leadership.[135] Athens under the reign of the Peisistratids had

---

[134] Cartledge (1979), 147 stresses the role of Athenian hostility toward the Spartan Kleomenes as smoothing the way for the implementation of Kleisthenes' reforms. For a similar argument in a different historical period, see Baron (1966) who put forward the now well-known thesis about the emergence of Florentine "civic humanism" as a response to the threat of Milanese domination in fourteenth-century (A.D.) Italy. An even closer historical parallel may be found in the role of the American colonies' War of Independence in developing the concept of American citizenship, as argued by Kettner (1978), 131–32:

The imperial crisis of the 1760s forced Americans to articulate their notions of allegiance and political obligation. In resisting the new British policies at the end of the Seven Years' War, the colonists began to give logical form and consistency to hitherto vague and disconnected assumptions concerning their rights and duties as British subjects.

[135] On the Spartan League, see Larsen (1932), (1933–34); de Ste. Croix (1972), 101ff. and 339ff.; Forrest (1980), 79ff. Kagan (1969), 13ff. offers some judicious warnings against constructing too legalistic a picture of the alliance. Though the Spartan League is "officially" visible by 506 or 505 when

been friendly with Argos, the bitter antagonist of Sparta. When the Spartan Kleomenes became king in c. 520, he was eager to undermine that alliance and, if possible, force Athens to join the new league.[136] In 519 Kleomenes campaigned in central Greece, and succeeded in setting the Boiotians against Athens.[137] About 517, the Spartans overthrew Peisistratos' old ally, Lygdamis of Naxos,[138] and in 511/10 they helped overthrow Peisistratos' son Hippias (Hdt. 5.64–65; *Ath. Pol.* 18.6). Later, in 507, Kleomenes took advantage of the dissension in Athens to ally with Isagoras; together they tried to take over the Athenian polis but were resisted successfully by the Council of 400 and other citizens (Hdt. 5.70–73; *Ath. Pol.* 20.2–3).[139]

Kleomenes had been humiliated in this effort but a year later he returned, and this time with a powerful army composed of contingents from most cities in the Peloponnese (Hdt. 5.74.1). In 506 Sparta stood at the head of a mighty alliance, and aimed to take over the Athenian polis newly founded by Kleisthenes. The armies advanced to Eleusis in western Attika,

---

Sparta convened the allies after the failed invasion of Attika (Hdt. 5.91ff.), it is reasonable to believe that Kleomenes began to plan it in the earliest years of his reign. Indeed, as many have pointed out, the League evolved from the series of alliances Sparta had forged in previous times.

[136] *Ath. Pol.* 19.4 claims that Peisistratid friendship with Argos (cf. 17.4; Hdt. 5.94) prompted Sparta to support the expulsion of Hippias. Cf. Forrest (1980), 79ff. who explains Spartan policy in the sixth century primarily motivated by hostility to this Peloponnesian rival. For another explanation of Kleomenes' actions, Cartledge (1979), 144ff. The date of Kleomenes' accession depends on the date of the Athenian-Plataian alliance which I take to be 519 (Thuc. 3.68.5; and see below, n. 141) and Herodotos' testimony (6.108.2–4) that the Spartans under his leadership advised the Plataians to seek the alliance, cf. Cartledge (1979).

[137] Hdt. 6.108.2–6, the date again depending on the reliability of Thucydides' tradition about the Athenian-Plataian alliance (below, n. 141).

[138] Plut. *Mor.* 859 D; schol. Aeschin. 2.77 with Huxley (1962), 74–75; Jeffery (1976), 181. For an earlier date, Cartledge (1979), 145.

[139] The sources for this event do not specify which *boulē* resisted the attack. I follow Rhodes (1981), 246 (and others) that the new Council of 500 had not yet been brought into existence, and the Areopagos should not be considered a candidate.

and the Athenians now stood at the brink of disaster. Their freedom and new institutions hung in the balance.

The situation was all the more urgent because the Athenians faced another external threat on their northwestern border. Since about 520 Thebes had also been forming a league—a federal state—of Boiotian cities.[140] The Theban efforts had been frustrated by the friendship of the Athenians with Plataia, which Thebes desperately wanted as a member of their league. In 519 Athens had become the protector of Plataia, and soon thereafter, in protest, the Thebans went to war against the Athenians.[141] The Thebans were beaten back and, like Kleomenes, were humiliated by the defeat (Hdt. 6.108). Now in 506 they were only too willing to launch another campaign in concert with the Spartans. The Boiotian army invaded Attika from the north (Hdt. 5.74.2, 5.77).

To make matters worse for the Athenians, the Euboian city of Chalkis added a third prong in the pincer movement formed by the Spartans and Boiotians. Crossing the straits, their army too moved into Attika and began to ravage territory (Hdt. 5.74.2, 5.77). In the end, however, through a com-

---

[140] For the date and discussion of this league, Buck (1972); cf. Larsen (1968), 26ff.

[141] The date given by Thucydides (3.68.5) has been challenged by many scholars on grounds varying from scribal error to the supposed good relations between the Peisistratids and the Thebans during this time: see recently, for example, Shrimpton (1984) who cites earlier scholarship. None of the usual arguments are compelling, and I accept the Thucydidean tradition, as per Gomme's succinct comments in (1945–81), 2:358.

The nature of this alliance is also controversial. Some scholars, on the basis of Thuc. 3.55.3 and 3.62, argue that as early as 519 (or 509, depending on one's resolution of the problem) the Plataians were granted citizenship by the Athenians; others have argued for some kind of *isopoliteia* or "honorary citizenship" that was extended to the Plataians in the sixth century, and later converted to "full" citizenship in the fifth (cf. Gomme [1945–81] 2:340; Amit [1973], 73ff.). The normally accepted date for the "enfranchisement" (sometime after 427), however, is not only firm enough in our sources (Dem. 59. 104–6; Isoc. 12.94), but also fits best with the establishment of procedures for formal grants that belongs to the fifth rather than sixth century: M. Osborne (1983), 160, 174ff. For treatment of *isopoliteia*, and a case against its existence here, Gawantka (1975), 165ff.

bination of luck and bravery, the Athenians were able to triumph over all foes. Kleomenes was forced to retreat with his Peloponnesian allies when the important Corinthian contingent suddenly withdrew (Hdt. 5.75–76). In the north, the Athenians repelled and humbled the Boiotians and Chalkidians in pitched battle, and went on to annex valuable lands from each of them (Hdt. 5.77).

Some scholars who have emphasized the daunting odds that Athens faced during this time have interpreted the Kleisthenic politeia as a primarily military reform. It is argued that under the tyranny mercenaries played the leading role in maintaining Athens' defense, and that during that period the citizen army was disarmed and rendered impotent through lack of practice and organization. By these views, Kleisthenes' real goals were to upgrade the civic force, and provide a new system for registering and deploying citizen hoplites—a system that proved itself handily in the victories of 506.[142]

This thesis is in some ways attractive, but ultimately not compelling. It is true that the Peisistratids had depended heavily on the military might of their mercenaries in both domestic and foreign affairs; it is also true that the Kleisthenic tribes provided the basis for organization of the Athenian army in the years after the reforms. But Athenians, not mercenaries, had fought and defeated the Thebans in 519, and their triumphant successes against Kleomenes in 507 and again against the Peloponnesians, Boiotians and Chalkidians in 506 suggest that the citizens' ability to fight was less tarnished than some historians have assumed.[143] As for the new military organization, it seems doubtful whether it could have

---

[142] See references cited above, n. 17.

[143] On the defeat of the Thebans in 519, Herodotus (6.108) speaks only of *hoi Athēnaioi*; in the fight against Kleomenes in 507, we hear of the council and "the rest of the Athenians" who united against the king (Hdt. 5.72.2–3). In the battles against the Boiotians and Chalkidians, Herodotus once again speaks only of "the Athenians." If my earlier interpretation of Kleisthenes' "enfranchisements" is correct, however, the citizen body (and thus the army) by then included some of the originally foreign mercenaries who had served the tyrants—but after 508/7 they fought as "Athenians."

been fully implemented in time for the crises of these years, so soon after the passage of Kleisthenes' legislation.[144] And even if it had been, it is still doubtful that the fact of men fighting in ten tribes rather than four in itself saved the day for Athens.

No, the citizens saved themselves, fighting gloriously against their foes, motivated by civic pride and joined together by the fear of failure. Failure meant loss of autonomy—even subjugation to a foreign league—and with that would vanish all that the polis had at last become.[145] The Kleisthenic organization and citizenship meant nothing if the community would be forced to give up its freedom and with it the newly found *isonomia*—equal order for all, on the basis of the people's own *nomoi*. Herodotus' words extolling the victory are justly famous: "Thus the Athenians waxed strong, and proved, not in one way, but in all ways what an excellent thing freedom (*isēgoria*) is" (Hdt. 5.78).[146]

[144] Rhodes (1983) further challenges the primarily military purpose of Kleisthenes with the point that not until 501/500 was the panel of ten generals, one from each of the new tribes, established. Cf. *Ath. Pol.* 22.2; and Rhodes (1981), 264–66 for interpretation of this passage, in itself highly controversial. See also Ostwald (1986), 315 n. 19.

[145] Some historians (e.g., Huxley [1962], 82; Bicknell [1972], 19) argue that after the expulsion of Hippias in 510, Athens became a member of the Spartan League; other than Kleomenes' demands of the Athenians to exile the accursed families (above, n. 83), there is no real proof of this. Even if Athens did become part of the League at this time, its "membership" clearly did not survive the expulsion of Kleomenes and Isagoras in 507 (Hdt. 5.72.2–4), though the experience doubtless underscored the desirability of maintaining independence thereafter. That Kleomenes intended to make Athens (once again?) a member of the Spartan League in 506 is certainly implied by Herodotus' account of his eagerness for revenge after the humiliation the year before (Hdt. 5.74.1).

[146] It is admittedly anomalous that Herodotus here uses the word *isēgoria* (literally "freedom of speech") rather than *isonomia* which was a central theme of the reforms of 508/7. Nonetheless, the two concepts were closely related, and this passage has been reasonably adduced in support of the belief that *isēgoria* too was an element of Kleisthenes' legislation (above, n. 123). In all events the context here requires us to take the term in the wider sense of "freedom," and understand the significance accordingly. See the comments of Ostwald (1969), 109 n. 2, 146–47, 157 n. 2.; cf. Lévêque and Vidal-Naquet (1964), 29–32; J. Lewis (1971); Raaflaub (1980).

Nakategawa (1988) reviews previous scholarship on the question and offers an interesting explanation linking *isēgoria* to the military victory and in-

This was a freedom worth preserving, and the struggle did not end with the victories of 506. Athenians knew that the Lacedaimonians and Thebans could return again, as could other enemies; it was not long in fact before both Sparta and Thebes resumed the attack, and the latter also encouraged Athens' old foe Aigina to ravage the coast of Attika (Hdt. 5.79ff.).[147] In the coming years, other threats to Athenian freedom would rise, but they would not undo the strength of the community now firmly established as a *koinōnia*. Against Thebes, Sparta, Aigina, against Persia, against other states Greek or barbarian, Athenians would fight again, successfully, to save the polis and politeia that had been born under Solon, nurtured by tyrants, and established for every individual in Attika by Kleisthenes.

In both spirit and law, then, citizenship at the end of the sixth century had become a fully developed institution. There now existed a central process for determining who was a citizen and who was not, and if all of its details were not instituted at once by Kleisthenes (probably unlikely), it would not be long before the essential procedures were in place.[148] One

deed the development of the Athenian polis consciousness. Ostwald (1986), 23 is dubious of any broad-based democratic mentality created by military success on the grounds that the hoplite army of Athenians would have excluded *thētes*, and thus a major segment of the population. Notwithstanding, the victory would have produced a widely felt civic response of citizens; one should not assume that only those who fought in the battle and won would have been proud of the outcome, and that freedom would not have been celebrated also by those who stayed at home.

[147] Herodotus' narrative needs untangling since he conflates several conflicts between Athens and Aigina, the earliest of which dates back to the early seventh century (see chapter 4, n. 58 and references cited there).

[148] For what follows, as earlier, I adopt the view of Whitehead (1986a), 34ff., 97ff. which seems the most plausible interpretation of the origins of registration procedures. M. Osborne (1983), 139ff. similarly stresses the importance of Kleisthenes' reforms in establishing the formal definition of citizenship. See also Morris (1987), 208ff., who suggests that Attic burial practices at the end of the sixth century reflect the integrative social structure indicative of the rise of the *polis* and a "citizen estate."

My emphasis on the advance implied by the establishment of systematic registrations does not deny, by the way, the inevitable problems and lapses that would occur in a process that still depended on the oath of a father and on the local opinions of different people who, like all human beings, often

can only guess how the various people of Attika were first registered and enrolled after 508/7, but certainly by the time that their children came of age every demesman had come to terms with the new rules. Candidates for registration were examined and voted upon by deme members to ensure that they met the requirements of age and legitimate birth, from an Athenian father; thereafter they were scrutinized by the new Council of 500. Whether the right to appeal to a jury for those rejected in the deme was also part of the original "Kleisthenic" procedure cannot be proven, but it accords well with that fundamental tenet of Athenian justice that was firmly established by then. And eventually, if not initially (which seems more likely), every deme kept a record of its enrollments in the form of a *lēxiarchikon grammateion*.

That citizenship was by now a well-articulated and realized concept is indicated by a few other contemporary developments. First is the analogous categorization of resident noncitizens by Athenians. By the second quarter of the fifth century, *metoikia* as a legal status is securely attested, existing as a formal identity for the foreigner who lived in Attika but was not a citizen.[149] This new status, if not included in the reforms of Kleisthenes, was certainly made possible by them,[150] and it is easy to understand why. Kleisthenes had "enfranchised" many people of "impure birth," effecting an amnesty for all who suffered through the *diapsēphismos*, and at the same time creating a new basis of belonging to the polis. If this system was to survive and have meaning, there had to be a way to keep track of those members of Attic society who were not citizens—or else the polis would cease to be anything more than a population and its land. The creation of the *metoikia* reinforced the boundary between "insider" and "outsider"—

---

contrived to do things their own way. What is important is that Athenians now had a standard. Even if not always adhered to, it did define the membership of the polis as first set out by Solon.

[149] *IG* i³ 244 C (= *IG* i² 188; before 460 B.C.) with Whitehead (1977), passim and (1986a), 81–82. Cf. also Meiggs and Lewis (1969), no. 23, lines 27–31 with Whitehead (1977), 83ff. (referring to 480 B.C.).

[150] Evidence and discussion in Whitehead (1977), 140ff.

and it is no surprise that *metoikoi* were required to register in demes, the keepers of citizenship for the polis.[151]

Categorization of another kind of non-citizen again tells a story of citizenship itself. During the same general period—and by 480 at the latest—another special class of foreigner was instituted by the Athenian polis: the *proxenos*.[152] A *proxenos* was a foreigner charged with the duty of looking after the interests of Athens in his native city; in return he was granted special privileges by the Athenian people. Those privileges might include legal safeguards for the *proxenos* and his family, the right to seek redress in Athens at the court of the polemarch,[153] and even an invitation to have dinner in the Athenian *prytaneion*. The *proxenos* was "placed, in short, on a par with Athenian citizens," according to one modern scholar,[154] but of course, he was never an exact equal. And the difference, even if it may seem negligible to us today, bears witness to the concrete and cherished institution that membership in the *polis* had become.[155]

As a third indication, other boundaries defining the citizen, and distinguishing him from the non-citizen, can be seen forming during this same period. At the end of the sixth century, Athenians established settlements beyond the borders of At-

[151] Whitehead (1977), 72–77, 145–46; (1986a), 81–85. Note, however, Whitehead's point ([1977], 77 and 145) that a centralized list of *metoikoi* was kept for the purpose of collection of the *metoikia*.

[152] On the origins and development of early proxenies, M. Wallace (1970); Gauthier (1972), 17–61; Walbank (1978), 2ff. Inscriptional evidence of *proxenoi* have been dated as early as the late seventh century, but the first attested Athenian cases belong to the period of the Persian Wars, e.g., Alexandros, king of Makedonia, and Arthmios of Zeleia. For sources and chronological arguments, see Walbank (1978), 63ff.

[153] In fairness, however, it should be noted that there is no evidence for the polemarch being anything other than a military leader until after 490. The argument for earlier judicial duties regarding non-Athenians is extrapolated from his role in later times. See MacDowell (1978), 222–23 who presents the view (including relevant sources and references) that is followed here.

[154] Walbank (1978), 6.

[155] Herman (1987), 130–56 similarly argues for the invention of the *proxenia* as a reflection of the "self-conscious community of the city-state," based on the model of pre-polis *xenia*.

tika which, for the first time, allowed the emigrants to maintain their citizenship at home. In earlier times, settlers preserved close ties with their mother city, but became members of an independent and autonomous "colony" (*apoikia*). This practice changed shortly after Kleisthenes' reforms. Thus Athenians who were dispatched to Lemnos and Imbros in about 504 formed not "colonies" but "klerouchies," which allowed them to continue to be Athenians.[156] The defeat of the Chalkidians in 506 provided an even earlier example of this new practice: the Athenians took over the rich farmland of the "hippobotai" across the straits in Euboia, and gave 4,000 of its own citizens shares (*klēroi*) of the seized estates (Hdt. 5. 77.2). In 490 the settlers returned to Attika and rejoined the ranks of the Athenian *dēmos* (Hdt. 6. 100–102).[157] Citizenship had become a tangible status, and those who had it now clearly wanted to keep it whenever they could.[158]

---

[156] In actual fact, the terminology of Athenian literary and inscriptional sources does not separate the *apoikia* from the *klērouchia* as neatly as I have implied here, especially with regard to those overseas settlements established at the end of the sixth century; to a large degree the distinction evolved in step with the evolution of citizenship itself, as I have argued heretofore. Nonetheless, later evidence suggests that, by about 500, foundations such as Imbros and Lemnos were composed of settlers who were still considered Athenian citizens, even though they resided beyond the boundaries of Attika. For the evidence and discussion of these cases, and treatment of the difficult problems of terminology see Ehrenberg (1946), 129–43. On the development of the institution of klerouchies, Will (1954).

[157] For this interpretation, and discussion of the evidence, Brunt (1966), 87.

[158] Further evidence of the concrete formulation of citizenship in opposition to non-citizen populations during this period may be found in contemporary cases of Athenians living in liminal Attic territories (above, n. 95). Thus, Salamis, under Athenian control but not part of the Kleisthenic system, looks to have been inhabited by klerouchs with obligations to the polis, datable to the end of the sixth century (Meiggs and Lewis [1969], no. 14 with commentary). Similarly, the people of Oropos, on the border with Boiotia, and which probably became "Athenian" after the victory of 506, were not made citizens, but some Athenians apparently lived there and registered elsewhere: Gomme et al. (1945–81), 2:80–81; Rhodes (1981), 253, cf. *IG* ii² 1125–28. Finally Eleutherai, annexed during the sixth century(?), but which also stood outside the Kleisthenic system: at least some of its inhabitants seem to have been considered Athenian citizens. See Gomme et al. (1945–81); Rhodes (1981), 768; cf. Meiggs and Lewis (1969), no. 48, col. ii, lines 96ff.

But perhaps the most obvious evidence that citizenship now existed as a full institution was the practice of awarding it as a lawful grant. By the end of the first quarter of the fifth century, the Athenian people began to make honored foreigners citizens; the process rapidly became a multistepped and formal procedure.[159] Not until something is formed and conceptualized can it be given away; and unless it is something valuable, its gift is not significant. After centuries of evolution, Athenian citizenship had become just that. A mere glimmer in the age of Drakon, born under Solon, nurtured by tyrants, and given full form by Kleisthenes, membership in the political community was now real, precious, and even alienable. Known by all, it now verged on being the center of the culture. If there is any short-hand description of the classical age, it can be said that it was a time when citizenship fully existed and embodied the meaning and life of the world of the polis.[160]

[159] For the date of the first formal grant to a foreigner (Menon of Pharsalos, in about 476: Dem. 23.199), and the development of the procedures thereafter, M. Osborne (1981), 6ff.; (1983), 139ff.

[160] Along similar lines, Sealey (1983b), 118–23 dates the emergence of citizenship to the period between Kleisthenes' reforms and the mid-fifth century, highlighted by the conflict between oikos and polis seen in Aeschylus' *Oresteia* and *Persians*.

Chapter Eight

CONCLUSION

THROUGHOUT history, people have pondered the relationship between themselves and the society to which they belong. Citizenship, as one form of that relationship, deserves such reflection; and ancient Greek citizenship provides a provocative case study for those who would look to the past to understand the ties between an individual and the world in which he or she lives. Unfortunately, most traditional treatments of Athenian citizenship describe the phenomenon as a static, timeless, and primarily legal institution. I have challenged such assumptions, and argued that citizenship in Athens was not simply a legal construct, but also crucially included important intangible qualities; moreover that it had not "always" existed during ancient times, but rather arose during a particular period of history. By my view, it was created by sixth-century political reformers, working together with a community of Athenians who increasingly defined themselves as just that—a community of citizens—as they rallied around their statesmen. By about the year 500, citizenship had become a fully formed institution and self-conscious ethos.

These conclusions emerged from an investigation that began with the perspective of the Athenians themselves: to be a citizen was "to share in the polis." As is clear from the evidence of the classical period, citizenship was membership in the polis, and that represented, simultaneously, a complement of formal obligations and privileges, and the behavior, feelings, and communal attitudes attendant upon them. To understand why that was so, and how the concept of membership in the polis came to be, I turned to earlier Athenian history, probing the origins of the polis itself. That task pointed to the need for another definition: what in fact was a polis? Describing its essential elements thus became the next challenge of this study.

Polis is typically translated "city-state," but I wanted to go beyond that description and at the same time skirt the general—and often ideological—issue of what makes a "state." Instead, recognizing that the ancient Greek city-state was a unique form of sociopolitical organization, I adapted a working definition from Aristotle's analyses of polis-type societies in the *Politics*, and his related discussion in the *Nicomachean Ethics*. Though any generic model necessarily implies some kind of ideal, I maintained that Aristotle's insights, based on his knowledge of actual Greek city-states, provide a valuable guide in the search for the historical polis.

Other scholars have used Aristotelian criteria to identify the origins of the polis, but they shy away from one of the most essential qualities set forth by the philosopher: its purpose and ability to provide justice, and thus morally to improve its citizens. Applying such a quality to a historical case is difficult, but to ignore it is to misunderstand the nature of the polis. Using a simple sense of the term "justice," as well as several other Aristotelian conditions, I argued that the Athenian polis first emerged with the reforms of Solon, in 594/3. And thus citizenship, as a formal institution and consciousness, is first recognizable only then.

A sixth-century date for the Athenian polis is later than those proposed by most historians, but my differences with them derive more from the definition that I brought to the ancient evidence than any deep disagreement about its array and meaning. And although I have marked the Solonian reforms as the true origin of the polis, and of citizenship, clearly a long period of development preceded their emergence. Borrowing a framework from political anthropologists, I have proposed that the Athenian city-state, and membership in it, were the products of a slow evolution whereby regional, autonomous units of a superficially homogeneous society were gradually brought into a centralized unity of law, formal organization, and "civic spirit."

The danger of an evolutionary model is that it may suggest

an inevitable outcome. The polis and citizenship at Athens were not the necessary results of anything we know about the history of early Attika. For that reason, I not only endeavored to date their appearance, but also to explain how and why they came to be. Historians have advanced many explanations for the social and political transformations that led to the rise of Greek poleis; without discounting wholly any of the most prominent hypotheses (and in fact acknowledging a variety of forces at work), I held that the Athenian case was particularly a response, led by Solon, to mounting population pressure at the end of the seventh century. Specifically, in the face of too many people working too little land (under a variety of statuses), the society enacted reforms that created or affirmed new boundaries. These boundaries—spatial, legal, political, and psychological—defined and set apart a community of citizens from a population of both existing and potential "outsiders."

Further, that community of citizens was truly a polis because Solon and his followers brought to the reforms the idea that justice and the goal of moral improvement belonged to, and would bind together, the "insiders." Solon's success was forged on the appeal to civic spirit whose core value was the Athenians' expectation of more uniform, centralized principles of governance and fairer resolution of disputes than had been known in the regionalized society of earlier years. Throughout the Solonian reforms, one sees a new consciousness about the role of the public sphere to better the lives of all members of the community.

But these favorable beginnings did not extend smoothly into the future. Another two generations would pass before Attic society achieved a tangible system of broad-based political membership. Soon after Solon's reforms the Athenian community again lapsed into regional and aristocratic strife; not until Peisistratos took control as a tyrant was stability restored. Thereafter, and through much of the sixth century, Peisistratos and his sons ruled the Athenians firmly, but their reign was more of a custodianship of the Solonic politeia than a radical departure from it. Along many dimensions, the polis thus further developed. The laws created in 594/3 remained intact, and the bodies of government continued to function, albeit in the shadow of a mercenary-supported dynasty. What "civic spirit" may have been lost in the absence of completely unfettered political activity was offset by the continuing centralization of society, the creation of pride-building institutions, festivals, and public works, and the expansion of Athenian power abroad. During the tyranny, patriotic sentiment and the world of the polis touched the lives of more men across Attika than ever before.

Nonetheless, citizenship in the Peisistratid state was not truly membership in a polis; full political freedom was lacking, and all-important boundaries between "insiders" and "outsiders" eroded due to evolutionary changes in the size, distribution, and makeup of the population. The fall of the tyranny set the stage for the next phase of citizenship's development. Thereupon, in the last decade of the sixth century, two major crises, the first stemming from the blurred social boundaries, and the second from a series of external threats to the political freedom of all Athenians, forced anew the question of what it meant to belong to the community. The ideals originally advanced by the Solonian reforms were desperately challenged. The fortunate resolution of both crises ultimately fostered the implementation of a citizenship with coherent legal and social force.

With the expulsion of Hippias in 511/10, and the subsequent reemergence of aristocratic factionalism, an unprecedented and brutal scrutiny—a *diapsēphismos*—of who was and who was not Athenian elevated membership in the polis to a literally life-and-death issue. Kleisthenes, backed by the *dēmos*, resolved this first crisis with a program of reforms that defined in fairer and more consistent terms the basis of Athenian identity. Soon thereafter, the new citizenship, with its more lucid legal boundaries, enhanced access to justice, and spirit of *isonomia*, was put to the test as the Athenians faced and beat back the attacks of several hostile neighbors. Victorious, the Athenians preserved for themselves the precious membership in a politically active and autonomous community. Their successes in both challenges, occurring in rapid succession, established firmly what may otherwise not have been: a concept of citizenship that was both practically operational and spiritually vigorous. By the beginning of the fifth century, it was meaningful in a legal, actual, and at least occasional manner for every adult male in Attica, worthy of preservation for those who settled abroad, and now even capable of being bestowed as a discrete honor upon deserving foreign benefactors. At about the same time, not coincidentally, Athenians began to classify substatuses of non-citizens (e.g., *metoikoi, proxenoi*) and to incorporate formal distinctions between themselves and non-Athenians into the organization of their community.

For these reasons, and the proof they represent of a defined citizenship, I have chosen the year 500 as a reasonable, if approximate, endpoint of this study. Arguably, however, the evolutionary model suggests that the institution and ethos of citizenship continued to develop through subsequent Athenian history. In certain ways, of course, the evolution did continue. In chapter 1, for the purpose of discussion, I characterized the classical polis by a broad continuity of laws and political culture. That deliberate oversimplification masks several changes that took place in the community and its constitution during the period of the full democracy, and ignores several others that occurred in its formative years in the first half of the fifth century. Parallel to our perspective about the preclassical age—that membership in the society and indeed the society itself were not static concepts—one can imagine that the many political, social, and intellectual developments of the classical age further shaped the definition and meaning of Athenian citizenship. This story, in other words, could be continued beyond the events and immediate aftermath of Kleisthenes' reforms.

Over the next sixty-odd years, to take two obvious examples, one can trace the effects of the rise of Athenian imperialism and the development of the polis' more advanced democratic institutions. The growth of Athenian power, built on military successes against the Persians, and the transformation of Athens' leadership in the Delian League of Greek allies to the sovereign head of a vast tribute-paying empire, added immeasurably to the material benefits and civic pride of being a member of the polis.[1] Similarly, with each incremental addition of privilege and responsibility to the *dēmos* during the 460s and 450s—the widening of the political role of the *boulē*, *dikastēria*, and *ekklēsia*; the introduction of pay for public service; increased sortition and accountability procedures for officials; and so on—an individual's citizenship became a more complete and meaningful representation of Athenian public life.[2] In general, for each subperiod one might identify within the classical age, one can hypothesize influences from internal and external events on the citizenship of that time. Whether one is discussing the nature of Athenian patriotism during and after the Peloponnesian War (431–404),[3] the efforts to restrict the politeia in the oligarchic revolutions of 411 and 404,[4] or the growth of governmental "professionalism" and the changing nature of the *ekklēsia*'s legislative powers in the fourth century,[5] the history of citizenship continued to mirror the history of the polis itself.

Not surprisingly, the classical age witnessed changes and refinements to laws relating directly to citizenship. Best known is Perikles' law of 451/50 which stipulated for the first time that citizens be born of not just an Athenian father but also an

[1] On the rise of Athens' imperial power, Kagan (1969), 31ff.; Meiggs (1972), 23ff.; on specific implications for citizenship, Frost (1976).

[2] For details and discussion of the "democratic revolution," Forrest (1966), 204ff.; Davies (1978), 63ff.; Ostwald (1986), 100ff.; Bleicken (1986), 13ff.; Sinclair (1988), 13ff.; Ober (1989), 75ff.

[3] Useful perspectives are offered by Meiggs (1972), 306–74; Kagan (1974), (1981), and (1987), passim; Krentz (1982), 28ff.; Strauss (1987), 86ff.; Farrar (1988), 153ff.; Ober (1989), 92ff.

[4] Thuc. 8.63.3ff.; *Ath. Pol.* 29–37; Xen. *Hell.* 2.3.11ff. with Gomme et al. (1945–81), 5:153–256; Rhodes (1981), 362–455; Krentz (1982), 23ff.

[5] On the fourth-century democracy's increasing reliance on paid and nonpaid "experts" in the realms of finance, military leadership, public works, and other areas of administration, Rhodes (1980) 307ff.; Sinclair (1988), 211–17. On changes in the *ekklēsia*'s legislative role, especially in connection with the development of *nomothesia*, Hansen (1979c) and (1985c); Rhodes (1980), 305ff.; Ostwald (1986), 480ff.

Athenian mother.[6] After a brief lapse during the Peloponnesian War (probably due to manpower shortages), the law was reaffirmed in 403 and subsequently strengthened by prohibitions against mixed marriages.[7] In addition, during the fifth and fourth centuries, new institutions and procedures were established to administer "outsiders," to maintain the integrity of the "insider" population, and to calibrate with increasing judicial exactitude the privileges and disabilities of various statuses of non-Athenians.[8] As we have seen, versions of a

[6] *Ath. Pol.* 26.4; Plut. *Per.* 37.2–5; Patterson (1981), and see chapter 6, n. 52.

[7] For evidence, including references on the lapse of the Periklean law, see chapter 1, n. 3, and Patterson (1981), 130ff. Additional measures in support of discouraging mixed marriages in the fourth century include the liability to prosecution by *graphē* and enslavement if convicted for any alien who married into the oikos of a citizen (Dem. 59.16); a 1,000-drachma fine for any male citizen who took an alien wife (Dem. 59.16); liability for prosecution and *atimia* and property confiscation if convicted for any citizen who acted as the guardian (*kyrios*) of an alien girl and gave her in marriage to a citizen (Dem. 59.52). Cf. Harrison (1968), 26–28; MacDowell (1978), 87; Whitehead (1986b), 109ff.

[8] New institutions and procedures regarding outsiders, and the maintenance of the integrity of the citizen population: establishment of the *graphē xenias* against aliens purporting to be citizens, and rights of prosecution against aliens born of two foreign parents who had become members of Athenian phratries (*FGrH* 324 F 4; other sources, previous scholarship, and discussion in MacDowell [1978], 70ff.; Patterson [1981], 108ff.); the changing role of the polemarch in judicial affairs concerning aliens, and the establishment of the *xenodikai*, and *nautodikai* (sources and arguments in Wade-Gery [1958], 180–92; Harrison [1971], 9ff.; Gauthier [1972], 132ff.; E. Cohen [1973], 166ff.; MacDowell [1978], 76, 221–22; Rhodes [1981], 652–55); other special arrangements in connection with *symbolai* between the Athenians and allies of the empire (de Ste. Croix [1961], 100ff.; Gauthier [1971] and [1972]).

Examples of increasing "status calibration": progressive addition of responsibilities and disabilities to the *metoikoi*, e.g., required military service, payment of *metoikion* tax, registration in demes, legal distinction between the visitor and the resident alien (Whitehead [1977], 72ff. for details); development of different categories of metic privilege such as *ateleia*, *isoteleia*, rights of *enktēsis* (Whitehead [1977], 7–14; MacDowell [1978], 78–79; Rhodes [1981], 653–54); development of increasing legal requirements for receiving grants of Athenian citizenship (M. Osborne [1981], 5ff.; [1983], 141ff.); de-

diapsēphismos were also conducted in 445/4 and 346/5 against the encroachments of aliens upon the membership of the polis.[9]

Such legal developments were in most cases responses to changes in the social composition of the Athenian community. Demographic analysis has shown that by the mid-fifth century the Athenian population included many more citizens than can be accounted for by natural growth after about 500;[10] similarly, the population of *metoikoi* and foreigners, drawn to the expanding opportunities in Athens and its port Peiraieus, increased substantially in the classical age.[11] Clearly, Athenians were more jealous about sharing the more robust privileges and prestige of their citizenship; amid a widening population of non-Athenians, including both residents in Attika and potential migrants from across the broader realm of Athenian influence in the Aegean, the polis took various measures to curb the assimiliation of outsiders into the civic body, and to strengthen distinctions between citizens and non-citizens.[12]

These interactions between law and social transformations are similar to that seen in the preclassical age, but there is one striking difference. Both the reforms of Solon and Kleisthenes were stimulated, at least partly, by demographic change, and resulted in the creation of boundaries between insiders and outsiders. In each case, however, the boundaries created represented an unprecedented demarcation of the community. The Solonian politeia established for the first time a system of *telē*, with accompanying rights and responsibilities, which em-

velopment of various kinds of partial *atimia* (Andoc. 1.73–76, with Manville [1980], 216–17; cf. MacDowell [1962], 106–13; Hansen [1976], 82–90).

[9] See chapter 7, discussion of the three known civic scrutinies.

[10] Patterson (1981), 51ff.; cf. Hansen (1982a), (1985b), (1988).

[11] Whitehead (1977), 97–98; Duncan-Jones (1980); Strauss (1987), 74–75; Sinclair (1988), 28–30; Hansen (1988), 10–11.

[12] For recent examples of this often stated view, Patterson (1981), 105ff.; Sinclair (1988), 24–27. As a relevant illustration, Sinclair notes the reluctance of the *dēmos* to award citizenship to the various non-Athenians among "the men from Phyle" who helped restore the democracy in 403/2. For details, and the debate about the limitation of the award indicated in *IG* ii² 10, see Krentz (1980); (1982), 110–12; (1986); cf. Whitehead (1984b).

braced the entire free male population of Attika and formalized the distinction between it and nonfree inhabitants. The Kleisthenic politeia established, for the first time, a practical implementation of the political community as defined by Solon's reforms; that system was built in the aftershock of the first attempt ever to expel "suspect" Athenians from the political community.

The attempt was, as we know, unsuccessful, and the free inhabitants of Attika became members of a system of demes that finally made real the ideal of the polis that Solon created, and bridged politically the societies of town and country. Thus, with Kleisthenes' reforms, the self-selecting members of the state and the state itself finally became one and the same. The Periklean law of citizenship of 451/50 tightened the definition of who might become a citizen but it is important to understand that by then the polis did have in place a centralized and standard definition which became the target of the modification. Likewise, the several other laws and institutions dealing with citizenship and non-citizenship brought forward during the classical age should be seen as refinements to a concept already firmly established, rather than as innovations in themselves.

It has been said that democracy represents the "perfection of the polis."[13] If so, then the "perfect polis" of classical Athenian democracy also represented a perfection of citizenship. With regard to a constitution, the rule of the people embodied in the fullest possible sense the unity of the state and its citizens; with regard to intangible civic spirit, the same, powerful themes seen in the Periklean funeral oration are visible (as generations of scholars have commented) throughout the drama, art and architecture, and political discourse of that "golden age."[14] But to be perfected, something must first exist, however imperfectly, and, for the reasons advanced in this book, I

[13] Ehrenberg (1969), 43–44.

[14] For some valuable recent treatments of civic ideology and classical Athenian culture, Pollitt (1972), 64ff.; Meiggs (1972), 273–90; Goldhill (1986); Farrar (1988), 153ff.; Ober (1989).

have made the case that citizenship had come into being in a reasonably well-formed way, by about 500.

Accordingly, although the evolutionary model I have employed provides the background of Solon's innovation in 594/3, and implies ongoing development long after the Kleisthenic reforms of 508/7, the sixth century must be seen as the pivotal era for the creation of membership in the polis, separating significantly in the historical record what had come before from that which followed after. Indeed, those years were both the true beginning and practical culmination of a process that can properly be called the origin of Athenian citizenship. If the events of later history serve to dignify the invention, those of us who reflect upon its achievement do so as well.

REFERENCES

NOTE: In the following citations, scholarly journals are abbreviated according to conventions in *L'Année Philologique*. For the benefit of the nonspecialist, abbreviations of the most commonly used English language journals are listed below.

ABSA	*Annual of the British School at Athens*
AJA	*American Journal of Archaeology*
AJAH	*American Journal of Ancient History*
AJPh	*American Journal of Philology*
AHR	*American Historical Review*
AncSoc	*Ancient Society*
C&M	*Classica et Mediaevalia*
CQ	*Classical Quarterly*
CJ	*Classical Journal*
CPh	*Classical Philology*
CR	*Classical Review*
CSCA	*California Studies in Classical Antiquity*
G&R	*Greece & Rome*
GRBS	*Greek, Roman, and Byzantine Studies*
HSCPh	*Harvard Studies in Classical Philology*
JHS	*Journal of Hellenic Studies*
LCM	*Liverpool Classical Monthly*
PCPhS	*Proceedings of the Cambridge Philological Society*
SO	*Symbolae Osloenses*
TAPhA	*Transactions of the American Philological Association*
YClS	*Yale Classical Studies*

Adeleye, G. 1983. "The Purpose of the Dokimasia." *GRBS* 24:295–306.

Adkins, A.W.H. 1960. *Merit and Responsibility: A Study in Greek Values*. Oxford.

———. 1972. *Moral Values and Political Behaviour from Homer to the End of the Fifth Century*. London.

Alföldy, G. 1969. "Der attische Synoikismos und die Entstehung des athenischen Adels." *RBPh* 47:15–36.

Alty, J. 1982. "Dorians and Ionians." *JHS* 102:1–14.

Amit, M. 1973. *Great and Small Poleis.* Brussels.

Anderson, C. W., F. von der Mehden, and C. Young, eds. 1974. *Issues of Political Development.* 2d ed. Englewood Cliffs, N.J.

Anderson, J. K. 1984. "Hoplites and Heresies: A Note." *JHS* 104:152.

Andrewes, A. 1956. *The Greek Tyrants.* London.

———. 1961a. "Phratries in Homer." *Hermes* 89:129–40.

———. 1961b. "Philochoros on Phratries." *JHS* 81:1–15.

———. 1967. *The Greeks.* London.

———. 1974. "The Survival of Solon's Axones." In *Phoros: Tribute to Benjamin D. Meritt,* edited by D. W. Bradeen and M. F. McGregor, pp. 21–28. Locust Valley, N.Y.

———. 1977. "Kleisthenes' Reform Bill." *CQ* 27:241–48.

———. 1981. "The Hoplite Katalogos." In *Classical Contributions: Studies in Honor of M. F. McGregor,* edited by G. S. Shrimpton and D. J. McCargar, pp. 1–3. Locust Valley, N.Y.

———. 1982a. "The Growth of the Athenian State." In *Cambridge Ancient History. See* Boardman and Hammond, eds. 1982.

———. 1982b. "The Tyranny of Peisistratus." In *Cambridge Ancient History. See* Boardman and Hammond, eds. 1982.

Andreyev, V. 1973. "Some Aspects of Agrarian Conditions in Attika in the Fifth to Third Centuries." *Eirene* 12:5–46.

Arnheim, M. T. 1977. *Aristocracy in Greek Society.* London.

Asheri, D. 1963. "Laws of Inheritance, Distribution of Land, and Political Constitutions of Ancient Greece," *Historia* 12:1–21.

———. 1966. *Distribuzioni di terre nelle antica Grecia.* Torino.

Austin, M. M. 1970. *Greece and Egypt in the Archaic Age.* Cambridge.

Austin, M. M., and P. Vidal-Naquet, eds. 1977. *Economic and Social History of Ancient Greece.* Berkeley, Calif.

Aymard, A. 1945. "L'Idée de travail dans la Grèce archaïque." *Journal de Psychologie* 41:29–45.

———. 1967. "Hierarchie du travail et autarcie individuelle dans la Grèce archaïque." In *Etudes d'histoire ancienne,* pp. 316–33. Paris.

Baba, K. 1984. "On Kerameikos INV. I 388 (SEG XXII, 79): A Note on the Formation of the Athenian Metic Status." *ABSA* 79:1–5.

Balme, M. 1984. "Attitudes to Work and Leisure in Ancient Greece." *G&R* 33:140–52.

Barker, E. 1918. *Greek Political Theory*. London.

———, ed. 1946. *The Politics of Aristotle*. Oxford.

———. 1959. *The Political Thought of Plato and Aristotle*. Reprint of 1906 ed. New York.

Baron, H. 1966. *The Crisis of the Early Italian Renaissance*. Vol. 2. 2d ed. Princeton.

Barth, F. 1969. "The System of Social Stratification in Swat, North Pakistan." In *Aspects of Caste in South India, Ceylon and Northwest Pakistan*, edited by E. R. Leach, pp. 113–46. Cambridge.

Baslez, M. 1984. *L'Etranger dans la Grèce antique*. Paris.

Beloch, K. J. 1912. *Griechische Geschichte*. 2d. ed. Strassburg, Berlin, and Leipzig.

Berghe, L. van den. 1969. "Pluralism and the Polity: A Theoretical Explanation." In *Pluralism in Africa*, edited by L. Kuper and M. G. Smith, pp. 67–81. Berkeley, Calif.

Beringer, W. 1982. "Servile Statuses in the Sources for Early Greek History." *Historia* 31:13–32.

———. 1985. "Freedom, Family, and Citizenship in Early Greece." In *The Craft of the Ancient Historian*, edited by J. W. Eadie and J. Ober, pp. 41–56. Lanham, Md. and London.

Bers, V. 1975. "Solon's Law Forbidding Neutrality and Lysias 31." *Historia* 24:507–8.

Berve, H. 1937. *Miltiades: Studien zur Geschichte des Mannes und Seiner Zeit*. Berlin.

———. 1967. *Die Tyrannis bei den Griechen*. Munich.

Beuscher, J., and C. von Dietze. 1956. "The Role of Inheritance in the Tenure Process." In *Land Tenure*, edited by K. Parsons et al., pp. 565–74. Madison, Wisc.

Bicknell, P. J. 1969a. "Whom Did Kleisthenes Enfranchise?" *PP* 24:34–37.

———. 1969b. "The Dates of the Archaic Owls of Athens." *AC* 38:175–80.

———. 1972. *Studies in Athenian Politics and Genealogy*. Wiesbaden.

———. 1976. "Clisthène et Kytherros." *REG* 89:599–603.

Biebuyck, D., ed. 1963a. *African Agrarian Systems*. London.

———. 1963b. "Introduction." In *African Agrarian Systems*, pp. 1–29. London.

Biebuyck, D., ed. 1963c. "Tenure foncière et valeurs religieuses." In *African Agrarian Systems*, pp. 35–41. London.

———. 1963d. "Droit foncière, pénurie et valorisation des terres." In *African Agrarian Systems*, pp. 30–35. London.

Billheimer, A. 1922. *Naturalization at Athens*. Gettysburg, Pa.

Billigmeier, J., and A. Dusing. 1981. "The Origins and Function of the Naukraroi at Athens: An Etymological and Historical Explanation." *TAPhA* 111:11–16.

Bleicken, J. 1986. *Die athenische Demokratie*. Paderborn.

Bloedow, E. F. 1975. "Corn Supply and Athenian Imperialism." *AC* 44:20–29.

Boardman, J. 1972. "Herakles, Peisistratos and Sons." *RA* 65:57–72.

———. 1974. *Athenian Black Figure Vases*. London.

———. 1975. "Herakles, Peisistratos, and Eleusis." *JHS* 95:1–12.

———. 1979. "The Athenian Pottery Trade." *Expedition* 21.4:33–39.

———. 1980. *The Greeks Overseas*. 3d ed. London.

———. 1982. "The Geometric Culture of Greece." In *Cambridge Ancient History*. See Boardman and Hammond, eds. 1982.

———. 1984. "*Signa Tabulae Priscae Artis.*" *JHS* 104:161–63.

Boardman, J., and N.G.L. Hammond, eds. 1982. *Cambridge Ancient History*. Vol. 3, pt. 3. 2d ed. Cambridge.

Boardman, J., N.G.L. Hammond, D. M. Lewis, and M. Ostwald, eds. 1988. *Cambridge Ancient History*. Vol. 4. 2d ed. Cambridge.

Boas, G. 1943. "A Basic Conflict in Aristotle's Philosophy." *AJPh* 64:187–93.

Boegehold, A. 1962. "The Nessos Amphora—A Note on the Inscription." *AJA* 66:405–6.

———. 1983. "A New Attic Black Figure Potter," *AJA* 87:89–90.

Boersma, J. S. 1970. *Athenian Building Policy from 561/0 to 405/4*. Groningen.

Bohannan, P. 1963. " 'Land,' 'Tenure,' and 'Land Tenure.' " In *African Agrarian Systems*. See Biebuyck. 1963a.

Bonner, R. J., and G. Smith. 1930–38. *The Administration of Justice from Homer to Aristotle*, Vols. 1–2. Chicago.

Bordes, J. 1980. "Aristote dans l'évolution de la notion de *Politeia.*" *Ktema* 5:249–56.

———. 1982. *Politeia dans la pensée grecque jusqu'à Aristote*. Paris.

Boserup, E. 1965. *The Conditions of Agricultural Growth*. Chicago.

Bourriot, F. 1976. *Recherches sur la nature du genos*. Paris.

———. 1984. "Le Concept grec de cité et la politique d'Aristote." *IH* 46:193–202.

Boutillier, J. 1963. "Les Rapports du système foncier Toucouleur et l'organisation sociale et économique traditionelle—leur évolution actuelle." In *African Agrarian Systems. See* Biebuyck. 1963a.

Bowra, C. M. 1961. *Greek Lyric Poetry.* 2d ed. Oxford.

Bradeen, D. W. 1955. "The Trittyes in Cleisthenes' Reforms." *TAPhA* 86:22–30.

Brandt, R. 1974. "Untersuchungen zur politischen Philosophie des Aristoteles." *Hermes* 102:191–200.

Brann, E. 1961. "Protoattic Well Groups from the Athenian Agora." *Hesperia* 30:305–71.

Bravo, B. 1977. "Remarques sur les assises sociales, les formes d'organisation et la terminologie du commerce maritime grec à l' époque archaïque." *DHA* 3:1–59.

———. 1983. "Le Commerce de céréales chez les grecs de l'époque archaïque." In *Trade and Famine in Classical Antiquity. See* Garnsey and Whittaker, eds. 1983.

Broneer, O. 1956. "Athens in the Late Bronze Age." *Antiquity* 30:9–18.

Brookfield, H. C., and P. Brown. 1963. *Struggle for Land.* Melbourne.

Brunnsåker, S. 1955. *The Tyrant Slayers of Kritios and Nesiotes.* Lund.

Brunt, P. 1966. "Athenian Settlements Abroad in the Fifth Century B.C." In *Ancient Society and Institutions: Studies Presented to Victor Ehrenberg*, pp. 71–92. Oxford.

Buchanan, J. J. 1962. *Theorika: A Study of Monetary Distributions to the Athenian Citizenry during the Fifth and Fourth Centuries B.C.* Locust Valley, N.Y.

Buck, R. J. 1972. "The Formation of the Boiotian League." *CPh* 67:94–101.

Burford, A. 1972. *Craftsmen in Greek and Roman Society.* London.

Burnet, J., ed. 1900. *The Ethics of Aristotle.* London.

Busolt, G. 1893–95. *Griechische Geschichte.* 2d ed. Gotha.

Busolt, G., and G. Swoboda. 1920–26. *Griechische Staatskunde.* Vols. 1–2. Munich.

Buxton, J. C. 1966. *Chiefs and Strangers.* Oxford.

Cadoux, T. J. 1948. "The Athenian Archons from Kreon to Hypsichides." *JHS* 68:70–123.

Cahn, H. A. 1975. "Dating the Early Coinage of Athens." In *Kleine Schriften zur Munzkunde und Archäologie*, pp. 81–89. Basel.

Camp, J. McK. 1979. "A Drought in the Late Eighth Century B.C." *Hesperia* 48:398–411.

——. 1983. Review of *Studies in Attic Epigraphy, History and Topography Presented to Eugene Vanderpool*. *AJA* 87:113–15.

——. 1986. *The Athenian Agora*. London.

Campbell, J. K. 1964. *Honour, Family, and Patronage*. Oxford.

Carlier, P. 1984. *La Royauté en Grèce avant Alexandre*. Strasbourg.

Carneiro, R. 1961. "Slash and Burn Cultivation among the Kuikuru and Its Implications for Cultural Development in the Amazon Basin." In *The Evolution of Horticultural Systems in Native South America*, edited by J. Wilbert, pp. 47–67. Caracas.

——. 1967. "On the Relationship Between Size of Population and Complexity of Social Organization." *Southwest Journal of Anthropology* 23:234–43.

——. 1970. "A Theory of the Origin of the State." *Science* 109:733–38.

Carter, L. B. 1986. *The Quiet Athenian*. Oxford.

Cartledge, P. 1977. "Hoplites and Heroes: Sparta's Contribution to the Techniques of Ancient Warfare." *JHS* 97:11–27.

——. 1979. *Sparta and Lakonia: A Regional History*. London.

——. 1980. "The Peculiar Position of Sparta in the Development of the Greek City-State." *Proceedings of the Royal Irish Academy* 80:91–108.

——. 1983a. "Trade and Politics Revisited: Archaic Greece." In *Trade in the Ancient Economy*. See Garnsey et al., eds. 1983.

——. 1983b. Review of P. J. Rhodes, *A Commentary on the Aristotelian Athēnaiōn Politeia*. *Hermathena* 134:77–85.

——. 1985. "Rebels and Sambos in Ancient Greece: A Comparative View." In *Crux: Essays Presented to G.E.M. de Ste. Croix*. See Cartledge and Harvey, eds. 1985.

Cartledge, P., and F. D. Harvey, eds. 1985. *Crux: Essays Presented to G.E.M. de Ste. Croix on his 75th Birthday*. London.

Cassola, F. 1964. "Solone, la terra, e gli ectemori." *PP* 19:25–67.

——. 1973. "La Proprietà del suolo fin a Pisistrato." *PP* 28:75–87.

Cataudella, M. 1966. *Atene fra il VII e il VI secolo*. Catania.

Cawkwell, G. L. 1988. "NOMOPHYLAKIA and the Areopagus." *JHS* 108:1–12.

Chadwick, J. 1975. "The Prehistory of the Greek Language." In *Cambridge Ancient History. See* Edwards et al., eds. 1975.

————. 1976. *The Mycenean World.* Cambridge.

Chandler, L. 1926. "The Northwest Frontier of Attica." *JHS* 46:1–21.

Cherry, J. 1984. "The Emergence of the State in the Prehistoric Aegean." *PCPhS* 30:18–48.

Chrimes, K.M.T. 1932. "On Solon's Property Classes." *CR* 46:2–4.

Claessen, H.J.M., and P. Skalnik. 1978. "The Early State: Theories and Hypotheses." In *The Early State. See* Claessen and Skalnik, eds. 1978.

————, eds. 1978. *The Early State.* The Hague.

Clairmont, C. W. 1983. *Patrios Nomos: Public Burial in Athens during the Fifth and Fourth Centuries B.C.* British Archaeological Reports, Int. Series 161. Oxford.

Clark, S.R.L. 1975. *Aristotle's Man.* Oxford.

Claus, D. 1977. "Defining Moral Terms in *Works and Days.*" *TAPhA* 107:73–84.

Cohen, E. E. 1973. *Ancient Athenian Maritime Courts.* Princeton.

Cohen, R. 1970. "Incorporation in Bornu." In *From Tribe to Nation in Africa. See* Cohen and Middleton, eds. 1970.

————. 1978a. "Introduction." In *Origins of the State. See* Cohen and Service, eds. 1978.

————. 1978b. "State Origins: A Reappraisal." In *The Early State. See* Claessen and Skalnik, eds. 1978.

————. 1978c. "State Foundations: A Controlled Comparison." In *Origins of the State. See* Cohen and Service, eds. 1978.

Cohen, R., and J. Middleton. 1970. "Introduction." In *From Tribe to Nation in Africa. See* Cohen and Middleton, eds. 1970.

————, eds. 1970. *From Tribe to Nation in Africa: Studies in the Incorporation Process.* Scranton, Pa.

Cohen, R., and E. R. Service, eds. 1978. *Origins of the State.* Philadelphia.

Coldstream, J. N. 1968. *Greek Geometric Pottery.* London.

————. 1976. "Hero-cults in the Age of Homer." *JHS* 96:8–17.

————. 1977. *Geometric Greece.* London.

————. 1983. "The Meaning of the Regional Styles in the Eighth Century B.C." In *The Greek Renaissance of the Eighth Century B.C. See* Hägg, ed. 1983.

————. 1984. *The Formation of the Greek Polis: Aristotle and Archaeology.* Opladen.

Cole, A. T. 1961. "The Anonymus Iamblichi and His Place in Greek Political Theory." *HSCPh* 65:127–63.

Cole, S. G. 1984. "The Social Function of Rituals of Naturalization: The *Koureion* and the *Arkteia*." *ZPE* 55:233–44.

Colson, E. 1963. "Land Rights and Land Use among the Valley Tonga of the Rhodesian Federation: The Background of the Kariba Resettlement Program." In *African Agrarian Systems. See* Biebuyck, ed. 1963a.

―――. 1970. "The Assimilation of Aliens among Zambian Tonga." In *From Tribe to Nation in Africa. See* Cohen and Middleton, eds. 1970.

Connor, W. R. 1970. "Theseus in Classical Athens." In *The Quest for Theseus*, pp. 143–74. London.

―――. 1971. *The New Politicians of Fifth-Century Athens*. Princeton.

―――. 1982. Review of M. Gagarin, *Drakon and Early Athenian Homicide Law. AHR* 87:1057.

―――. 1986. "The New Classical Humanities and the Old." *CJ* 81:337–47.

―――. 1987. "Tribes, Festivals, and Processions: Civic Ceremonial and Political Manipulation in Archaic Greece." *JHS* 107:40–50.

Cook, J. M. 1975. "Greek Settlement in the Eastern Aegean and Asia Minor." In *Cambridge Ancient History. See* I. Edwards et al., eds. 1975.

Cook, R. M. 1972. *Greek Painted Pottery*. 2d ed. London.

Cornelius, F. 1929. *Die Tyrannis in Athen*. Munich.

Coulton, J. J. 1977. *Greek Architects at Work*. London.

Cox, C. A. 1988. "Sisters, Daughters, and the Deme of Marriage." *JHS* 108:185–88.

Crawford, M. H. 1972. "Solon's Alleged Reform of Weights and Measures." *Eirene* 10:5–8.

Crome, J. 1935–36. "Hipparcheioi Hermai." *AM* 60–61:300–13.

Damaskenides, A. N. 1965. "Problems of the Greek Rural Economy." *Balkan Studies* 6:21–34.

Dantwala, M. L. 1956. "Problems in Countries with Heavy Pressure of Population on Land: The Case of India." In *Land Tenure. See* Parsons et al., eds. 1956.

David, E. 1984. "Solon, Neutrality and Partisan Literature of Late 5th-Century Athens." *MH* 41:129–38.

―――. 1986. "A Preliminary Stage of Cleisthenes' Reforms." *ClAnt* 5:1–13.

Davies, J. K. 1971. *Athenian Propertied Families*. Oxford.

———. 1977–78. "Athenian Citizenship: The Descent Group and the Alternatives." *CJ* 73:105–21.

———. 1978. *Democracy and Classical Greece*. Glasgow.

———. 1981. *Wealth and the Power of Wealth in Classical Athens*. New York.

Davison, J. A. 1958. "Notes on the Panathenaia." *JHS* 78:22–41.

———. 1962. "Addenda." *JHS* 82:141–42.

DeLaix, R. A. 1973. *Probouleusis at Athens*. Berkeley, Calif.

De Sanctis, G. 1912. *Atthis: Storia della Repubblica Ateniese*. 2d ed. Turin.

Desborough, V.R.d'A. 1964. *The Last Mycenaeans and Their Successors*. Oxford.

———. 1972. *The Greek Dark Ages*. London.

Detienne, M. 1968. "La phalange: Problèmes et controverses." In *Problèmes de la guerre en Grèce ancienne*, edited by J.-P. Vernant, pp. 119–42. Paris.

Develin, R. 1979. "The Election of Archons from Solon to Telesinos." *AC* 48:455–68.

Diamant, S. 1982. "Theseus and the Unification of Attica." In *Studies in Attic Epigraphy, History and Topography Presented to Eugene Vanderpool* (*Hesperia* Supp. 19), pp. 38–47. Princeton.

Dickie, M. W. 1978. "*Dike* as a Moral Term in Homer and Hesiod." *CPh* 73:91–101.

Diller, A. 1937. *Race Mixture among the Greeks*. Urbana, Ill.

Dodds, E. R. 1951. *The Greeks and the Irrational*. Berkeley, Calif.

———, ed. 1959. *Plato. Gorgias*. Oxford.

Donlan, W. 1985. "The Social Groups of Dark Age Greece," *CPh* 80:293–308.

Dontas, G. 1983. "The True Aglaurion." *Hesperia* 52:48–63.

Dover, K. J. 1974. *Greek Popular Morality in the Time of Plato and Aristotle*. Oxford.

Drerup, H. 1969. *Griechische Baukunst in der geometrischer Zeit*. In *Archaeologia Homerica. Die Denkmäler und das frühgriechische Epos*, edited by F. Matz and H. G. Buchholz, bd. ii, Lief. O. Göttingen.

Drews, R. 1983. *Basileus: The Evidence for Kingship in Geometric Greece*. New Haven, Conn.

Droegemueller, H. P. 1970. "Stadtischer Raum und politischer Machtbereich in der Entwicklung der griechischen Polis." *Gymnasium* 77:484–507.

Du Boulay, J. 1974. *Portrait of a Greek Mountain Village.* Oxford.

Dummond, D. E. 1965. "Population Growth and Cultural Change." *Southwest Journal of Anthropology* 21:302–24.

———. 1972. "Population Growth and Political Centralization." In *Population Growth. See* Spooner, ed. 1972a.

Dunbabin, T. J. 1936–37. "*Echthrē Palaiē.*" *ABSA* 37:83–91.

———. 1950. "An Attic Bowl." *ABSA* 45:193–202.

Duncan-Jones, R. P. 1980. "Metic Numbers in Periclean Athens." *Chiron* 10:101–9.

Duthoy, R. 1986. "Qu'est-ce qu'une POLIS?" *LEC* 54:3–20.

Edwards, I.E.S., C. J. Gadd, N.G.L. Hammond, and E. Sollberger, eds. 1975. *Cambridge Ancient History.* Vol. ii.2. 3d ed. Cambridge.

Effenterre, H. van. 1976. "Clisthène et les mesures de mobilisation." *REG* 89:1–17.

———. 1977. "Solon et la terre d'Eleusis." *RIDA* 24:91–130.

———. 1985. *La Cité grecque: Des origines à la défaite de Marathon.* Paris.

Ehrenberg, V. 1937. "When Did the Polis Rise?" *JHS* 57:147–59.

———. 1946. "Early Athenian Colonies." In *Aspects of the Ancient World,* pp. 116–43. Oxford.

———. 1969. *The Greek State.* 2d ed. London.

Eliot, C.W.J. 1962. *Coastal Demes of Attika: A Study in the Policy of Kleisthenes.* Toronto.

Engels, D. 1984. "The Use of Historical Demography in Ancient History." *CQ* 34:386–93.

Engels, F. 1891. *The Origin of the Family, Private Property, and the State.* Reprinted ed., E. B. Leacock, ed. 1972. New York.

Farrar, C. 1988. *The Origins of Democratic Thinking: The Invention of Politics in Classical Athens.* Cambridge.

Ferguson, W. S. 1936. "The Athenian Law Code and Old Attic Trittyes." In *Classical Studies Presented to Edward Capps,* pp. 144–58. Princeton.

———. 1938. "The Salaminioi of Heptaphylai and Sounion." *Hesperia* 7:1–74.

———. 1944. "The Attic Orgeones." *HThR* 37:62–140.

Figueira, T. J. 1981. *Aegina.* New York.

———. 1984. "The Ten Archontes of 579/8 at Athens." *Hesperia* 53:447–74.

———. 1986. "Xanthippos, Father of Perikles, and the Prytaneis of the Naukraroi." *Historia* 35:257–79.

Fine, J.V.A. 1951. *Horoi: Studies in Mortgage, Real Security and Land Tenure in Ancient Athens*. Baltimore.

Finley, M. I. 1951. *Studies in Land and Credit in Ancient Athens 500–200 B.C.* New Brunswick, N.J.

———. 1957. "The Mycenaean Tablets and Economic History." *Economic History Review* 10:128–41.

———. 1965. "La Servitude pour dettes." *RD* 4.43:159–84.

———, ed. 1979. *The Bücher-Meyer Controversy*. New York.

———. 1980. *Ancient Slavery and Modern Ideology*. New York.

———. 1981a. "The Freedom of the Citizen in the Greek World." In *Economy and Society in Ancient Greece*, edited by B. D. Shaw and R. Saller, pp. 77–94. New York.

———. 1981b. "The Ancient City: From Fustel de Coulanges to Max Weber and Beyond." In *Economy and Society in Ancient Greece*, edited by B. D. Shaw and R. Saller, pp. 3–23. New York.

———. 1981c. "Land, Debt, and the Man of Property in Classical Athens." In *Economy and Society in Ancient Greece*, edited by B. D. Shaw and R. Saller, pp. 62–76. New York.

———. 1981d. "Between Slavery and Freedom." In *Economy and Society in Ancient Greece*, edited by B. D. Shaw and R. Saller, pp. 116–32. New York.

———. 1981e. "The Athenian Empire: A Balance Sheet." In *Economy and Society in Ancient Greece*, edited by B. D. Shaw and R. Saller, pp. 41–61. New York.

———. 1983. *Politics in the Ancient World*. Cambridge.

———. 1985. *The Ancient Economy*. 2d ed. London.

———. 1986a. "Anthropology and the Classics." In *The Use and Abuse of History*, 2d ed., pp. 102–19. New York.

———. 1986b. "Max Weber and the Greek City State." In *Ancient History: Evidence and Models*, pp. 88–103. New York.

———. 1986c. "The Alienability of Land in Ancient Greece." In *Use and Abuse of History*, 2d ed., pp. 153–60. New York.

Fisher, N.R.E., ed. 1976. *Social Values in Classical Athens*. London.

Forrest, W. G. 1956. "The First Sacred War." *BCH* 80:33–52.

———. 1966. *The Emergence of Greek Democracy*. London.

———. 1980. *A History of Sparta 950–192 B.C.* 2d ed. London.

Forrest, W. G., and D. L. Stockton. 1987. "The Athenian Archons: A Note." *Historia* 36:235–40.

Fortes, M. 1940. "The Political System of the Tallensi of the Northern Territories of the Gold Coast." In *African Political Systems*. See Fortes and Evans-Pritchard, eds. 1940.

Fortes, M. 1949. *The Dynamics of Clanship among the Tallensi.* London.

———. 1969. *Kinship and the Social Order.* Chicago.

Fortes, M., and E. E. Evans-Pritchard, eds. 1940. *African Political Systems.* London.

Fox, R. L. 1985. "Aspects of Inheritance in the Greek World." In *Crux: Essays Presented to G.E.M. de Ste. Croix. See* Cartledge and Harvey, eds. 1985.

Francis, E. D., and M. J. Vickers. 1983. "*Signa priscae artis:* Eretria and Siphnos." *JHS* 103:49–67.

Freeman, K. 1926. *The Work and Life of Solon.* Cardiff.

Frei, P. 1981. "Politik im Spiegel griechischer Worbildungslehre." *MH* 38:205–13.

French, A. 1956. "The Economic Background to Solon's Reforms." *CQ* 50:11–25.

———. 1961. "A Note on Thucydides iii 68.5." *JHS* 81:191.

———. 1964. *The Growth of the Athenian Economy.* London.

———. 1984. "Solon's Act of Mediation." *Antichthon* 18:1–12.

Fried, M. H. 1967. *The Evolution of Political Society.* New York.

———. 1978. "The State, the Chicken, and the Egg." In *Origins of the State. See* Cohen and Service, eds. 1978.

Fritz, K. von, and E. Kapp. 1950. *The Constitution of Athens and Aristotle's Political Philosophy.* New York.

Frost, F. J. 1976. "Tribal Politics and the Civic State." *AJAH* 1:67–73.

———. 1984. "The Athenian Military Before Cleisthenes." *Historia* 33:283–94.

Gabrielsen, V. 1981. *Remuneration of State Officials in Fourth-Century B.C. Athens.* Odense.

———. 1985. "The Naukrariai and the Athenian Navy." *C&M* 36:21–51.

Gagarin, M. 1973. "Dike in the *Works and Days.*" *CPh* 68:81–94.

———. 1974. "Dike in Archaic Greek Thought." *CPh* 69:186–97.

———. 1981a. "The Thesmothetai and the Earliest Athenian Tyranny Law." *TAPhA* 111:71–77.

———. 1981b. *Drakon and Early Athenian Homicide Law.* New Haven, Conn.

———. 1986. *Early Greek Law.* Berkeley and Los Angeles.

———. 1987. "Morality in Homer." *CPh* 82:285–306.

Gallant, T. W. 1982. "Agricultural Systems, Land Tenure, and the Reforms of Solon." *ABSA* 77:11–124.

Garbett, G. K. 1963. "The Land Husbandry Act of Southern Rhodesia." In *African Agrarian Systems. See* Biebuyck, ed. 1963a.

Garlan, Y. 1982. *Les Esclaves en Grèce ancienne.* Paris.

Garner, R. 1987. *Law and Society in Classical Athens.* London.

Garnsey, P. 1985. "Grain for Athens." In *Crux: Essays Presented to G.E.M. de Ste. Croix. See* Cartledge and Harvey, eds. 1985.

———. 1988. *Famine and Food Supply in the Graeco-Roman World.* Cambridge.

Garnsey, P., K. Hopkins, and C. R. Whittaker, eds. 1983. *Trade in the Ancient Economy.* Berkeley, Calif.

Garnsey, P., and C. R. Whittaker, eds. 1978. *Imperialism in the Ancient World.* Cambridge.

———. 1983. *Trade and Famine in Classical Antiquity.* Cambridge.

Gauthier, P. 1971. "Les XENOI dans les textes athéniens de la seconde moitié du Ve siècle av. J.-C." *REG* 84:44–79.

———. 1972. *Symbola.* Nancy.

———. 1974. Générosité romaine et avarice grecque." In *Mélanges d'historie ancienne offerts à W. Seston*, pp. 207–15. Paris.

———. 1981. "La Citoyenneté en Grèce et à Rome: Participation et integration." *Ktema* 6:167–79.

Gawantka, W. 1975. *Isopolitie.* Munich.

———. 1985. *Die sogennante Polis.* Stuttgart.

Geertz, C. 1973. "Thick Description: Toward an Interpretative Theory of Culture." In *The Interpretation of Cultures*, pp. 3–30. New York.

Gernet, L. 1920. "La Création du testament." *REG* 23:123–68, 249–90.

———. 1921. "Sur l'épiclerat." *REG* 34:337–79.

———. 1968. *Anthropologie de la Grèce antique.* Paris.

———. 1983. "La Famille dans l'antiquité grecque. Vue générale." *AION* (arch.) 5:173–95.

Gettys, L. 1934. *The Law of Citizenship in the United States.* Chicago.

Gigante, M. 1956. *Nomos Basileus.* Naples.

Gilliard, C. 1907. *Quelques réformes de Solon.* Lausanne.

Glass, D. V., and D.E.C. Eversley. 1965. *Population in History.* London.

Glotz, G. 1904. *La Solidarité de la famille dans le droit criminel en Grèce.* Paris.

———. 1930. *The Greek City and Its Institutions.* New York.

Gluckman, M. 1965. *Politics, Law, and Ritual in Tribal Society*. Chicago.

Golden, M. 1979. "Demosthenes and the Age of Majority at Athens." *Phoenix* 33:25–38.

———. 1981. *Aspects of Childhood in Classical Athens*. Ph.D. dissertation, University of Toronto.

———. 1985. "Donatus and Athenian Phratries." *CQ* 35:9–13.

Goldhill, S. 1986. *Reading Greek Tragedy*. Cambridge.

Gomme, A. W. 1933. *The Population of Athens in the Fifth and Fourth Centuries B.C.* Oxford.

———. 1934. "Two Problems of Athenian Citizenship Law." *CPh* 29:123–40.

———. 1937. "The Speeches on Thucydides." In *Essays on Greek History and Literature*, pp. 156–89. Oxford.

———. 1962. "The Working of Athenian Democracy." In *More Essays in Greek History and Literature*, pp. 177–93. Oxford.

Gomme, A. W., K. J. Dover, and A. Andrewes, eds. 1945–81. *A Historical Commentary on Thucydides*. Vols. 1–5. Oxford.

Goody, J. 1970. "Marriage Policy and Incorporation in Northern Ghana." In *From Tribe to Nation in Africa. See* Cohen and Middleton, eds. 1970.

———. 1976. *Production and Reproduction: A Comparative Study of the Domestic Domain*. Cambridge.

Gould, J. P. 1980. "Law, Custom, and Myth: Aspects of the Social Position of Women in Classical Athens." *JHS* 100:38–59.

Grace, E. 1973. "Status Distinctions in the Draconian Law." *Eirene* 11:5–30.

Graham, A. J. 1971. "Patterns in Early Greek Colonisation," *JHS* 91:33–47.

———. 1982. "The Colonial Expansion of Greece." In *Cambridge Ancient History. See* Boardman and Hammond, eds. 1982.

Greenhalgh, P.A.L. 1973. *Early Greek Warfare*. Cambridge.

Griffith, G. T. 1966. "Isegoria in the Assembly at Athens." In *Ancient Society and Institutions: Studies Presented to Victor Ehrenberg*, pp. 115–38. Oxford.

———. 1978. "Athens in the Fourth Century." In *Imperialism in the Ancient World. See* Garnsey and Whittaker, eds. 1978.

Grigg, D. 1980. *Population Growth and Agrarian Change: An Historical Perspective*. Cambridge.

Guarducci, M. 1937. "L'Istituzione della fratria nella Grecia antica e nelle colonie greche." *MAL* 6.6:5–108.

Guiraud, P. 1893. *La Propriété foncière en Grèce jusqu'à la conquête romaine.* Paris.

Guthrie, W.K.C. 1965. *The Presocratic Tradition from Parmenides to Democritus.* Vol. 2 of *A History of Greek Philosophy.* Cambridge.

———. 1969. *The Fifth-Century Enlightenment.* Vol. 3 of *A History of Greek Philosophy.* Cambridge.

———. 1979. "Reply to R. G. Mulgan." *JHI* 40:128.

Gutkind, E. 1969. *Urban Development in Southern Europe: Italy and Greece.* New York.

Gutkind, P.C.W., ed. 1970. *The Passing of Tribal Man in Africa.* Leiden.

Gwynn, A. 1918. "The Character of Greek Colonization." *JHS* 38:88–123.

Haas, J. 1985. "Athenian Naval Power." *Historia* 34:29–46.

Haas, Jonathan. 1982. *The Evolution of the Prehistoric State.* New York.

Hägg, R., ed. 1983. *The Greek Renaissance of the Eighth Century B.C.: Tradition and Innovation.* Proceedings of the Second International Symposium at the Swedish Institute in Athens. Stockholm.

Hahn, I. 1983. "Foreign Trade and Foreign Policy in Archaic Greece." In *Trade and Famine in Classical Antiquity. See* Garnsey and Whittaker, eds. 1983.

Hammond, N.G.L. 1956. "The Philaids and the Chersonese." *CQ* 50:113–29.

———. 1961. "Land Tenure and Solon's Seisachtheia." *JHS* 82:76–98.

———. 1986. *A History of Greece.* 3d ed. Oxford.

Hammond, N.G.L., and G. T. Griffith. 1976. *A History of Macedonia 550–336 B.C.* Vol. 2. Oxford.

Hampl, F. 1939. "Poleis ohne Territorium." *Klio* 32:1–60.

Hansen, M. H. 1975. *Eisangelia: The Sovereignty of the People's Court in Athens in the Fourth Century B.C. and the Impeachment of Generals and Politicians.* Odense.

———. 1976a. *Apagoge, Endeixis, and Ephegesis against Kakourgoi, Atimoi and Pheugontes.* Odense.

———. 1976b. "How Many Athenians Attended the *Ecclesia?*" *GRBS* 17:115–34.

———. 1977a. "How Often Did the *Ecclesia* Meet?" *GRBS* 18:43–70.

Hansen, M. H. 1977b. "How Did the Athenian *Ecclesia* Vote?" *GRBS* 18:123–37.

———. 1978. *"Demos, Ecclesia,* and *Dicasterion* in Classical Athens." *GRBS* 19:127–46.

———. 1979a. "The Duration of a Meeting of the Athenian *Ecclesia.*" *CPh* 74:43–49.

———. 1979b. "Misthos for Magistrates in Classical Athens." *SO* 54:5–22.

———. 1979c. "Did the Athenian *Ecclesia* Legislate after 403/2 B.C.?" *GRBS* 20:27–53.

———. 1979d. "How Often Did the Athenian *Dicasteria* Meet?" *GRBS* 20:243–46.

———. 1979e. *"Ekklesia sygkletos* in Hellenistic Athens." *GRBS* 20:149–56.

———. 1980a. "Perquisites for Magistrates in Fourth-Century Athens." *C&M* 32:105–25.

———. 1980b. "Seven Hundred *Archai* in Classical Athens." *GRBS* 21:151–73.

———. 1980c. "Eisangelia in Athens: A Reply." *JHS* 100:89–95.

———. 1981. "The Number of Athenian Hoplites in 431." *SO* 56:19–32.

———. 1981–82. "The Athenian Heliaia from Solon to Aristotle." *C&M* 33:9–47.

———. 1982a. "Demographic Reflections on the Number of Athenian Citizens 451–309 B.C." *AJAH* 7:172–89.

———. 1982b. "The Athenian *Ecclesia* and the Assembly-Place on the Pnyx." *GRBS* 23:241–49.

———. 1983a. "The Athenian Politicians 403–322 B.C." *GRBS* 24:33–56.

———. 1983b. "Political Activity and the Organization of Attica in the Fourth Century B.C." *GRBS* 24:227–38.

———. 1985a. "The History of the Athenian Constitution." Review of P. J. Rhodes, *A Commentary on the Aristotelian Athēnaiōn Politeia. CPh* 80:51–66.

———. 1985b. *Demography and Democracy: The Number of Athenian Citizens in the Fourth Century B.C.* Herning.

———. 1985c. "Nomothesia in Fourth-Century Athens." *CQ* 35:55–60.

———. 1987a. "The Political and Constitutional Powers of the Athenian *Dikasteria.*" Lecture at Princeton University, January 6 (unpublished).

———. 1987b. *The Athenian Assembly in the Age of Demosthenes.* Oxford.

———. 1988. "Three Studies in Athenian Demography." *Historisk-filosofiske Meddelelser* (Royal Danish Academy of Sciences and Letters) 56:2–28.

Hardie, W.F.R. 1980. *Aristotle's Ethical Theory.* 2d ed. Oxford.

Harner, M. J. 1970. "Population Pressure and the Social Evolution of Agriculturalists." *Southwest Journal of Anthropology* 26:67–86.

Harris, E. M. 1986. "How Often Did the Athenian Assembly Meet?" *CQ* 36:363–77.

Harrison, A.R.W. 1968. *The Law of Athens.* Vol. 1, *The Family and Property.* Oxford.

———. 1971. *The Law of Athens.* Vol. 2, *Procedure.* Oxford.

Hasebroek, J. 1933. *Trade and Politics in Ancient Greece.* Engl. trans. of *Griechische Wirtschafts- und Gesellschaftsgeschichte.* London.

Haussoullier, B. 1884. *La Vie municipale en Attique.* Paris.

Havelock, E. A. 1969. "Dikaiosyne: An Essay in Greek Intellectual History." *Phoenix* 23:49–70.

———. 1978. *The Greek Concept of Justice from Its Shadow in Homer to Its Substance in Plato.* Cambridge.

Hedrick, C. W. 1983. "Old and New on the Attic Phratry of the Therrikleidai." *Hesperia* 52:299–302.

———. 1984. *The Attic Phratry.* Ph.D. dissertation, University of Pennsylvania.

———. 1988a. "The Thymaitian Phratry." *Hesperia* 57:81–83.

———. 1988b. "An Honorific Phratry Inscription." *AJPh* 109:111–17.

———. 1988c. "The Temple and Cult of Apollo Patroos in Athens." *AJA* 92:185–210.

———. 1989. "Phratry Shrines of Attica and Athens." *Hesperia* 58: in press.

Herington, C. J. 1955. *Athena Parthenos and Athena Polias.* Manchester.

Herman, G. 1987. *Ritualised Friendship and the Greek City.* Cambridge.

Higgins, R. A. 1969. "Early Greek Jewellery." *ABSA* 64:143–53.

Hignett, C. 1952. *A History of the Athenian Constitution.* Oxford.

Hobhouse, L. T., G. Wheeler, and M. Ginsburg. 1915. *The Material Culture and Social Institutions of Simpler Peoples.* London.

Holladay, A. J. 1977. "The Followers of Peisistratos." *G&R* 24:40–56.

———. 1982. "Hoplites and Heresies." *JHS* 102:94–103.

Hollingsworth, T. H. 1969. *Historical Demography*. Ithaca, N.Y.

Holmes, S. T. 1979. "Aristippus In and Out of Athens." *American Political Science Review* 73:113–28.

Homan, F. 1963. "Land Consolidation and Redistribution of Population in the Imenti Sub-Tribe of the Meru (Kenya)." In *African Agrarian Systems. See* Biebuyck, ed. 1963a.

Hommel, H. 1939. "Trittys." In Pauly-Wissowa, *Real-Encyclopaedie der classischen Altertumswissenschaft* 13:334–35.

Hooker, J. T. 1976. *Mycenaean Greece*. London.

Hopper, R. J. 1957. *The Basis of the Athenian Democracy*. Sheffield.

———. 1961. " 'Plain,' 'Shore,' and 'Hill' in Early Athens." *ABSA* 56:189–219.

———. 1976. *The Early Greeks*. London.

———. 1979. *Trade and Industry in Classical Greece*. London.

How, W. W., and J. Wells. 1928. *A Commentary on Herodotus*. Corrected ed. Vols. 1–2. Oxford.

Humphreys, S. C. 1974. "The Nothoi of Kynosarges." *JHS* 94:88–95.

———. 1978. *Anthropology and the Greeks*. London.

———. 1983a. "Oikos and Polis." In *The Family, Women, and Death*, pp. 1–21. London.

———. 1983b. "Women in Antiquity." In *The Family, Women, and Death*, pp. 33–50. London.

———. 1983c. "Public and Private Interests in Classical Athens." In *The Family, Women, and Death*, pp. 23-32. London.

———. 1983d. "The Family in Classical Athens: Search for a Perspective." In *The Family, Women, and Death*, pp. 55–78. London.

———. 1983e. "Family Tombs and Tomb Cult in Ancient Athens: Tradition or Traditionalism?" In *The Family, Women, and Death*, pp. 79–130. London.

———. 1983f. "Introduction." In *The Family, Women, and Death*, pp. ix–xiv. London.

———. 1983g. "Greeks and Others." In *The Family, Women, and Death*, pp. 51–54. London.

———. 1983h. "The Evolution of Legal Process in Ancient Attica." In *Tria Corda: Scritti in onore di Arnaldo Momigliano*, edited by E. Gabba, pp. 229–56. Como.

———. 1985a. "Law as Discourse." *History and Anthropology* 1:241–64.

———. 1985b. "Social Relations on Stage." *History and Anthropology* 1:331–69.

Hussey, E. 1972. *The Presocratics.* London.

———. 1985. "Thucydidean History and Democritean Theory." In *Crux: Essays Presented to G.E.M. de Ste. Croix. See* Cartledge and Harvey, eds. 1985.

Huxley, G. L. 1962. *Early Sparta.* London.

———. 1979. *On Aristotle and Greek Society: An Essay.* Belfast.

Iliopoulos, P. J. 1951. *L'Attique au point de vue physique et économique.* Athens.

Immerwahr, H. R. 1986. "Early Greek Literacy." Abstract of paper read at 87th General Meeting of Archaeological Institute of America. *AJA* 90:178–79.

Irwin, T. 1985. "Moral Science and Political Theory in Aristotle." In *Crux: Essays Presented to G.E.M. de Ste. Croix. See* Cartledge and Harvey, eds. 1985.

Jacoby, F. 1944. "*GENESIA*: A Forgotten Festival of the Dead." *CQ* 38:65–75.

———. 1949. *Atthis: The Local Chronicles of Ancient Athens.* Oxford.

Jaeger, W. 1946. *Paideia.* 2d ed. Oxford.

Jameson, M. 1965. "Notes on the Sacrificial Calendar from Erchia." *BCH* 89:154–72.

———. 1977–78. "Agriculture and Slavery in Classical Athens." *CJ* 73:122–45.

———. 1983. "Famine in the Greek World." In *Trade and Famine in Classical Antiquity. See* Garnsey and Whittaker, eds. 1983.

Jeffery, L. H. 1962. "The Inscribed Gravestones of Archaic Attika." *ABSA* 57:115–53.

———. 1976. *Archaic Greece: The City States c. 700–500 B.C.* London.

Johnson, C. 1984. "Who Is Aristotle's Citizen?" *Phronesis* 29:73–90.

Johnston, A. W. 1972. "The Rehabilitation of Sostratos." *PP* 27:416–23.

———. 1979. *Trademarks on Greek Vases.* Warminster.

Johnston, A. W., and R. E. Jones. 1978. "The 'SOS' Amphorae." *ABSA* 73:103–41.

Jones, A.H.M. 1957. *Athenian Democracy.* Oxford.

Jones, A.H.M. 1974. "Taxation in Antiquity." In *The Roman Economy: Studies in Ancient Economic and Administrative History*, edited by P. Brunt, pp. 151–85. Oxford.

Jordan, B. 1970. "Herodotus 5.71.2 and the Naukraroi of Athens." *CSCA* 3:153–75.

———. 1979. *Servants of the Gods*. Göttingen.

Kagan, D. 1960. "The Origin and Purpose of Ostracism." *Hesperia* 30:393–401.

———. 1963. "The Enfranchisement of Aliens by Cleisthenes." *Historia* 12:41–46.

———. 1965. *The Great Dialogue*. New York.

———. 1969. *The Outbreak of the Peloponnesian War*. Ithaca, N.Y.

———. 1974. *The Archidamian War*. Ithaca, N.Y.

———. 1975. "The Speeches in Thucydides and the Mytilene Debate." *YClS* 24:71–94.

———. 1981. *The Peace of Nicias and the Sicilian Expedition*. Ithaca, N.Y.

———. 1982a. "Pericles' Vision of Athens." Paper delivered to the Yale College Chapter of Phi Beta Kappa, December 17 (unpublished).

———. 1982b. "The Dates of the Earliest Coins." *AJA* 86:343–60.

———. 1987. *The Fall of the Athenian Empire*. Ithaca, N.Y.

Keaney, J. J. 1970. "The Text of Androtion F 6 and the Origin of Ostracism." *Historia* 19:1–11.

———. 1980. "Hignett's HAC and the Authorship of the *Athēnaiōn Politeia*." *LCM* 5:51–56.

Kearns, E. 1985. "Change and Continuity in Religious Structures after Kleisthenes." In *Crux: Essays Presented to G.E.M. de Ste. Croix. See* Cartledge and Harvey, eds. 1985.

Kerferd, G. B. 1981. *The Sophistic Movement*. Cambridge.

Kettner, J. 1978. *The Development of American Citizenship 1608–1870*. Chapel Hill, N.C.

Keynes, J. M. 1930. *A Treatise on Money*. Vols. 1–2. New York.

Kinzl, K. 1977. "Athens: Between Tyranny and Democracy." In *Greece and the Eastern Mediterranean in Ancient History and Prehistory* (Studies for F. Schachermeyr), edited by K. Kinzl, pp. 199–223. New York and Berlin.

———. 1987. "On the Consequences of Following AP 21.4 (On the Trittyes of Attika)." *Ancient History Bulletin* 1:25–33.

Kirchner, J., and S. Dow. 1937. "Inschriften vom attischen Lande." *AM* 6:1–3.

Kirk, G. 1977. "The Hektemoroi of pre-Solonian Athens Reconsidered." *Historia* 26:369–70.

Kirsten, E. 1956. *Die griechische Polis als historisch-geographisches Problem des Mittelmeeraumes.* Bonn.

Kluwe, E. 1976. "Die soziale Zusammensetzung der athenischen Ekklesia." *Klio* 58:295–333.

Köbben, A. 1963. "Land as an Object of Gain in a Non-literate Society: Land Tenure among the Bete and Dida (Ivory Coast, West Africa)." In *African Agrarian Systems. See* Biebuyck, ed. 1963a.

Kolb, F. 1977. "Die Bau-, Reigions-, und Kulturpolitik der Peisistratiden." *JDAI* 92:99–138.

Koppers, W. 1963. *L'Origine de l'état. Sixth International Congress of Anthropological and Ethnological Sciences, 1960. Paris.* 1:159–68.

Kornemann, E. 1908. "Stadtstaat und Flachenstaat der Altertums in ihren Wechselbeziehungen." *Neue Jahrbucher für das Klassische Altertum Geschichte und deutsche Literatur und für Pädagogik* 21:233–53.

Kraay, C. 1956. "The Archaic Owls of Athens." *NC* 16:43–68.

———. 1962. "The Early Coinage of Athens." *NC* 22:417–23.

———. 1968. "An Interpretation of *Ath. Pol.* 10." In *Essays in Greek Coinage Presented to Stanley Robinson,* edited by C. M. Kraay and G. K. Jenkins, pp. 1–9. Oxford.

———. 1976. *Archaic and Classical Greek Coins.* London.

Krader, L. 1968. *The Formation of the State.* Englewood Cliffs, N.J.

Kränzlein, A. 1963. *Eigentum und Besitz im griechischen Recht des fünften und vierten Jahrhunderts v. Chr.* Berlin.

Kraut, R. 1984. *Socrates and the State.* Princeton.

Krentz, P. 1980. "Foreigners Against the Thirty: IG ii² 10 Again." *Phoenix* 34:298–306.

———. 1982. *The Thirty at Athens.* Ithaca, N.Y.

———. 1985. "The Nature of Hoplite Battle." *ClAnt* 4:50–61.

———. 1986. "The Rewards for Thrasyboulos' Supporters," *ZPE* 62:201–4.

Kretschmer, P. 1894. *Griechische Vaseninschriften.* Gutersloh.

Kroll, J. H., and N. M. Waggoner. 1984. "Dating the Earliest Coins of Athens, Corinth and Aegina." *AJA* 88:325–40.

Kuper, L. 1969. "Strangers in Plural Societies: Asians in South Africa and Uganda." In *Pluralism in Africa,* edited by L. Kuper and M. G. Smith, pp. 247–62. Berkeley, Calif.

Kurtz, D., and J. Boardman. 1971. *Greek Burial Customs.* London.

Labarbe, J. 1953. "L'Age correspondant au sacrifice du koureion et les données du sixième discours d'Isée." *BAB* 5.39:358–93.

Lacey, W. K. 1968. *The Family in Classical Greece*. Ithaca, N.Y.

Lambert, S. D. 1986. "Herodotus, the Cylonian Conspiracy and the *prytaneis ton naukraron.*" *Historia* 35:105–12.

Lang, M. 1967. "Kylonian Conspiracy." *CPh* 62:243–49.

Langdon, M. 1985. "The Territorial Basis of the Attic Demes." *SO* 60:5–16.

Larsen, J.A.O. 1932. "Sparta and the Ionian Revolt: A Study of Spartan Foreign Policy and the Genesis of the Peloponnesian League." *CPh* 27:136–50.

———. 1933–34. "The Constitution of the Peloponnesian League." *CPh* 28:256–76; 29:1–19.

———. 1949. "The Origins and Significance of the Counting of Votes." *CPh* 44:164–81.

———. 1955. *Representative Government in Greek and Roman History*. Chicago.

———. 1962. "Freedom and Its Obstacles in Ancient Greece." *CPh* 57:230–34.

———. 1968. *Greek Federal States*. Oxford.

Latacz, J. 1977. *Kampfparänase, Kampfdarstellung, und Kampfwirklichkeit in der Ilias, bei Kallinos und Tyrtaios*. Munich.

Latte, K. 1920a. "Phyle." In Pauly-Wissowa, *Real-Encyclopaedie der classischen Altertumswissenschaft* 20:994–1011.

———. 1920b. "Phratrie." In Pauly-Wissowa, *Real-Encyclopaedie der classischen Altertumswissenschaft* 20:746–56.

———. 1968. *Kleine Schriften zu Religion, Recht, Literatur und Sprache der Griechen und Römer*. Munich.

Lauter, H. 1985. *Lathuresa: Beiträge zur Architektur und Siedlungsgeschichte im spätgeometrischer Zeit*. Mainz.

Layton, R. 1972. "Settlement and Community. Gemeinschaft and Gesellschaft." In *Man, Settlement, and Urbanism. See* Ucko et al., eds. 1972.

Leach, E. 1982. *Social Anthropology*. Oxford.

Ledl, A. 1907–8. "Das attische Bürgerrecht und die Frauen." *WS* 29:173–227; 30:1–46, 173–230.

Lepore, E. 1969. "Osservazioni sul rapporto tra fatti economici e fatti di colonizzazione in Occidente." *DArch* 3:175–212.

Lévêque, P. 1978. "Formes des contradictions et voies de développement à Athènes de Solon à Clisthène." *Historia* 27:522–49.

———. 1981. "La Genèse de la cité grecque: Société archaïque et cité-état." *La Pensée* 217–18: 24–32.

Lévêque, P., and P. Vidal-Naquet. 1964. *Clisthène l'Athenien*. Paris.

Levi, M. A. 1964. "Aspetti della società micenea e dello stato miceneo." *NRS* 48:91–99.

Levine, R. A. 1964. "The Gusii Family." In *The Family Estate in Africa*, edited by R. F. Graynand and P. H. Gulliver, pp. 63–82. London.

Lévy, E. 1980. "Cité et citoyen dans la Politique d'Aristote." *Ktema* 5:223–48.

Levy, H. L. 1972. "Inheritance and Dowry in Classical Athens." In *Mediterranean Countrymen*, edited by J. A. Pitt-Rivers, pp. 137–43. Westport, Conn.

Lewellen, T. 1983. *Political Anthropology: An Introduction*. South Hadley, Mass.

Lewis, D. M. 1963a. "Cleisthenes and Attica." *Historia* 12:22–40.

———. 1963b. Review of C.W.J. Eliot, *Coastal Demes of Attica*. *Gnomon* 35:723–25.

———. 1973. "The Athenian Rationes Centesimarum." In *Problèmes de la terre en Grèce ancienne*, edited by M. I. Finley, pp. 187–212. Paris.

———. 1988. "The Tyranny of the Peisistratidae." In *Cambridge Ancient History*. See Boardman et al., eds. 1988.

Lewis, I. M. 1985. *Social Anthropology in Perspective*. 2d ed. Cambridge.

Lewis, J. D. 1971. "Isegoria at Athens: When Did It Begin?" *Historia* 20:129–40.

Lewis, N. 1941. "Solon's Agrarian Legislation." *AJPh* 62:144–56.

Linforth, I. 1919. *Solon the Athenian*. Berkeley, Calif.

Littman, R. J. 1979. "Kinship in Athens." *AncSoc* 10:5–31.

Lloyd, G.E.R. 1968. *Aristotle: The Growth and Structure of His Thought*. Cambridge.

Lloyd-Jones, H. 1985. *The Justice of Zeus*. 2d ed. Berkeley, Calif.

———. 1987. "A Note on Homeric Morality." *CPh* 82:307–10.

Loraux, N. 1981. *Les Enfants d'Athéna: Idées athéniennes sur la citoyenneté et la division des sexes*. Paris.

———. 1984. "Solon au milieu de la lice." In *Aux origines de l'Hellénisme, La Crète, et La Grèce. Hommage à Henri van Effenterre*, pp. 199–214. Paris.

———. 1986. *The Invention of Athens: The Funeral Oration in the*

Classical City. Engl. trans. of *L'Invention de Athènes: Histoire de l'oraison funèbre dans la 'cité classique.'* Cambridge.

Lord, C. 1982. *Education and Culture in the Political Thought of Aristotle.* Ithaca, N.Y.

———, ed. 1984. *Aristotle. The Politics.* Chicago.

Lotze, D. 1981. "Zwischen Politen und Metoiken. Passivbürger im klassischen Athen?" *Klio* 63:159–78.

Lowie, R. H. 1927. *The Origin of the State.* New York.

Luce, J. V. 1978. "The Polis in Homer and Hesiod." *PRIA* 78:1–15.

Luzzi, G. 1980. "I nuovi cittadini di Clistene." *ASNP* 10:71–78.

MacDowell, D. M., ed. 1962. *Andokides. On the Mysteries.* Oxford.

———. 1963. *Athenian Homicide Law in the Age of the Orators.* Manchester.

———. 1978. *The Law in Classical Athens.* Ithaca, N.Y.

McGregor, M. F. 1973. "Athenian Policy, at Home and Abroad." In *Lectures in Memory of Louise Taft Semple,* pp. 53–66. Norman, Okla.

Maio, D. P. 1983. "*Politeia* and Adjudication in Fourth-Century B.C. Athens." *American Journal of Jurisprudence* 28:16–45.

Manville, P. B. 1979. *The Evolution of Athenian Citizenship: Individual and Society in the Archaic Age.* Ph.D. dissertation, Yale University.

———. 1980. "Solon's Law of Stasis and Atimia in Archaic Athens." *TAPhA* 110:213–21.

Markle, M. M. 1985. "Jury Pay and Assembly Pay at Athens." In *Crux: Essays Presented to G.E.M. de Ste. Croix. See* Cartledge and Harvey, eds. 1985.

Marshall, T. H. 1964. "Citizenship and Social Class." In *Class, Citizenship, and Social Development: Essays,* pp. 65–122. Garden City, N.Y.

Martin, R. 1975. *L'Urbanisme dans la Grèce antique.* 2d ed. Paris.

Masaracchia, A. 1958. *Solone.* Florence.

Meek, C. K. 1946. *Land Law and Custom in the Colonies.* New York.

Meier, C. 1973. "Clisthène et le problème politique de la polis grecque." *RIDA* 20:115–59.

———. 1977. "Der Wandel der politisch-sozialen Begriffswelt im 5.Jahrhundert v. Chr." *ABG* 21:7–41.

———. 1978. "Enstehung und Besonderheit der Griechischen Demokratie." *Zeitschrift für Politik* 25:1–31.

———. 1980. *Die Entstehung des Politischen bei den Griechen.* Frankfurt.

———. 1984. *Introduction à l'anthropologie politique de l'antiquité classique.* Paris.

Meiggs, R. 1972. *The Athenian Empire.* Oxford.

Meiggs, R., and D. M. Lewis. 1969. *A Selection of Greek Historical Inscriptions to the End of the Fifth Century B.C.* Oxford.

Mele, A. 1979. *Il Commercio greco arcaico.* Naples.

Meritt, B. D., H. T. Wade-Gery, and M. F. McGregor, eds. 1939–53. *The Athenian Tribute Lists.* Vols. 1–4. Princton.

Meyer, E. 1892–99. *Forschungen zur alten Geschichte.* Vols. 1–2. Halle.

———. 1921–25. *Geschichte des Altertums.* Vols. 1–2. Berlin and Stuttgart.

Middleton, J. 1970. "Political Incorporation among the Lugbara of Uganda." In *From Tribe to Nation in Africa. See* Cohen and Middleton, eds. 1970.

Mikalson, J. D. 1975. *The Sacred and Civil Calendar of the Athenian Year.* Princeton.

Miller, M. H. 1968. "The Accepted Date for Solon: Precise but Wrong?" *Arethusa* 2:62–86.

Miller, S. G. 1978. *The Prytaneion: Its Function and Architectural Form.* Berkeley, Calif.

Momigliano, A., and S. C. Humphreys, eds. 1980. *N. D. Fustel de Coulanges: The Ancient City.* Baltimore.

Moore, J. M. 1983. *Aristotle and Xenophon on Democracy and Oligarchy.* 2d ed. Berkeley, Calif.

Morgan, L. H. 1877. *Ancient Society.* Reprinted ed. E. B. Leacock, ed., 1963. Cleveland.

Morpurgo, A. 1963. *Mycenaeae Graecitatis Lexicon.* Rome.

Morris, I. 1987. *Burial and Ancient Society.* Cambridge.

Morrow, G. 1937. "The Murder of Slaves in Attic Law." *CPh* 32:210–27.

Mossé, C. 1964. "Classes sociales et regionalisme à Athènes au debut du VIe siècle." *AC* 33:401–13.

———. 1967. "La Conception du citoyen dans la Politique d' Aristote." *Eirene* 6:17–21.

———. 1968. "Le Rôle politique des armées dans le monde grecque à l'époque classique." In *Problèmes de la guerre en Grèce ancienne,* edited by J. Vernant, pp. 221–30. Paris.

———. 1973. *Athens in Decline.* London.

Mossé, C. 1979a. "Citoyens actifs et citoyens 'passifs' dans les cités grècques." *REA* 81:241–49.

———. 1979b. "Comment s'élabore un mythe politique: Solon 'père fondateur' de la démocratie athénienne." *Annales ESC* 34:425ff.

Moulinier, L. 1946. "La Nature et la date du crime des Alcmeonides." *REA* 48:189–97.

Mulgan, R. G. 1977. *Aristotle's Political Theory*. Oxford.

———. 1979. "Lycophron and Greek Theories of Social Contract." *JHI* 40:121–28.

Müller, O. 1899. "Untersuchungen zur Geschichte des attischen Bürger und Eherechts." *Jahrbuch für Classische Philologie*, Suppl. 25:663–865.

Murray, O. 1980. *Early Greece*. London.

———. 1983. "The Symposion as Social Organization." In *The Greek Renaissance of the Eighth Century B.C. See* Hägg, ed. 1983.

Musiolek, P. 1981. "Zum Begriff u. Bedeutung des Synoikismos." *Klio* 63:207–13.

Mylonas, G. 1961. *Eleusis and the Eleusinian Mysteries*. Princeton.

———. 1969. "The Wanax of the Mycenaean State." In *Classical Studies Presented to B. E. Perry*, pp. 66–79. Urbana and Chicago.

Nakategawa, Y. 1988. "Isegoria in Herodotus." *Historia* 37:257–75.

Nemes, Z. 1980. "The Public Property of Demes in Attica." *ACD* 16:3–8.

Netting, R. McC. 1972. "Sacred Power and Centralization: Aspects of Political Adaptation in Africa." In *Population Growth. See* Spooner, ed. 1972a.

Newman, W. L., ed. 1887–1902. *The Politics of Aristotle*. Vols. 1–4. Oxford.

Noonan, T. S. 1973. "The Grain Trade of the Northern Black Sea in Antiquity." *AJPh* 94:231–42.

Ober, J. 1987. Review of H. Lauter, *Lathuresa. Gnomon* 59:183–85.

———. 1989. *Mass and Elite in Democratic Athens: Rhetoric, Ideology, and the Power of the People*. Princeton.

Ober, J., and B. Strauss. 1990. "Drama, Political Rhetoric, and the Discourse of Athenian Democracy." In *Nothing to Do with Dionysos? The Social Meanings of Athenian Drama*, edited by J. J. Winkler and F. Zeitlin, pp. 237–68. Princeton.

O'Connor, D. 1972. "A Regional Population in Egypt, to *circa* 600 B.C." In *Population Growth. See* Spooner, ed. 1972a.

Oliver, J. H. 1935. "Greek Inscriptions." *Hesperia* 4:1–70.

———. 1960. "Reforms of Kleisthenes." *Historia* 9:503–7.

———. 1980. "From Gennetai to Curiales." *Hesperia* 49:30–56.

Osborne, M. J. 1972. "Attic Citizenship Decrees: A Note." *ABSA* 67:128–58.

———. 1978. "Athenian Grants of Citizenship after 229 B.C. Again." *AS* 9:75–81.

———. 1981. *Naturalization in Athens.* Vol. 1. Brussels.

———. 1982. *Naturalization in Athens.* Vol. 2. Brussels.

———. 1983. *Naturalization in Athens.* Vol. 3–4. Brussels.

Osborne, R. 1985a. *Demos: The Discovery of Classical Attika.* Cambridge.

———. 1985b. "Law in Action in Classical Athens." *JHS* 105:40–58.

———. 1985c. "The Erection and Mutilation of the Hermai." *PCPhS* 31:47–31.

Ostwald, M. 1955. "The Athenian Legislation Against Tyranny and Subversion." *TAPhA* 86:103–28.

———. 1969. *Nomos and the Beginnings of the Athenian Democracy.* Oxford.

———. 1973. "Ancient Greek Ideas of Law." In *Dictionary of the History of Ideas,* 2:673–85. New York.

———. 1982. *Autonomia: Its Genesis and Early History.* Chico, Calif.

———. 1986. *From Popular Sovereignty to the Sovereignty of Law: Law, Society, and Politics in Fifth-Century Athens.* Berkeley, Calif.

———. 1988. "The Reform of the Athenian State by Cleisthenes." In *Cambridge Ancient History. See* Boardman et al., eds. 1988.

Paden, J. P. 1970. "Urban Pluralism, Integration, and Adaptation of Communal Identity in Kano, Nigeria." In *From Tribe to Nation in Africa. See* Cohen and Middleton, eds. 1970.

Padgug, R. A. 1972. "Eleusis and the Union of Attica." *GRBS* 13:135–50.

Page, D. L. 1959a. *Sappho and Alcaeus.* 2d ed. Oxford.

———. 1959b. *History and the Homeric Iliad.* Berkeley, Calif.

———, ed. 1962. *Poetae Melici Graeci.* Oxford.

Paoli, U. E. 1930. *Studi di diritto Attico.* Florence.

———. 1976. "Cittadinanza e nazionalità nell'antica Grecia." In *Ugo Enrico Paoli. Altri Studi di Diretto Greco e Romano,* edited by A. Biscardi, pp. 197–200. Milan.

Parke, H. W. 1933. *Greek Mercenary Soldiers from the Earliest Times to the Battle of Ipsus.* Oxford.

———. 1977. *Festivals of the Athenians.* Ithaca, N.Y.

Parsons, K. H. 1956. "Land Reform and Agricultural Development." In *Land Tenure. See* K. H. Parsons et al., eds. 1956.

Parsons, K. H., R. J. Penn, and P. Raup, eds. 1956. *Land Tenure.* Madison, Wisc.

Patterson, C. 1981. *Pericles' Citizenship Law of 451/0 B.C.* New York.

———. 1985. "Not Worth Rearing: The Causes of Infant Exposure in Ancient Greece." *TAPhA* 115:103–23.

Pearson, L. 1962. *Popular Ethics in Ancient Greece.* Stanford, Calif.

Pečírka, J. 1963. "Land Tenure and the Development of the Athenian Polis." In *Geras: Studies for G. Thomson on the Occasion of His Sixtieth Birthday,* pp. 183–201. Prague.

———. 1966. *The Formula for the Grant of Enktesis in Attic Inscriptions.* Prague.

———. 1967. "A Note on Aristotle's Conception of Citizenship and the Role of Foreigners in Fourth-Century Athens." *Eirene* 6:23–26.

Pélékidis, C. 1962. *Histoire de l'éphébie attique des origines à 31 avant J.C.* Paris.

Philippi, A. 1870. *Beiträge zu einer Geschichte des attischen Bürgerrechtes.* Berlin.

Pickard-Cambridge, A. W. 1962. *Dithyramb, Tragedy, and Comedy.* 2d ed. Oxford.

———. 1968. *The Dramatic Festivals of Athens.* 2d ed. Oxford.

Podlecki, A. J. 1966. "The Political Significance of the Athenian 'Tyrannicide' Cult." *Historia* 15:129–41.

Pohlenz, M. 1924. "Anonymous *peri nomōn.*" In *Nachrichten der königlichen Gesellchaft der Wissenschaften,* pp. 19–37. Gottingen.

Polignac, F. de. 1984. *La Naissance de la cité grecque.* Paris.

Pollitt, J. J. 1972. *Art and Experience in Classical Greece.* Cambridge.

Pritchett, W. K. 1971–85. *The Greek State at War.* Vols. 1–4. Berkeley, Calif.

Raaflaub, K. 1980. "Des freien Bürgers Recht der freien Rede. Ein Beitrag zur Befriffs und Sozialgeschichte der athenischen Demokratie." In *Studien zur antiken Sozialgeschichte, Festschrift Fried-*

rich Vittinghoff, edited by W. von Eck, H. Galsterer, and H. Wolff, pp. 7–57. Cologne.

———. 1985. *Die Entdeckung des Freiheit. Zur historischen Semantik und Gesellschaftsgeschichte eines politischen Grundbegriffs der Griechen.* Munich.

Rahe, P. 1984. "The Primacy of Politics in Classical Greece." *AHR* 89:265–93.

Raubitschek, A. (with L. H. Jeffery). 1949. *Dedications from the Athenian Akropolis.* Cambridge.

Renfrew, C. 1972. *The Emergence of Civilisation.* London,.

Rhodes, P. J. 1972a. *The Athenian Boule.* Oxford.

———. 1972b. "The Five Thousand in the Athenian Revolutions of 411 B.C." *JHS* 92:115–27.

———. 1975. "Solon and the Numismatists." *NC* 15:1–11.

———. 1979. "EISANGELIA in Athens." *JHS* 99:103–14.

———. 1980. "Athenian Democracy after 403." *CJ* 75:305–23.

———. 1981. *A Commentary on the Aristotelian Athēnaiōn Politeia.* Oxford.

———. 1982. "Problems in Athenian Eisphora and Liturgies." *AJAH* 7:1–19.

———. 1983. Review of P. Siewert, *Die Trittyen Attikas und die Heeresreform des Kleisthenes. JHS* 103:203–4.

———. 1984a. "Members Serving Twice in the Athenian Boule and the Population of Athens Again." *ZPE* 57:200–202.

———, trans. 1984b. *Aristotle: The Athenian Constitution.* Harmondsworth.

Richards, A. 1963. "Some Effects of the Introduction of Individual Freehold into Buganda." In *African Agrarian Systems. See* Biebuyck, ed. 1963a.

Ridley, R. T. 1979. "The Hoplite as Citizen: Athenian Military Institutions in Their Social Context." *AC* 48:508–48.

Robertson, M. 1975. *A History of Greek Art.* Vols. 1–2. Cambridge.

Robertson, N. 1985. "The Origin of the Panathenaia." *RhM* 128:231–95.

———. 1986. "Solon's Axones and Kyrbeis and the Sixth-Century Background." *Historia* 35:147–76.

Roebuck, C. 1974. "Three Classes (?) in Early Attika." *Hesperia* 43:485–93.

Roussel, D. 1976. *Tribu et cité.* Paris.

Runciman, W. G. 1982. "Origins of States: The Case of Archaic Greece." *CSSH* 24:351–77.

Ruschenbusch, E. 1966. *Solonos Nomoi*. Wiesbaden.

———. 1968. *Untersuchungen zur Geschichte des Athenischen Strafrechts*. Cologne.

———. 1978. "Die soziale Herkunft der Epheben um 330." "Die soziale Zusammensetzung des Rates der 500 in Athen im 4. Jh." *ZPE* 35:173–80.

———. 1981. "Epheben, Buleuten und die Bürgerzahl von Athen um 300 v. Chr." *ZPE* 41:103–5.

———. 1985. "Die Sozialstruktur der Bürgerschaft Athens im 4.Jhr. v. Chr." *ZPE* 59:249–51.

Ruzé, F. 1984. "*Plethos*: Aux origines de la majorité politique." In *Aux Origines de l'Hellénisme, La Crète, et La Grèce. Hommage à Henri van Effenterre*, pp. 247–64. Paris.

Sahlins, M., and E. R. Service. 1960. *Evolution and Culture*. Ann Arbor, Mich.

Ste. Croix, G.E.M. de. 1953. "Demosthenes' *Timema* and the Athenian Eisphora in the Fourth Century B.C." *C&M* 14:30–70.

———. 1956. "The Constitution of the Five Thousand." *Historia* 5:1–23.

———. 1961. "Jurisdiction in the Athenian Empire." *CQ* 11:94–112, 268–80.

———. 1966. Review of R. Thomsen, *Eisphora: A Study of Direct Taxation in Ancient Athens*. *CR* 16:90–93.

———. 1970. "Some Observations on the Property Rights of Athenian Women." *CR* 20:273–78.

———. 1972. *The Origins of the Peloponnesian War*. Ithaca, N.Y.

———. 1981. *The Class Struggle in the Ancient Greek World*. Ithaca, N.Y.

Sakellariou, M. 1976–77. "La Situation politique en Attique et en Eubée de 1100 à 700 avant JC." *REA* 78–79:11–21.

Salmon, J. B. 1977. "Political Hoplites?" *JHS* 97:84–101.

Sanders, I. T. 1962. *The Rainbow in the Rock: The People of Rural Greece*. Cambridge.

Sarkady, J. 1966. "Attika im 12 bis 10 Jahrhundert. Die Anfänge des athenischen Staates." *ACD* 2:9–27.

———. 1975. "Outlines of the Development of Greek Society in the Period Between the 12th and 8th C. B.C." *AAntHung* 23:107–25.

Sartre, M. 1979. "Aspects économiques et aspects religieux de la frontière dans les cités grecques." *Ktema* 4:213–24.

Schenkl, H. 1883. "Zur Geschichte des attischen Burgerrechtes." *WS* 5:52ff.

Schlesinger (Jr.), A. 1989. "How Goes the Cycle Now?" *Wall Street Journal*, January 4, p. 8A.

Sealey, R. 1960. "Regionalism in Archaic Athens." *Historia* 9:155–75.

———. 1976. *A History of the Greek City States ca. 700–338 B.C.* Berkeley, Calif.

———. 1983a. "The Athenian Courts for Homicide." *CPh* 78:275–96.

———. 1983b. "How Citizenship and the City Began in Athens." *AJAH* 8:97–129.

———. 1987. *The Athenian Republic.* University Park, Pa., and London.

Service, E. R. 1975. *Origins of the State and Civilization: The Process of Cultural Evolution.* New York.

Shear, T. L. 1978. "Tyrants and Buildings in Archaic Athens." In *Athens Comes of Age: From Solon to Salamis*, pp. 1–19. Princeton.

Shrimpton, G. 1984. "When Did Plataia Join Athens?" *CPh* 79:294–304.

Siewert, P. 1977. "The Ephebic Oath in the Fifth Century." *JHS* 97:102–11.

———. 1982. *Die Trittyen Attikas und die Heeresreform des Kleisthenes.* Munich.

Simms, R. 1983. "Eumolpos and the Wars of Athens." *GRBS* 24:197–208.

Sinclair, R. K. 1988. *Democracy and Participation in Athens.* Cambridge.

Skinner, E. P. 1970. "Processes of Political Incorporation in Mossi Society." In *From Tribe to Nation in Africa. See* Cohen and Middleton, eds. 1970.

Smith, C. F. 1906–7. "What Constitutes a State?" *CJ* 2:299–302.

Smith, M. G. 1972. "Complexity, Size, and Urbanism." In *Man, Settlement, and Urbanism. See* Ucko et al., eds. 1972.

Smith, R. C. 1985. "The Clans of Athens and the Historiography of the Archaic Period." *EMC* 29:51–61.

Smithson, E. L. 1968. "The Tomb of a Rich Athenian Lady ca. 850 B.C." *Hesperia* 37:77–116.

Snodgrass, A. M. 1965. "The Hoplite Reform and History." *JHS* 85:110–22.

———. 1971. *The Dark Age of Greece.* Edinburgh.

Snodgrass, A. M. 1977. *Archaeology and the Rise of the Greek State.* Cambridge.

———. 1980. *Archaic Greece: The Age of Experiment.* London.

———. 1982. "Central Greece and Thessaly." In *Cambridge Ancient History. See* Boardman and Hammond, eds. 1982.

———. 1983a. "Heavy Freight in Archaic Greece." In *Trade in the Ancient Economy. See* Garnsey et al., eds. 1983.

———. 1983b. "Two Demographic Notes." In *The Greek Renaissance of the Eighth Century B.C. See* Hägg, ed. 1983.

———. 1986a. "Interaction by Design: The Greek City-State." In *Peer Polity Interaction and Socio-Political Change,* edited by C. Renfrew and J. Cherry, pp. 47–58. Cambridge.

———. 1986b. Review of H. van Effenterre, *La Cité grecque,* and F. de Polignac, *La Naissance de la cité grecque. CR* 26:261–65.

Solders, S. 1931. *Die ausserstadtische Kulte und die einigung Attikas.* Lund.

Soret, M. 1963. "La Propriété foncière chez les Kongo du nord-ouest: Charactéristiques générales et évolution." In *African Agrarian Systems. See* Biebuyck, ed. 1963a.

Sourvinou-Inwood, C. 1973. "Movements of Populations in Attica at the End of the Mycenaean Period." In *Bronze Age Migrations in the Aegean,* edited by R. A. Crossland and A. Birchall, pp. 215–21. London.

———. 1983. "A Trauma in Flux: Death in the 8th Century and After." In *The Greek Renaissance of the Eighth Century B.C. See* Hägg, ed. 1983.

Southall, A. 1970. "Ethnic Incorporation among the Alur." In *From Tribe to Nation in Africa. See* Cohen and Middleton, eds. 1970.

Spencer, H. 1896. *Principles of Sociology.* New York.

Spooner, B., ed. 1972a. *Population Growth: Its Anthropological Implications.* Cambridge.

———. 1972b. "Introduction." In *Population Growth. See* Spooner ed. 1972a.

Stahl, M. 1987. *Aristokraten und Tyrannen im archaischen Athen.* Stuttgart.

Stanton, G. R. 1984. "The Tribal Reforms of Kleisthenes the Alkmeonid." *Chiron* 14:1–44.

Starr, C. 1958. "An Overdose of Slavery." *Journal of Economic History* 18:17–30.

———. 1961. *The Origins of Greek Civilization, 1100–650 B.C.* New York.

———. 1977. *The Economic and Social Growth of Early Greece, 800–500 B.C.* New York.

———. 1982. "Economic and Social Conditions in the Greek World." In *Cambridge Ancient History. See* Boardman and Hammond, eds. 1982.

———. 1986. *Individual and Community: The Rise of the Polis 800–500 B.C.* New York.

Staveley, E. S. 1972. *Greek and Roman Voting and Elections.* London.

Stevenson, R. F. 1968. *Population and Political Systems in Tropical Africa.* New York.

Stinton, T.C.W. 1976. "Solon, Fragment 25." *JHS* 96:159–62.

Strauss, B. 1987. *Athens after the Peloponnesian War: Class, Faction, and Policy 403–386.* Ithaca, N.Y.

———. 1989. "Political Anthropology and Ancient Greek History." Paper delivered at the First Joint Archaeological Congress, Baltimore, January 7.

Stroud, R. S. 1968. *Drakon's Law on Homicide.* Berkeley and Los Angeles.

———. 1971. "Theozotides and the Athenian Orphans." *Hesperia* 40:280–301.

———. 1978. "State Documents in Archaic Athens." In *Athens Comes of Age: From Solon to Salamis*, pp. 20–42. Princeton.

———. 1979. *The Axones and Kyrbeis of Drakon and Solon.* Berkeley, Calif.

Stubbings, F. H. 1975a. "The Expansion of the Mycenaean Civilization." In *Cambridge Ancient History. See* Edwards et al., eds. 1975.

———. 1975b. "The Recession of Mycenaean Civilization." In *Cambridge Ancient History. See* Edwards et al., eds. 1975.

Swoboda, H. 1905. "Beiträge zur griechischen Rechtsgeschichte." *ZRG* 26:9ff.

Szanto, E. 1892. *Das griechische Bürgerrecht.* Freiburg.

Taeuber, C., and I. Taeuber. 1956. "Population and the Land Tenure Problem." In *Land Tenure. See* Parsons et al., eds. 1956.

Thiel, J. 1950. "Solon's Property Classes." *Mnemosyne* 4.3:1–11.

Thomas, C. G. 1977. "Literacy and the Codification of Law." *Stud. Doc. Hist. Juris* 43:455–58.

———. 1979. "The Territorial Imperative of the Polis." *AncW* 2:35–39.

Thomas, C. G., and R. Griffeth, eds. 1981. *The City-State in Five Cultures*. Santa Barbara, Calif.

Thomas, L. V. 1963. "Essai sur quelques problèmes relatifs au régime foncier des Diola de Basse-Casamance (Senegal)." In *African Agrarian Systems*. *See* Biebuyck, ed. 1963a.

Thompson, H. 1982. "The Pnyx in Models." In *Studies in Epigraphy, History, and Topography Presented to Eugene Vanderpool* (*Hesperia* Suppl. 19), pp. 133–47. Princeton.

Thompson, H. A., and R. E. Wycherley. 1972. *The Athenian Agora*. Vol. 14. Princeton.

Thompson, K. 1963. *Farm Fragmentation in Greece*. Athens.

Thompson, W. E. 1964. "Three Thousand Acharnian Hoplites." *Historia* 13:400–413.

———. 1970. "Regional Distribution of Athenian Pentakosiomedimnoi." *Klio* 52:137–51.

———. 1971. "The Deme in Kleisthenes' Reforms." *SO* 46:72–79.

———. 1982. "The Athenian Entrepreneur." *AC* 51:53–85.

Thomsen, R. 1964. *Eisphora: A Study of Direct Taxation in Ancient Athens*. Copenhagen.

———. 1972. *The Origin of Ostracism*. Copenhagen.

Tod, M. N., ed. 1933–48. *A Selection of Greek Historical Inscriptions*. Vols. 1–2. Oxford.

Toepffer, J. 1889. *Attische Genealogie*. Berlin.

Traill, J. S. 1975. *The Political Organization of Attika: A Study of the Demes, Trittyes, and Phylai and their Representation in the Athenian Council*. Princeton.

———. 1978. "Diakris, the Inland Trittys of Leontis." *Hesperia* 47:89–109.

Ucko, P., R. Tringham, and G. W. Dimbleby, eds. 1972. *Man, Settlement, and Urbanism*. London.

Vamvoukos, A. 1979. "Fundamental Freedoms in Athens of the Fifth Century." *RIDA* 26:89–124.

Vanderpool, E. 1970. *Ostracism at Athens*. Cincinnati.

———. 1974. "The Date of the Pre-Persian City Wall of Athens." In *Phoros: Tribute to B. D. Meritt*, pp. 156–60. New York.

Van Groningen, B. A., ed. 1966. *Theognis. Le premier Livre*. Amsterdam.

Vansina, J. 1966. *Kingdoms of the Savanna*. Madison, Wis.

Vatin, C. 1984. *Citoyens et non-citoyens dans le monde grec*. Paris.

Vernant, J. P. 1973. "Le Mariage en Grèce archaïque." *PP* 28:51–74.

———. 1982. *The Origins of Greek Thought*. Ithaca, N.Y.

————. 1986. *Mythe et pensée chez les Grecs.* 3d ed. Paris.

Vidal-Naquet, P. 1968. "La Tradition de l'hoplite athénien." In *Problèmes de la guerre en Grèce ancienne,* edited by J.-P. Vernant, pp. 171–82. Paris.

————. 1981. "The Black Hunter and the Origin of the Athenian *ephebeia.*" In *Myth, Religion, and Society,* edited by R. L. Gordon, pp. 147–62. Cambridge.

Vlastos, G. 1946. "Solonian Justice." *CPh* 41:65–83.

————. 1953. "Isonomia." *AJPh* 74:337–60.

————. 1964. "*Isonomia Politikē.*" In *Isonomia,* edited by J. Mau and E. Schmidt, pp. 1–35. Berlin.

Wade-Gery, H. T. 1932–33. "Studies in Attic Inscriptions of the Fifth Century B.C.; B. Charter of the Democracy, 410 B.C. = IG i² 114." *ABSA* 33:113–22.

————. 1958. *Essays in Greek History.* Oxford.

Walbank, M. B. 1978. *Athenian Proxenies of the Fifth Century B.C.* Toronto.

————. 1983a. "Leases of Sacred Properties in Attica. Part I." *Hesperia* 52:100–135.

————. 1983b. "Leases of Sacred Properties in Attica. Parts II–IV." *Hesperia* 52:177–231.

————. 1984. "Leases of Sacred Properties in Attica. Part V." *Hesperia* 53:361–68.

Wallace, M. B. 1970. "Early Greek *Proxenoi.*" *Phoenix* 24:196–204.

Wallace, R. W. 1983. "The Date of Solon's Reforms." *AJAH* 8:81–95.

————. 1987. "The Origins of Electrum Coinage." *AJA* 91:385–97.

————. 1989. *The Areopagus Council, to 307 B.C.* Baltimore and London.

Wallace, W. 1962. "The Early Coinages of Euboia and Athens." *NC* 22:23–42.

Walters, K. R. 1979. "Political Codes and Cultural Contradictions in Attic Mythology." *AncW* 2:75–77.

————. 1983. "Pericles' Citizenship Law." *CA* 2:314–36.

————. 1984. "FGrH 324 F6: A New Conjecture." *RhM* 127:223–26.

Waters, K. H. 1960. "Solon's Price Equalization." *JHS* 80:181–90.

Weidauer, L. 1975. *Probleme der frühen Elektronprägung.* Fribourg.

Weil, R. 1960. *Aristote et l'histoire: Essai sur la Politique.* Paris.

————. 1964. "Philosophie et histoire: La vision de l'histoire chez

Aristote." In *Entretiens sur l'antiquité classique*, 4:159–89. Geneva.

Welwei, K. W. 1967. "Der Diapsephismos nach dem Sturz der Peisistratiden." *Gymnasium* 74:423–37.

———. 1983. *Die griechische Polis: Verfassung und Gesellschaft in archaischer und klassischer Zeit.* Stuttgart.

West, M. L., ed. 1978. *Hesiod. Works and Days.* Oxford.

———, ed. 1980. *Delectus Ex Iambis et Elegis Graecis.* Oxford.

Westermann, W. 1955. *The Slave Systems of Greek and Roman Antiquity.* Philadelphia.

Wheatley, P. 1972. "The Concept of Urbanism." In *Man, Settlement, and Urbanism. See* Ucko et al., eds. 1972.

White, C. 1963. "Factors Determining the Content of African Land Tenure Systems in Northern Rhodesia." In *African Agrarian Systems. See* Biebuyck, ed. 1963a.

Whitehead, D. 1977. *The Ideology of the Athenian Metic.* Cambridge.

———. 1981. "The Archaic Athenian *Zeugitai.*" *CQ* 31:282–86.

———. 1982–83. "Sparta and the Thirty Tyrants." *AS* 13/14:105–30.

———. 1983. "Competitive Outlay and Community Profit: *Philotimia* in Democratic Athens." *C&M* 34:55–74.

———. 1984a. "Immigrant Communities in the Classical Polis: Some Principles for a Synoptic Treatment." *AC* 53:47–59.

———. 1984b. "A Thousand New Athenians." *LCM* 9:8–10.

———. 1986a. *The Demes of Attica 508/7—ca. 250 B.C.* Princeton.

———. 1986b. "Women and Naturalization in Fourth-Century Athens: The Case of Archippe." *CQ* 36:109–14.

Whitley, J. 1988. "Early States and Hero Cults: A Reappraisal." *JHS* 108:173–82.

Wilamowitz-Möllendorff, U. von. 1893. *Aristoteles und Athen.* Vols. 1–2. Berlin.

———. 1910. *Staat und Gesellschaft der Griechen und Romer.* Berlin.

Will, E. 1954. "Sur l'évolution des rapports entre colonies et métropoles en Grèce à partir du VIe siècle." *La Nouvelle Clio* 6:413–60.

———. 1969. "Soloniana." *REG* 82:104–16.

Wilson, M. 1963. "Effects on the Xhosa and Nyakyusa of Scarcity of Land." In *African Agrarian Systems. See* Biebuyck, ed. 1963a.

Winkler, J. J. 1985. "The Ephebes' Song: Tragôidia and *Polis.*" *Representations* 11:26–62.

Wolff, H. J. 1944. "Marriage Law and Family Organization in Ancient Athens." *Traditio* 2:43–95.

———. 1946. "The Origin of Judicial Legislation among the Greeks." *Traditio* 4:31–87.

Wood, E. M. 1983. "Agricultural Slavery." *AJAH* 8:1–47.

———. 1988. *Peasant-Citizen and Slave*. London.

Woodhead, A. G. 1967. "Isegoria and the Council of 500." *Historia* 16:129–40.

Woodhouse, W. J. 1938. *Solon the Liberator*. Oxford.

Worsley, P. M. 1956. "The Kinship System of the Tallensi: A Revaluation." *Journal of the Royal Anthropological Institute* 86:37–75.

Wright, H. T., and G. Johnson. 1975. "Population, Exchange, and Early State Formation in Southwestern Iran." *American Anthropologist* 77:267–89.

Wrigley, E. A. 1969. *Population and History*. New York.

Wüst, F. R. 1957. "Zu den prytaneis ton naukraron und zu den alten attischen Trittyen." *Historia* 6:126–91.

Wycherley, R. E. 1957. *The Athenian Agora*, vol. 3. Princeton.

———. 1966. "Archaia Agora." *Phoenix* 20:285–93.

———. 1978. *The Stones of Athens*. Princeton.

Wyse, W. 1904. *The Speeches of Isaeus*. Cambridge.

Yalman, N. 1963. "On the Purity of Women in the Castes of Ceylon and Malabar." *Journal of the Royal Anthropological Institute* 93:25–58.

Young, D., ed. 1961. *Theognis*. Leipzig.

INDEX

Aeschylus: *Oresteia* and *Persians*, 209n.160
agora, 91n.76, 154–55, 167–69, 194
agroikoi, 158n.2
Aigikoreis, 59
Aigina, 87, 205
Akropolis, 36, 77, 88–89, 167–69
Alexandros of Makedonia (*proxenos*), 207n.152
alienability of land. *See* land and land tenure
aliens. *See xenoi*
aliens, resident. *See metoikoi*
Alkibiades, 26
Alkmeonidai, 81, 141n.48, 160n.8, 163n.18, 172–73, 183n.83, 190n.101
anchisteia, 107
Anonymus Iamblichi, 49
anthropology: and historical methodology, 28–34, 137–39, 211–12
Antiphon, 47–48
Apatouria, 62
apoikia. See colonization
Apollo Patroos, 25, 167
archai, 9, 19, 40. *See also* archons; *boulē; strategoi*; and other offices by name
archons, 25, 73–77, 152–53n.76, 158
Areopagos, 12, 73–76, 151, 162n.16, 181, 196n.122, 201n.139
Argadeis, 59
Argos, 88n.67, 140n.45, 201
aristocracy: early origins of, 71–77; effects of Solonian reforms on, 144; and land tenure, 110–17,

123; marriage patterns of, 142n.42; relationship of, with *genē*, 61; social and political roles of, in sixth century, 83, 158–61, 166n.31, 172–77, 183–84, 200; *xenia* of, 26. *See also* Eupatridai
Aristogeiton, 172–73
Aristotle: and authorship of *Athēnaion Politeia*, xiii; and portrayal of early Attic social and political organization, 64–65, 75; as source for definition of "ownership," 94; as source for definition of *polis*, 38–54, 211
army, Athenian. *See* hoplite phalanx; military and military service
Artemis Brauronia, 167n.36
Arthmios of Zeleia (*proxenos*), 207n.152
artisans. *See* manufacture and trade
assembly. *See ekklēsia*
asylia, 11n.42
ateleia, 11n.42, 216n.8
Athena Phratria, 62
Athena Polias, 168–69
atimia, 4n3, 147–48, 183–84, 216–17nn. 7 and 8
Attika: as depicted in *Iliad*, 155n.78; in modern times, 105–6; Mycenaean kingdom of, 57; social and economic life of, 30–31, 55–92, 106–23, 128–44, 158–59, 178–82, 192–94, 212, 218; territory of, 9, 11, 25, 35, 39, 55–56, 80–81, 93, 107–18, 126–32, 196, 201–3, 208
autarkeia, 41–43
autochthony, 14, 35, 103, 140–41
autonomia, 41, 204, 213

THE ORIGINS OF CITIZENSHIP IN ANCIENT ATHENS

PHILIP BROOK MANVILLE

"There can be no questioning the value and validity of Manville's patient unraveling of the strands that . . . make up the close weave of classical Athenian citizenship: corporate identity, territoriality, population density, personal freedom, and landownership above all. It is one of the many strengths of Manville's quietly persuasive approach that he can deploy comparative ethnographic evidence from so-called 'primitive' states with telling sensitivity."
—*Paul Cartledge, The Times Literary Supplement*

"An enlightened and enlightening study."
—*P. J. Rhodes, The Classical Review*

"This book well repays the attention of anyone, whether historian, literary critic, or archaeologist, who is interested in the wider context of preclassical Athenian society."
—*Gregory Crane, Bryn Mawr Classical Review*

"A very thorough, intelligent investigation. Manville knows the ancient evidence well and has an extensive grasp of the modern literature. . . . This book is a real contribution to the perennial debate on the Athenian way of life. I would recommend it strongly to all who are also interested in the origins of our own society and our own brand of citizenship."
—*Harold B. Mattingly, History*

"The strength of the book lies in its concentration on citizenship itself, rather than the polis in general, and in his teasing out of the implications of Solon's and Kleisthenes' reforms for the development of a sense of community."
—*Rosalind Thomas, Journal of Hellenic Studies*

Philip Brook Manville is Director of Knowledge Management at McKinsey & Company, an international management consulting firm based in New York City. In his earlier career he taught classics and ancient history at Northwestern University. He holds degrees in classics from Yale University and Oxford University, and a Ph.D. in history from Yale University.

PRINCETON PAPERBACKS

Cover illustration: Drawing adapted from a sixth-century B.C. Athenian vase painting by the painter Sophilos (Athens National Museum 15499). Drawn by Margarita Egan.

ISBN 0-691-01593-7

90000

9 780691 015934